Undercover

MEMOIRS OF AN AMERICAN SECRET AGENT

Undercover

Memoirs of an American
Secret Agent

by E. Howard Hunt

Published by
BERKLEY PUBLISHING CORPORATION
Distributed by
G. P. PUTNAM'S SONS

For my children

A man may defend himself against all enemies save those who are resolved that such a man as he should not exist.

—TACITUS

Contents

PROLOGUE

BREATHILY through the walkie-talkie came the urgent query: *"Any of your guys wearing hippie clothes?"*

Gordon Liddy sat bolt upright, grabbed the W/T and barked, "One to Three. Repeat."

"Any of your guys wearing hippie clothes?"

I exchanged glances with Liddy. He said, "One to Three, negative. Our guys are in business suits. Why? Over."

"Three here," came the voice of James McCord's monitor from the balconied Listening Post in the Howard Johnson Motel across Virginia Avenue. "There's four, maybe five guys running around the sixth floor. Lights are going on. One's wearing a cowboy hat, another a sweat shirt. Oh, oh, they've got guns. Looks like trouble."

"Keep reporting," Liddy told him and stood up. "One to Two," he snapped, calling the entry team in Democratic National Committee headquarters. "Two, come in. There are lights on your floor. Any trouble?"

From the W/T only the low rushing sound of the carrier current. "One to Two," Liddy repeated, voice louder now. "Come in. This is an order. Repeat: *Come in!*"

My throat and mouth were dry, my stomach hard. By now I realized the entry team was in trouble. I looked around our Command Post—Room 214 in the Watergate Hotel—automatically cataloguing what we would have to take with us. The monitor again: "I can see our guys now, hands in the air. Must be cops with them."

1

Galvanized, Liddy gripped the W/T in one hand. Then a disembodied voice spoke: *"They've got us."* The entry team had responded at last.

Stepping onto the balcony, I looked up at the rear windows of DNC headquarters in the adjacent office building. Lights were on but no one was in sight. The two upper floors were also lighted. I returned to Liddy, who was receiving a moment-by-moment description from the monitor across the street: ". . . filing out with them now, guns drawn. Police wagon pulling up at the entrance below, also some marked police cars. . . ."

"Keep talking," Liddy told him as I began opening suitcases. Together we began throwing in operational litter, forcing McCord's surplus electronic gear into his black attaché case.

To Liddy I said, "Let's go; the police will be here any minute."

"Why?"

"Barker has our room key."

From the W/T the monitor's voice: "What should I do?"

Liddy grunted. I picked up the W/T and pressed the transmit button. "Keep your lights out and stay out of sight. I'll come over as soon as I can. We're signing off."

I retrieved the long automobile antenna from the balcony, telescoped it and tossed it on the bed, where Liddy was packing the most incriminating items into a handbag. "That's most of it," he said, "except for that damn antenna. Leave it here?"

"Hell no." I thrust it down inside my trouser leg and turned off the lights. "Let's go."

Down the elevator, hearts pounding, we walked past the drowsing desk clerk. Then my leg antenna began to slide onto the floor. Hitching it back under my belt, I kept on going without looking back.

We reached the street, half a block from an assemblage of police cars, flashers playing eerily through the darkness. We got inside my Firebird, which I had parked at the entrance—just in case. . . .

As I started the engine, Liddy said, "My jeep's up the street."

"I'll take you there."

He gestured at the dark Listening Post windows across the street. "What about *him*?"

"I'll come back. Go home and get yourself an alibi."

Silently we drove four blocks toward the city, and Liddy got out. "Got the emergency money?"

"I'm going to get it now."

"Okay." He swallowed. "Goodnight, Howard. I'll be in touch tomorrow." We shook hands and he walked toward his green jeep. I made a U-turn and parked two blocks from the motel. Within pistol range of the police cars, I reflected.

From the motel lobby I took the elevator to the seventh floor and knocked on the L/P door. It opened a crack and I saw a man with a crew cut indistinctly against the dark background. "Are you—?" he asked, but I handed him the W/T and went inside, locking the door behind me. Offering me binoculars, he said, "Hey, take a look; the cops are leading them out."

"Listen," I said, "it's all over. Pack up and get going."

He looked around uncertainly. "Lotta heavy gear here. What do I do with it?"

"Load the goddamn van and shove off."

"Where should I go—McCord's house?"

I stared at him incredulously. "That's the *last* place to go. I don't care if you drive the van into the river; just get the stuff out of here. Understood?" Turning, I strode toward the door.

Plaintively he called, "What's going to happen?"

"I don't know—but you'll be contacted." From the room I took the elevator to the lobby and walked casually to the sidewalk. On the far side of the street police were loading the last of the five-man entry team into a white paddy wagon. It seemed so damned final, I thought as I walked back to my car.

From there I drove to the White House annex—the Old Executive Office Building, in bygone years the War Department and later the Department of State.

Carrying three heavy attaché cases, I entered the Pennsylvania Avenue door, showed my blue-and-white White House pass to the uniformed guards and took the elevator to the third floor. I unlocked the door of 338 and went in. I opened my two-drawer safe, took out my operational notebook, found a telephone number and dialed it.

The time was 0213 on the morning of June 17, 1972, and five of my companions had been arrested and taken to the maximum-security block of the District of Columbia jail. I had recruited four of them

and it was my responsibility to try to get them out. That was the sole
focus of my thoughts as I began talking on the telephone.

But with those five arrests the Watergate Affair had begun.

*   *   *

It has been said authoritatively that no catastrophe since Pearl
Harbor has so shocked and traumatized the nation as the series of
events and revelations that have come to be known collectively as
Watergate.

Because I was involved in many of the episodes that culminated in
Watergate and have suffered their heavy consequences, and because I have been depicted as at best a fumbler and at worst a
pathological criminal, I am writing my personal record of events as I
saw them develop, and so illuminate the truth of these events which
for all time must bear the scrutiny of history.

Few Watergate participants were subjected to such intensive
press scrutiny as I was. Much of the media speculation concerning
me and certainly many of the conclusions about me not only lack
substance in fact but in many cases were nothing more than fabrications.

At the time my five companions were arrested in the Watergate
offices of the Democratic National Committee I had been happily
married for nearly twenty-three years. I had four children, two of
whom were in college and one in private school. I had a comfortable
home in suburban Maryland with horses, paddocks and a stable. I
had a well-paying and absorbing position as vice president of a
leading Washington public-relations firm, and for nearly a year I had
been employed as a consultant to the Executive Office of the President of the United States.

Yet within nine months I was a prisoner in solitary confinement in
a filthy, rat-infested jail, with little hope of release within my
lifetime. The classic element of tragedy is the fall from high place to
low. By that definition, as well as other personal circumstances,
including the death of my wife, my role has been a tragic one indeed.
Moreover, I was and still am enmeshed in the larger national
tragedy of Watergate.

As I begin this book, my future is uncertain. A few weeks ago the United States Court of Appeals in Washington released me from the Federal Prison Camp at Allenwood, Pennsylvania, pending a hearing on my appeal from my conviction and sentence of eight years in jail imposed upon me by District Judge John J. Sirica, *Time*'s Man of the Year for 1973. Five civil suits have been filed against me for heavy damages, all because I was involved in Watergate and a variety of events of which Watergate was the culmination. These civil suits demand payment of heavy monetary damages. Meanwhile, I have been summoned back to testify before one or more of the several Watergate grand juries. Investigators from the Ervin committee came unannounced to my home and subjected me to further questioning. I anticipate that sometime in the not-too-distant future I will be called upon to testify in the anticipated trials of many former members of the Nixon Administration who now stand under indictment.

During World War II I served in the armed forces, both the Navy and the Air Force, for nearly five years. For a time I was a press aide to Ambassador Averell Harriman in Paris. Subsequently I served uninterruptedly as an officer of the Central Intelligence Agency for twenty-one years until my retirement in May of 1970. In 1971 I joined the White House staff. Beginning in 1942 I managed to write an average of about two popular novels each year. During all my long years of government service I was never so much as fined for a moving traffic violation, much less arrested for anything more serious.

The emergent and persisting question seems to be: How could a man like myself be a participant in the greatest national scandal of modern times and end up a prisoner in one of the country's most notorious jails?

To supply even a partial answer to this question and to reveal why I was disposed to lend my talents and acquired skills to surreptitious entries in Los Angeles and at Watergate, an examination of my life from its beginning must be made. Accordingly, what follows will be my personal story and accounting—to my knowledge the first detailed autobiography of a career CIA operations officer since the Agency's inception.

1 ANCESTORS AND EDUCATION

I was born in October, 1918, in the Buffalo suburb of Hamburg, a semirural community of 5,000 or so in western New York not far from Lake Erie. The physician who delivered me was my Great-Uncle Howard, who drove by horse and buggy from the nearby town of Orchard Park. My father, Everette, was then a captain in the Air Service stationed on Long Island and awaiting shipment to France. Because of the flu epidemic, he was denied leave to be with my mother at the time of my birth.

I am half English, one-quarter German and one-quarter Welsh. The Hunts emigrated from England, settled in Vermont and made their way south and west. One of my ancestors, Captain James Hunt, served in the Revolutionary Army and was a landholder of means in northern Manhattan. It is after him that Hunt's Point, now New York's municipal market area, is named.* My father's mother was a Von Dietrich, a Lutheran family that emigrated to the United States from Germany to avoid religious persecution. The mother of my mother, Jenny Prosser, was the daughter of a civil engineer in Pennsylvania. Her husband, and the father of my mother, was

---

*Among other English Hunts was Leigh, essayist, poet and political radical who suffered official persecution and political imprisonment from 1813 to 1815. Henry the "Orator" Hunt also served two years in prison, then became a member of Parliament. Imprisonment may even have enhanced his subsequent career.

William Totterdale, who, as a boy, fled the Welsh mining town of
Swansea and worked his passage to the United States as cabin boy on
a sailing vessel. When the ship docked at Philadelphia, my grandfather jumped ship and found work in the steel mills, work he was to
follow for the rest of his life. He was almost entirely self-educated,
but his Spencerian handwriting was beautiful to behold, and he was
an avid student of Shakespeare. My mother, Ethel Jean Totterdale,
studied at a Pittsburgh music conservatory for a career as a concert
pianist. My father also had musical talents. He had a fine baritone
voice and both sang in the Cornell Glee Club and played in the
Cornell Mandolin Club. But before reaching Cornell, where he
received his law degree in 1911, my father spent two years at Hobart
College in central New York State, because Cornell's minimum
admission age was sixteen, and my father graduated from Hamburg
High School at fourteen. Linguistically he was gifted and had a flair
for mathematics. Curiously, he planned to become an electrical
engineer when he went to college, shifting to law studies after
leaving Hobart for Cornell. As a young student he was accounted
something of a prodigy and mastered Latin, Classical Greek, Italian,
Spanish, French and German.

My mother and father met at Hamburg's Methodist Episcopal
Church, where my mother was organist and my father was guest
baritone soloist. Although only a few years out of law school, my
father had an active practice in Buffalo, and after honeymooning in
Bermuda, they moved into a new house at 35 Maple Avenue,
where, a year or so later, I was born.

An attractive and affluent young couple, my mother and father led
an active social life. My father was a thirty-second degree Mason and
a Shriner, and they belonged to two country clubs and the Buffalo
Athletic Club, of which my father was a founding member, along
with another contemporary Buffalo lawyer, William J. Donovan.
My father's mother had been a founder of Buffalo's Twentieth
Century Club, and in later years my father was also to be a member
of the Buffalo Club. During his lifetime he belonged to the Banker's
Club in New York, New York's Drug and Chemical Club, the Lake
Placid Club, Albany's Fort Orange Club, the Albany Country Club
and a small private hunting and conservation club in the Adiron-
dacks, the Adirondack League Club. Gregarious by nature, my

father enjoyed these social associations, some of which I was later to share and enjoy with him.

At the end of World War I my father was discharged from the Air Service and returned to Buffalo only to find his law practice largely vanished. At the request of now Colonel "Wild Bill" Donovan of the Fighting Sixty-ninth, my father became an active organizer of the New York Department of the American Legion. Within a short time he was approached by a Northern financial consortium which retained him to incorporate and establish what became the Biscayne Kennel Club of Miami, Florida. On behalf of this same consortium, my father also became active in Canadian gold and silver mining and in Oklahoma oil. By 1924, when I was six years old, my father was practicing law in both Florida and New York State. He was early aware of the potential that Florida represented to the Northern investor, and he arranged his professional life so that he could devote winters to his law practice in Florida and spring, summer and early autumn to affairs in New York State.

Although convenient for my parents, this arrangement caused me scholastic difficulties.

Each September I would begin school in Hamburg, and by mid-October I was entering another school in Ft. Lauderdale, Hollywood or Miami Beach. By Easter we usually headed north, where I would reenter the class I had abandoned the previous September.

Even earlier, though, I had found reading difficult.* Accordingly, I was given special Saturday morning tutoring by Miss Alice Robbins, principal of the Hamburg Elementary School and the lady who had taught my father to read. Each Saturday when I arrived at Miss Robbins' cottage near the school, she would have ready for me fresh-made cookies and hot chocolate; if the weather was cold, there would be a roaring fire. With me her technique was as simple as it was effective. She would begin reading from a book a story calculated to appeal to me and when my interest heightened unbearably, Miss Robbins would stop. "Now you read to me, Howard," she would say and hand me the book. So with this gently applied stimulus, I was brought into the world of books, the world of

---

*With the exception of my father, nearly all Hunt males, including my own two sons, have been afflicted with dyslexia. Its extreme form, which I did not have, is so-called mirror vision—i.e., reversal of words and letters.

imagination and adventure that was to occupy so large a portion of my later years.

My early schooling in Florida was pleasant, if casual. My classmates seemed evenly divided between children of vacationing Northerners and Florida Crackers. I remember distinguishing myself in spelldowns and in mental addition of fractions. Simultaneously, I was learning how to play football barefoot, and swimming every afternoon and weekend, either in the ocean or at a pool. My father, having been a varsity fencer at Cornell, wanted me to become proficient in at least one sport. I was a good swimmer, but the boys who lived year around in Florida and swam competitively every day had the advantage over me, and I was still too small to hold a tennis racket and become proficient at tennis, as was my father's brother, Horace, a tennis star at Mercersburg Academy and Hobart College.

When my father became a Ft. Lauderdale municipal judge, my Cracker classmates began beating up on me regularly. To put an end to this my father hired former boxing champion Young Stribling to coach me, and by the time I was twelve I was boxing occasionally in preliminary fights at the local American Legion arena.

My father taught me how to fish and took me fishing regularly either along the canals or waterways or deep-sea fishing in the Gulf Stream for bluefish, Spanish mackerel, dolphin and shark. When I was ten, he gave me my first .22 repeating rifle. One day, after a particularly heavy rain, my father drove me into the Everglades. There, lying across the road, was a large rattlesnake torpid with its recent kill. Because the rifle was too large for me to both aim and pull the trigger, my father sighted the .22 on the rattler's head and allowed me to pull the trigger. Forty-odd years later that rattler's skin still adorns my wall.

I remember my parents' social life as being divided between bridge, which they both played exceedingly well, and musical evenings during which my mother played piano and my father sang. Frequently my mother accompanied a guest artist. They played golf together and in those Prohibition days went frequently to Havana for long weekends with friends, returning well laden with illegal liquor. During their absences, I was left in the charge of a delightful Scotswoman, Mrs. Abele. She and her husband were childless, and while my parents were in Havana, Gulfport or St. Petersburg, she indulged me in every possible way: movies, car trips, and culinary delights.

But with each spring came return to my Northern school and my frantic race to catch up with my Northern classmates, particularly my first cousin, Amos Minkel, the school's outstanding student. Amos, now a doctor in Hamburg, was the son of my father's sister Leigh. My father's other sister, Hollis, was and is a physician who married a medical-school classmate, Dr. Richard DeNiord. My father's brother, Norris, was attending law school when he joined the Army in World War I and was one of that small detachment of United States soldiers who were sent to Vladivostok at the time of the Bolshevik Revolution.

The 1929 Wall Street crash, the bank holiday and the ensuing Depression profoundly altered my parents' way of life. We were in Ft. Lauderdale when the crash occurred and my father had just $400 in cash. All other money in savings and checking accounts was lost when the banks failed to reopen. And my father had made heavy investments in a hotel and an office building then under construction along Las Olas Boulevard in Ft. Lauderdale. As financing dried up, construction on the buildings ceased, and in time they were simply sold for taxes. One of the purchasers, we were later to learn, was my Scots nurse, Mrs. Abele, who had a high opinion of my father's acumen and optimistically invested her savings in land and incomplete construction that today must be worth many millions of dollars.

When it became evident to my father that he would not soon be able to repair his fortunes in Florida, we moved back North. I remember the long trek north in our Buick convertible, a vehicle that was to be our principal source of family transportation for the remainder of the Depression years. Although my father was heavily in debt, he never declared bankruptcy or, as far as I know, seriously considered it. Instead he applied himself to what remained of his law practice in Buffalo while we lived in Hamburg and he commuted to his office in Buffalo.

Through connections on the German side of my father's family he was retained by the heirs of Jacob Wurlitzer to reorganize the company, there being little demand for high-priced pianos and organs in those Depression days. His legal work completed, my father was asked if he preferred a cash fee or whether he might not want to accept at least a portion in Wurlitzer stock. Hard pressed financially, my father took cash to pay old bills. Had he known that within a few years the Wurlitzer Company would develop and market the jukebox, he would, of course, have taken stock.*

In later years my father was to remark that that decision plus his earlier one to accept money for his legal work in incorporating the Biscayne Kennel Club (greyhound racing) rather than accepting a stock participation had probably cost him millions of dollars. He was a philosophical man, though, and usually optimistic. He believed that opportunities presented themselves in the course of a man's life and if they were not seized, in all likelihood they would not come again.

Meanwhile, I was losing my Florida Cracker accent at Hamburg High School, where my grades showed startling discrepancies. In spelling, English and humanities I usually excelled; geometry was the course I remember disliking the most.

But if not an outstanding scholar, I was one of the school's leading musicians. Wind instruments had fascinated me, and after a brief brush with piano instruction I acquired a trumpet from the high school music department and my father found an excellent teacher for me in Buffalo. He was Harold Austin, then the leader of a large dance orchestra which played in an Austin-owned dance hall. By age fourteen I was able to play stock orchestra arrangements and soon became trumpet soloist in the high school band and symphony orchestra. Other high school musicians were interested in dance music, and so we formed a dance orchestra, which, as we gained experience, played for high school dances and other social events in Hamburg, East Aurora, Orchard Park, Williamsville and Buffalo itself.

As a sideline to this steady source of income, I ran a trap line along the Eighteen Mile Creek trapping muskrats in the wintertime, skinning them, stretching and salting their hides and shipping them in the spring to Sears, Roebuck for, I think, about thirty-five cents a pelt. Usually I would service the trap line before dawn on my way to school, often passing the ruins of the first foundry in western New York, which had been established by my forebears. These Quaker Hunts had not insured their foundry out of respect for God's will. So

*In 1974 the Wurlitzer Company ceased manufacturing jukeboxes.

when lightning struck and destroyed the foundry, my ancestors abandoned industry and took up farming in the Hamburg area. My father's grandmother is remembered as "the Angel of Hamburg" for having given many hundreds of acres of choice farmland to the area's poor. All that remains today to recall her benefactions is a short street in Hamburg named Hunt Avenue.

Having learned to drive in Florida when I was twelve, I gradually took over my mother's Chevrolet convertible and used it for dance-job transportation and for weekend forays to the lakeshore. Around my dance band developed a vocal group in which I sang tenor lead. Soon we were singing in a Buffalo radio station, and in this musical milieu I became acquainted with and, for a brief while, sang with the vocal quartet that went on, without me, to become the Modernaires of lasting memory.

My final high school marks were sufficiently good to bring me a Regents scholarship at any college or university in New York State that I chose to attend. My father, of course, had long made it clear that he could not afford full tuition for me at any institution, though his constant hope was that I attend either Hobart or Cornell as he had and, of course, join his fraternity, Theta Delta Chi. However, I had become interested in Brown University from reading catalogues in the high school library; of particular interest to me was the degree of bachelor of philosophy then offered by Brown. Thanks to my father's tutoring, I had passed three years of Latin, which was then one of the prerequisites for entrance into Brown. I applied for admission, was interviewed by alumni and the dean of admissions, and over the summer of 1936 was accepted for the fall class.

Among my classmates, I remember that Howard Osborn,* director of security for the Central Intelligence Agency, went to the University of Michigan, where he played football during the epic days of all-American Tom Harmon.

---

*In 1974 Osborn retired from CIA. Columnist Jack Anderson termed him a victim of Watergate. James McCord had been a subordinate of Osborn's, and while McCord was in jail following his arrest at DNC headquarters, his wife was assisted by an employee of Osborn's in burning McCord's files, typewriter ribbons and papers. A memorandum recording this incident was buried in CIA files until early 1974—just before Osborn's retirement.

2 BROWN UNIVERSITY AND WORLD WAR II

EARLIER that spring my Grandfather Hunt and his second wife had been killed in an automobile accident while en route from their winter home at Lake Worth, Florida, to their summer home on Lake Erie. As the accident was reconstructed by state police, their chauffeur fell asleep at the wheel while driving at night and the car hurtled over an embankment. Because my grandfather was survived by his second wife for several minutes, his wealth and property passed from the Hunt family to his wife's heirs.

At the time of his death my grandfather was retired from a long string of political offices in New York State. At one time he had been commissioner of charities and corrections, having under his control such institutions as Sing Sing Prison. While I was myself a prisoner, I was often to reflect on this irony of fate. So neither my father nor his siblings inherited from their father, and I entered Brown University on a half-tuition scholarship, the balance to be paid by my father while my living and miscellaneous expenses were to be met by me out of any undergraduate employment I might be able to find.

At Brown I suffered my first cultural shock. Even the fine public education I had received at Hamburg High School was no match for what had been provided my classmates by such Eastern boarding schools as Andover and Exeter. Nor did I then dress in approved Ivy League fashion. However, within a few weeks I acquired button-down shirts, foulard ties, a Shetland tweed jacket, gray flannel

14

trousers and white bucks. Now I was indistinguishable from the rest of the undergraduates except for those unfortunate townies who brown-bagged it daily up the hill and wore that shameful badge of parochialism, black leather shoes.

I was rushed by a number of fraternities, including my father's, but chose Zeta Psi. For that era I had thought myself a comparatively well-traveled young man, and I had lived in Florida and New York. But for the first time I was exposed to classmates from every state in the Union and parts of Europe besides. Through them I became familiar with and learned to appreciate the society and life-styles of Honolulu, Beverly Hills, San Francisco, Dallas, Milwaukee and Chicago. On weekends when I was not playing a dance job, I journeyed with classmates to nearby Wheaton College, girls' schools in Boston, Smith College in Northampton and Wellesley College, where I had a second cousin from Cleveland.

Freshman placement examinations had established me in the honors program. There were two prime advantages to honors courses: first, no large lecture classes, but small seminars. The second advantage was that none of the seminars was held before noon. Thus I could play a dance job until one or two in the morning, get a full night's sleep, study and prepare myself for the seminars that were to follow for the balance of the day.

Even so, I did not really know how to study. That, plus the combination of social activity and nocturnal employment, produced a not surprising result: At the end of the first semester the dean placed me on academic probation.

Returning to campus, I was given friendly academic counseling by my favorite professor, Dr. Israel J. Kapstein.* "Kappy" apparently discerned qualities in me that he felt worth saving, and in me he had a predisposed pupil, for I admired him tremendously. I knew that Kappy had been a classmate of humorist S. J. Perelman** and that following graduation, they had lived together in New York, where Kappy worked for a time as an editor for Alfred A. Knopf.

But most impressive to me was the fact that Kapstein's novella† had been selected by the Book-of-the-Month Club. Here, obvi-

---

*Alive, well and still my valued friend at this writing.
**Who, with me, gave the principal speeches at Kapstein's retirement banquet.
†*The Song the Summer Evening Sings*.

ously, was a man of parts who transcended the narrow confines of the campus.

Under his aegis my marks improved respectably and I ended my freshman year if not in a blaze of glory, at least without probationary status. Even so, I lost my half-tuition scholarship.

In the winter of my sophomore year I was called upon to recite in Spanish class. I rose and opened my mouth but no words came out; when I finally forced myself to speak, I stammered. That day I consulted the university's (sole) physician, Dr. MacDonald, who invited me to lunch at the University Club. After drinks and lunch, during which no reference was made to my problem, the doctor led me into the library, where there was a pleasant fire. He asked me to pick up a poker and stir the logs, then seat myself. Finally, he told me to cross my legs and handed me the poker.

"Ever do any shooting, Howard?"

"Yes."

"Then sight down it as though it were a rifle."

After I had followed his instructions, MacDonald sat back and allowed himself a slight smile. "You don't have a real problem," he told me.

"I don't?"

"No. Were you ever forced to use your right hand—writing for example?"

"I was discouraged from using my left."

He shrugged. "That explains it. The two sides of your brain are still warring for control—dominance, we call it. You have mixed dominance. Don't worry about it and you'll outgrow the problem." He beckoned to the waiter for brandy refills. "Meanwhile, think through a sentence before you say it. Avoid words that begin with M, N, S or T—until you're calm enough to enunciate quite clearly." He sipped from his snifter glass. "Ever think of taking Ben Brown's public-speaking course?"

I shook my head. "Hell, no."

"Well, you should. In fact, I'll sign you up for it. Not as 'treatment,' of course, but because every educated man should be able to stand up and deliver himself lucidly of whatever opinions he has. Any other problems, Howard?"

"I guess not."

"Come in and see me anytime."

Despite the doctor's invitation I never revisited him, for his sympathetic one-to-one therapy produced the anticipated cure.

In those halcyon prewar days university life was hardly all work and no play. As a change from Smith excursions, one wintry Saturday a group of us drove to New London for a white-tie prom at Connecticut College for Women, perched high above the frozen Thames. Dance over, I lingered overlong in the entrance of my date's dormitory, sheltered from the cruel wind, but also out of sight of my companions, who, they later swore, passed by in their car and then sped back to Providence, under the impression I had made other return arrangements.

Until three I waited for them in the freezing darkness, then began trudging downhill over icy paths and frozen roads. My feet were covered by black silk stockings and thin-soled patent-leather shoes which readily transmitted the frigid temperature to my feet. New London's sole hotel—an old frame structure—offered my only possible refuge, so I pounded the desk bell, roused the night clerk and asked lodging for the night. I remember sitting on the edge of my bed fully clothed until circulation revived. But the overheated room, plus residual alcohol in my blood, so disoriented me that I placed my patent-leather shoes outside my door, European style, then sought surcease under thick down comforters.

Came dawn and I dressed: tails and piqué shirt, Chesterfield and top hat, reached for my shoes and found—nothing. I called the desk to inquire their whereabouts and received a testy reply in the negative. So, setting my teeth, I descended the stairs in my thin silk socks, breakfasted and waited in the hotel lobby for the arrival of the morning bus to Providence. Most of the expectant passengers were honest New England burghers en route church who stared at me as though I were Count Dracula.

Waiting in the warm lobby until the bus was ready to leave, I dashed across the icy sidewalk and swung aboard. As it rumbled over ice-rutted roads, I tried to immunize myself from the scandalized whispers and stares of my fellow pilgrims by dozing until the bus reached Providence.

In my absence Providence had received an additional six inches of snow, and neither trolleys nor taxis were running. This meant a half-mile walk to College Hill, breaking trail as I mushed on numb feet over powder snow and frozen crust. When I finally reached the

warmth and security of my room, I drank several ounces of medici-
nal whiskey and immersed myself in a steaming tub until drowsy.
But even that sovereign procedure failed to ward off a lousy cold that
clung relentlessly to me for the balance of the winter.

In addition to my scholarship I was paid for singing in the chapel
choir and, on Sunday mornings, at a large Episcopal church near
campus. Ever alert for other income supplements, I welcomed a call
for undergraduate extras at a downtown theater performance of
Julius Caesar. When I applied and was accepted, I learned that this
was no ordinary performance of the Shakespearian classic, but a
modern dress antifascist drama staged by Orson Welles' famed
Mercury Theatre players.

Welles rehearsed mob-scene extras Sunday afternoon before the
Monday opening. Crowd noises, I discovered, were orchestrated by
having half the extras mutter, "Hubba-hubba," while the other half
growled, "Rutabaga-rutabaga." This charge seemed elementary
enough. Welles told us that we would be grouped in front of Marc
Antony, during the funeral oration, muttering ominously at the
conspirators, and when M.A. shouted, "Cry 'Havoc!' and let slip the
dogs of war," we were to rush offstage, half to stage right, the rest
stage left, ostensibly to root out Caesar's murderers.

Performance night I arrived at the theater in the required black
raincoat, black hat—and galoshes, for it was a cold and rainy night.
As the drama reached the climactic oration scene, we extras were
positioned across the stage, backs to the audience, staring worship-
fully at a vibrant Marc Antony. And when Marc let slip the dogs of
war, I followed my fellow extras in a frantic stage-left exit.

I was last man offstage, but unfortunately my open galoshes
hooked on a scenery guy wire, and I slammed forward, poleaxed.
My chin struck the stage hard enough to knock me out, and as
unkind undergraduates later described the scene to me, stagehands
had to come onstage and carry me off, to the wild amusement of the
audience.

In 1966 I was perched on a bar stool in Madrid's Castellana-Hilton
taking a prelunch sherry when I became aware of a rotund presence
at my right. Turning, I made out the features of a matured and
bearded Orson Welles.

Instantaneously my mind reverted to my one brush with the
legitimate theater, and I made myself known to the onetime boy

genius of the American radio, stage and cinema. Welles smiled, confessed not recalling our former association, and permitted me to buy him a glass of Manzanilla by way of overdue apology. On parting, we shook hands and maintained a nodding acquaintance whenever we spotted each other in the hotel.

While I was at Brown, one of my classmates, Frank Rollins, played piano in his own dance orchestra. I had played with him occasionally my freshman year, and as classes resumed, he told me of a fabulous summer spent traveling through Europe. He and several others had formed a dance band for one of the transatlantic passenger liners. In addition to free first-class passage, the band members were paid. Rollins said he was planning to take a band to Havana and Nassau over the Christmas and New Year's holidays and asked if I were interested. I was.

For us, at least, the cruise was a huge success, and from that time on my school vacations were spent aboard ship visiting Bermuda, Havana, Nassau, and finally when our junior year classes ended, we boarded the Norwegian liner *Oslofjord* for a summer-long North Cape cruise.

Although the band was billed as coming from Brown, our drummer was a non-U townie, and other musicians were from Amherst, Wesleyan, Williams and Yale. Our first stop was Bermuda, then north to Iceland, whose quiet fjords* we cruised, spending part of a day in the capital, Reykjavik. Two years later I was to find myself part of the naval occupying force that took over control of Iceland from the British. Norway next, and a climb to the top of the North Cape, where I watched the midnight sun and fell in love with a young girl from St. Louis.

Stockholm next, then Copenhagen and France. In Copenhagen we visited the Tuborg and Carlsberg breweries on alternate days, ending the tours in their great dining halls, where we stuffed our pockets with bread, cheese and cold meats and samples of their brew. Through this economy we were able to take our dates nightly to dine in the Tivoli Gardens.

---

*In one, I boarded a German destroyer with a group and, unnoticed, took a number of photographs. In 1942 I sent the films to the Office of Naval Intelligence. Until my photographs, ONI had known little about that particular destroyer class. It was my first venture in espionage.

In Paris, at Harry's New York Bar, we encountered other class-mates just in from Germany with hair-raising tales of persecution of the Jews. In prewar Paris bars you could pay a few pennies for a beer and eat as many hard-boiled eggs as you could hold. For lunch a plate of *haricots verts* and a demicarafe of table wine, then sight-seeing and dinner at a good Paris restaurant.

Early one September morning I was sipping beer and breaking hard-boiled eggs at Harry's New York Bar when I heard Neville Chamberlain announce by radio a state of war between Great Britain and Germany.

Our ship was due to sail in a few days from Boulogne for South-ampton. As the French Army mobilized, hysteria swept Paris. At the Café de la Paix we were offered large sums of money for our return tickets to America. Two of our classmates lived in France and were determined to serve in the French Ambulance Corps, in-spired, no doubt, by Ernest Hemingway, William Faulkner and John Dos Passos. The idea appealed to me and I cabled my father for permission. His response was a telegram that miraculously arrived at my hotel urging me to return, finish my senior year and take my degree. After that, he said, I could do as I pleased. So on the appointed day we entrained from Paris to Boulogne and crossed to Southampton, taking the train to London.

There I stayed in an inexpensive temperance hotel in Russell Square and was witness to the feverish activity of Londoners prepar-ing for the oncoming German blitz. Strolling with my girl through Hyde Park, I saw trenches being dug, sandbag emplacements hastily erected for antiaircraft guns, while barrage balloons drifted in the sky.

The *Oslofjord* crossed to New York in darkened-ship condition. On the return voyage to Oslo it was torpedoed in mid-Atlantic, with all hands lost.

Having seen the great nations of Europe marshal themselves for the war, I was determined to become part of it. In June, 1940, I graduated on the day France capitulated, and although I had been accepted as a playwriting student at Yale Drama School, I set about finding a way to prepare myself for the war my father told me he was certain would involve the United States. Six weeks later I enlisted in the United States Naval Reserve, an applicant for the V-7 program. After qualifying on the battleship *New York* during a cruise to

Guantánamo Bay, Cuba, I entered the United States Naval Academy at Annapolis as a midshipman in February, 1941.

Because most of us had college degrees, we were given an accelerated program of seamanship, navigation and gunnery: average nightly reading four hundred pages. About a third of our Reserve midshipman class failed to qualify, but the passage of time had alleviated my earlier difficulties with mathematics, and I graduated somewhere toward the center of my class.

One outstanding midshipman had completed only two years at Harvard: Morton B. "Tony" Jackson, who graduated third in our class, became a Navy pilot during the war and was discharged a full commander. He is now a successful lawyer in Beverly Hills, California, and figured early in my Watergate involvement.

Although I had requested assignment aboard a capital ship of the Pacific fleet, I was assigned to destroyers, Atlantic. Most of my classmates envied me but I was displeased. I had been thinking seriously of marrying a Smith freshman, but knew that destroyer duty, based at Norfolk as was my ship, was incompatible with married life.

With regard to the discipline I learned at the Naval Academy, I remember very clearly the three possible answers accorded a midshipman or a junior naval officer: Yes, sir; No, sir; or No excuse, sir. These replies formed part of the indoctrination that led to unquestioning obedience to orders; otherwise, no naval unit could function effectively in combat. My indoctrination was thorough and lasting.

My destroyer was the *Mayo* (DD422). I boarded her at Charleston, South Carolina, during final outfitting, and our shakedown cruise under Captain Campbell Dallas Emory took us north toward Boston. We went through the Cape Cod Canal at such a high rate of speed that the canal management complained of subsequent silting. It was a good ship, but unfortunately designed for service in the Pacific Ocean. Another 400 tons of ballast had to be added to the keel to prevent capsizing in the rougher North Atlantic waters. I was assistant first lieutenant on the *Mayo* and my battle station was in the range finder at the topmost part of the ship.

During the summer of 1941 German U-boats were operating with appalling success along the convoy routes between Britain and the United States. Covertly, our destroyer squadron was ordered to meet incoming convoys at a mid-ocean meeting point (MOMP) and escort them into American waters. This we did a few times before being ordered to stand by in Casco Bay off Portland, Maine. Most of us assumed we would be there for a week, so I went ashore with a liberty party and telephoned my fiancée at Smith. She was to come immediately to Portland, where, I hoped, we could be married before the squadron had to leave. I had barely completed the call when, through the hotel page system, I heard an order that all officers and men of the *Mayo* should return to ship immediately. Before doing so, I telephoned Smith again and canceled wedding plans. For many months I was not to have a similar opportunity.

Sailing under sealed orders, we took a course north and east and at a mid-ocean meeting point in the eastern Atlantic saw a new British battleship hull down on the horizon. Our squadron escorted HMS *Prince of Wales* to Little Placentia Bay off Argentia, Newfoundland. There, while we stood guard duty, the Atlantic Charter Conference was held. From fifty yards away we watched the historic morning church services, saw President Roosevelt and his staff of senior military officials and a tall civilian adviser named Averell Harriman. Later, as the conference ended, Winston Churchill boarded a captain's gig and made a tour of the harbor waving to each American ship and displaying his famous V-for-Victory sign.

We escorted the *Prince of Wales* back to mid-Atlantic, where we were relieved by British escort destroyers and corvettes. From there we picked up an eastbound convoy, wallowing toward Britain's western approaches at four or five knots. Earlier we had escorted Marine troop ships to Iceland and off-loaded them to take over the island in the hope of keeping it out of German hands. Several old British battleships were stationed in Iceland's long, deep fjords, among them *Hood*. We took delight in renaming the British vessels HMS *Vanquished*, HMS *Conquered*, HMS *Vainglory*, the *Recreant* and so forth. There for a few days I attended a British-run school for antisubmarine detection, learning sonar ranging and other aspects of the new sonar art.

Over the next few months we made many escort trips back and forth across the North Atlantic. Winter approached, weather worsened and from time to time there would be antisubmarine alarms and calls to general quarters. One night a U-boat wolf pack attacked our convoy sinking several cargo ships and badly damaging a sister destroyer, the USS *Kearney*, which we helped shepherd back to Iceland. At least once a week we would come across empty rafts from sunken merchant vessels and occasionally a German sailor's corpse. These we would hoist aboard and search for documents before returning "Herman the German" to the deep.

By now the USS *Reuben James* had been sunk, and with the attack on the *Kearney*, the United States was engaged in a full-scale war in the North Atlantic, although only those directly involved were aware of it. I resented Roosevelt's secret and undeclared war in the North Atlantic but I was in awe of Presidential power and came to believe that in the North Atlantic at least, given Britain's desperate plight, the end probably justified the means. This philosophical question was put to me during my televised appearance before the Ervin committee in September, 1973. Too tired to cite the Roosevelt precedent of thirty-odd years ago, I settled for a soft demurrer which seemed to appease my questioner.

One night in early December while we were at sea a general-quarters Klaxon sounded. Pulling on my life jacket, I stepped into bedroom slippers, then bolted for my battle station. The rungs of the turret ladder I had to climb were ice-coated, as was the deck below. The ship rolled wildly, and my body swung like a pendulum. Reaching for the next rung, I missed and fell to the ice-covered deck below. The fall caused groin injuries which hospitalized me at Boston Naval Hospital. There I was operated on and underwent a long convalescence. I had been at sea at the time of Pearl Harbor, and now I was out of action, much to my disgust. At Pearl Harbor and at Wake Island I had lost a lot of Academy classmates, and Boston Hospital was filling with our wounded. My class was automatically promoted from ensign to lieutenant junior grade, but because I was not fit for full duty, I was surveyed by a medical board and offered two alternatives: shore duty as a supply officer or an honorable medical discharge. I chose the latter.

While the paperwork was under way, I joined my parents at their new home in Albany, where my father was lobbyist for the insurance industry at the State Capitol. In a few weeks I wrote my first novel, *East of Farewell*, and sent it to Knopf, the publishing house that once had employed my mentor, Dr. Kapstein. My book, a fictionalized account of convoy duty in the North Atlantic, was the first book published about World War II by an American who had taken part in the war. The novel was a satisfying critical success, but sales were disappointing.

Soon after its publication I received a phone call from Louis de Rochemont, producer of the news film, *The March of Time*. A former Navy man himself, De Rochemont hired me at a then substantial salary to help turn out his monthly documentaries and to work on Navy training films. So I moved to Manhattan and took a comfortable apartment just off Park Avenue on Murray Hill. I soon became familiar with 21, the Copacabana, Le Ruban Bleu, and other fashionable night spots. On weekends my apartment was the focus for parties involving my uniformed classmates and their girls. I was enjoying my job and life as a Manhattan bachelor, but as casualty lists grew, I became obsessed with the desire to somehow return to action.

The opportunity evolved from a budgetary dispute between De Rochemont and the parent corporation, Time Inc. Predictably, De Rochemont lost and summoned me to his office. He had been invited by Darryl Zanuck to join him in Hollywood as a producer. Would I go with him?

Having always viewed De Rochemont as charming and voluble but unreliable, I declined, a decision which, in retrospect, was probably wrong.

At De Rochemont's suggestion, I consulted Dan Longwell at *Life* magazine and was named South Pacific war correspondent, to replace novelist John Hersey, already famous for his book *Into the Valley*.

Uniformed by Abercrombie & Fitch, I flew to San Francisco, where I had a brief reunion with Tony Jackson, who had completed flight training as a naval aviator. I had hoped to fly to Honolulu, but instead the Navy put me aboard a slow cargo vessel loaded with cement destined to help repair bomb damage at Pearl Harbor. Aside from the Merchant Marine crew, there were only half a dozen civilian passengers, one a diamond merchant from Honolulu who had been in New York at the time of the Japanese attack. From San Francisco to Honolulu the voyage lasted fourteen days.

On several occasions the crew staged a belowdecks entertainment which we were permitted to watch through the cargo hatch. The high point of these shows was a dance by several young homosexuals in hula skirts to the accompaniment of loud applause. I was shocked and later reflected on this when I observed the prevalence of homosexuality in prison.

At Honolulu I took half of a duplex at the Halekulani on Waikiki Beach. The duplex was divided vertically by sliding doors, and occasionally I could hear through the partition the sound of a reed instrument. But it was not until I took an early-morning stroll that I met my neighbor: a dark-haired, taciturn man whom I recognized at once as band leader and clarinetist Artie Shaw. Now a Navy chief petty officer, Shaw led a dance orchestra that played every afternoon not far from the Halekulani. It was an all-star band, most of whose members resented Shaw's higher rating and the fact that he was allowed to live in private quarters.

Once rapport was established between us, Shaw and I pooled our resources: He had a station wagon and I had access to liquor from the officers' mess at Pearl Harbor. Daily, long lines of girls formed outside the Halekulani, hoping for a glimpse of Shaw. From among them we selected appropriate nightly companions and enjoyed life to the full until I was ordered to board a bomber bound for the South Pacific.

In Nouméa, New Caledonia, I reported to Admiral William "Bull" Halsey, chief of naval forces in the South Pacific, and his chief of staff, Miles Browning, the legendary hero at the decisive battle of Midway for his direction of the Navy's carrier fighter. The corps of war correspondents attached to Halsey's headquarters averaged between thirty and forty men, most of whom possessed slim journalistic skills and a burning desire to avoid being drafted. They ate exceedingly well at Halsey's mess, and their laundry was done aboard the aircraft carrier *Saratoga*, then in port. In Nouméa I was bored and disgruntled, anxious to join the fighting at least as an observer, and finally my pleas were answered. I was put aboard a cargo ship heading for a forward base in the New Hebrides. Facilities were cramped, so a young Navy lieutenant generously shared his cabin with me. His father was then governor of Georgia, a post my roommate would one day occupy before going on to Washington as Senator Herman Talmadge. (During my two-day grilling by the Ervin committee thirty years later, I often wondered if Senator Talmadge remembered our voyage together.)

In the New Hebrides the rainy season had set in. The naval base was a sea of mud, and water often rose to the level of our cots, carrying away shoes, boots and baggage. Soon space was found for me aboard a Marine-piloted C-47, and I landed at Guadalcanal's Henderson Field in the wake of a Japanese bombing attack. A few hardy war correspondents were on Guadalcanal, among them Dick Tregaskis, and we lived in tents not far from that of Admiral Marc Mitscher, who was in charge of operations.

Every night a Japanese recon plane, "Washboard Charlie," flew over our area dropping nuisance bombs. This meant hasty abandonment of cots for water-filled slit trenches and general wonderment over why our night fighters were unable to shoot down so predictable a target.

I was allowed to fly surface-level weather missions up "The Slot" to Bougainville and back aboard unarmed Lockheed Hudsons piloted by New Zealanders. I flew on rescue missions conducted by the Marine "Black Cat" Squadron, whose aircraft were Catalina amphibian bombers painted dull black to avoid visual detection.

On a typical mission we would climb to ten to twelve thousand feet, cut off the engines and glide down to a prearranged point off one of the Solomon Islands. There, if we were lucky, an Australian intelligence officer, a "coast watcher," would paddle out in a rubber raft and tell us how many passengers to expect. Usually we had no more than half a dozen missionaries: nuns and priests, mostly of French origin. But one night a coast watcher pressed on us some thirty evacuees, most of them Chinese copra workers who had been hiding from the Japanese since the Solomons' occupation. Their children came with them, of course, and the pilot decided not to risk taking off overloaded as the amphibian was. Instead he let the big plane drift seaward and, when we were nearly out of sight of the island, started the twin engines and we taxied slowly and bumpily back to Guadalcanal.

From Henderson Field I flew dive-bombing and torpedo-bombing missions with VTB143, often serving as rear cockpit gunner, an action strictly against the Geneva Convention. However, there was simply no other way to go. Among those officers with whom I flew was Lieutenant George Gay, the lone survivor of Torpedo Eight, which was wiped out at the Battle of Midway.

Thanks to pilot friends, I learned to fly both land and sea planes and in a small informal ceremony was given Navy Wings by Admiral Marc Mitscher,* whose tent was adjacent to mine.

I spent a couple of weeks aboard the light cruiser *St. Louis*, which, along with the *Helena* and *Louisville*, sailed nightly up The Slot to bombard Japanese shore positions. A few nights after I had left the *St. Louis*, the cruisers, making their predictable run, were attacked by Japanese destroyers. It was on this occasion that Jack Kennedy's fast PT boat was run down by a slower Japanese destroyer.

The PT-boat squadron was based at Tulagi, across Iron Bottom Bay from Guadalcanal, and its executive officer had been a classmate of mine at Brown. The skipper was Walter Kohler,** and we arranged a friendly accommodation through which I would occasionally fly bags of Seabee ice cubes to Tulagi and bring back a five-gallon tin of 200-proof torpedo alcohol together with a few cans of grapefruit juice.

So popular were these "torpedo cocktails" that from time to time some of us, deep in sleep, would be blissfully unaware of Washboard Charlie's nightly call.

Hitherto in the South Pacific I had suffered only dengue fever, perhaps the most painful illness I had ever undergone. On Guadalcanal mosquitoes seemed to avoid me—perhaps the result of protective body odor. In any case, while shaving one morning, I became aware that an anopheles mosquito had settled on my left hand. Since it was the one mosquito bite I recall, it must have been the one that gave me tertian malaria. I felt no effects because all of us were taking Atabrine, the malaria suppressant which colored our skin and eyeballs a hideous yellow. But the torpedo-bombing squadron to which I had attached myself was ready for rest and recreation in Australia, and I was invited to accompany them. At this point our staple diet on Guadalcanal consisted of cornflakes and powdered milk, flapjacks and molasses. For dessert or to accompany us while flying we had a caked mass of Christmas sugar candy which had to be chipped apart with a hatchet to reduce it to pocket-size proportions.

Two C-47's were to fly the squadron to Sydney, Australia, and my

---

*As skipper of the *Hornet*, Mitscher had carried Doolittle's Tokyo Raiders and later went on to lead Task Force Fifty-eight, one of the most awesome assemblages of naval power the world has ever seen.
**Later governor of Wisconsin.

name appeared with those men who were to fly in the second aircraft. Just before takeoff, however, Squadron Commander F. L. Ashworth invited me to join him in the first echelon. We flew at night, blacked out, and maintaining radio silence from Guadalcanal to Sydney, where we landed early in the morning. It was bitter cold in Sydney, and most of us were wearing khaki shorts, combat boots and short-sleeved shirts. An Australian Red Cross bus picked us up and deposited us at our downtown hotel, where we unpacked our few belongings, shaved and made a beeline for the dining room. There, while breakfasting on steak, eggs and beer, we learned that our companions would never join us: The second C-47, on which I was to have flown, barely cleared the end of Henderson before plunging into the water, killing all aboard, including Commander Weldon L. Hamilton, commander of Carrier Group 11. The tragedy dampened our spirits, and it was several days before we were able to begin to enjoy the pleasures of man-short wartime Sydney.

As required, I reported to the Sydney branch of General MacArthur's headquarters, where neatly uniformed press-relations officers stared at me with horror. I was yellow, unkempt and out of uniform. A tailor quickly made me proper uniforms, and I decided to let my system rid itself of yellow pigmentation by stopping daily Atabrine pills. No sooner had I done so than I began suffering violent chills and fever.

I moved into a furnished apartment, met an Australian Red Cross girl and was determined not to let malaria interfere with the diversions of Sydney. So when chills began, I got under the shower and turned on the hot water. When fever later struck, I would return to the shower, this time turning on the cold water, and so through this field expedient was able to enjoy life to the full.

Among the local celebrities was Australian war photographer George Silk, whom I was instrumental in hiring for *Life* magazine. Other correspondents I knew well were the late George Moorad, killed during the war, and Martin Agronsky, who survived to become a TV news analyst.

Because I had served my allotted span in the South Pacific, and also because my dispatches, owing to severe censorship, were next to useless, *Life* sent a replacement to Sydney and I was told to return to New York. MacArthur's headquarters in Brisbane, however, controlled stateside transportation, and I was ordered to Brisbane.

There I reported to MacArthur's press-relations officers, of whom I particularly remember "Fumbling Phil" LaFollette. I pointed out to Major LaFollette that I was not accredited to the Army in the Southwest Pacific, but only to the Navy in the South Pacific. Even so, said LaFollette, I was to report for the day's press briefing, at which General MacArthur would appear; otherwise it might be very difficult to find me homeward-bound transportation.

The briefing was farcical: We were handed mimeographed press releases, the colonel in charge made a few remarks, and General MacArthur entered the room. Having glanced at the press handout, I rose and made so bold as to ask General MacArthur a question. Correspondents and officers alike glared at me. MacArthur eyed me as though I were a representative of some alien race, shook his head and stalked offstage. Major LaFollette and his superior took me to task for lese majesty while the other correspondents dashed for the cable room to file their unaltered press handouts.

Within a day or so I was homeward bound aboard a B-24 Liberator, which, after refueling at Hickam Field, Hawaii, lost an engine while we were airborne and made the rest of the trip to the California coast in a long flat glide.

In New York I showed Dan Longwell my uncensored dispatches, and though he admired their quality, he pointed out that they were no longer timely. It was suggested that I work on *Fortune* for a while, since that magazine was putting out a special Pacific War issue.

During the summer of 1943 I was able to return to my former apartment, and after working all day at *Fortune*, I began typing my second novel, *Limit of Darkness*, a fictionalized account of life and death at Henderson Field. After Random House agreed to publish the book, I decided, as I had once before, that I did not want to live as a civilian safe in the United States while the war went on abroad. Accordingly, I visited the recruiting offices of the Royal Canadian Air Force at the Waldorf Astoria. The recruiting officers encouraged me, particularly because I had already mastered navigation in the Navy. It was their suggestion that I become a bombardier-navigator, to which I readily agreed. This interview took place on a Friday afternoon, and I was told to return Monday morning to fill out the final forms. On Monday when I returned, I was startled to see furniture being moved out of the RCAF offices. The recruiting officer was gone, but a secretary told me that a bilateral treaty between the United States and Canada had just gone into effect: No longer would the two countries accept each other's nationals in their armed service.

Dejectedly, I made my way to Grand Central Station and enlisted as a private in the Army Air Force.

After basic training at Fort Dix and Miami Beach, I qualified for Officer Candidate School and was commissioned, with none other than Navy Lieutenant George Gay pinning on my second lieutenant's bars. After being commissioned the second time, I was sent to the Air Force Intelligence School at Orlando, Florida, where, after two weeks as a student, I was placed on the faculty.

Life at the Orlando air base was pleasant and easy: In the morning I read intelligence reports and briefed the commanding general. For the rest of the day, in effect, my time was my own. There was a fine officers' club on the shores of the lake, and I was allowed to take a private apartment in town.

Among other officers at the base was a former dean at Brown, with whom I had had several run-ins. He was a humorless disciplinarian, furious at some of my undergraduate pranks, and now a major at Orlando. Meanwhile, I had fallen in love with the stepdaughter of a senior officer on the base. By chance, the young lady was a Smith classmate of my former fiancée and had heard of me beforehand.

One night as I was walking toward the outdoor dance floor with my date, the dean-major appeared in the surrounding bushes and said, "Oh, there you are, Hunt. With one of your whores, I suppose."

Without hesitating, I punched his jaw and he dropped back into the barberries. Wide-eyed, my date said, "Who, in God's name, is he?"

"A Harvard fairy," I told her, for the dean had gone to Harvard Law. I never again saw him around the base and remained dry-eyed when, years later, the alumni magazine announced his death. The dean was not only a sour old bachelor, but worse, a miserable horse's ass.

Over the summer we had an idyllic romance, but when she

returned to Northampton in September, it ended. Again I was at loose ends.

I applied for overseas duty, but was refused on the grounds that I had already served overseas twice, the Air Force counting my South Pacific tour as war correspondent as my second tour.

Through the base grapevine I heard about the presence on the base of several officers who were screening candidates for a hush-hush organization. Of it nothing was known, although I heard the name of General "Wild Bill" Donovan mentioned. A little more digging, and I learned the recruiters came from an all-volunteer outfit that specialized in unorthodox, behind-the-lines warfare. The thought appealed to me, and I telephoned my father to explain the situation and enlist his aid in making contact with General Donovan.

A day or so later I was in Washington, talking with General Donovan, who by now I knew to be the head of the Office of Strategic Services. Donovan was cordial, remembered me as a child and spoke highly of my father. He said that although he would like to have me with his organization, it was a select, elite force, and I must qualify for it as any other candidate. I told him I wouldn't have it any other way, and he said he would have me transferred, at least temporarily, to OSS. By the time I returned to Orlando, the base adjutant was looking for me agitatedly. Teletype orders had arrived for me and I was to return immediately to Washington.

Thus began my long association with the clandestine services of the United States.

3 OSS DETACHMENT 202 (CHINA)

PROVISIONALLY assigned to the Office of Strategic Services, I took a small apartment at the Wardman-Park Hotel, where I made myself comfortable in wartime Washington. I was given OSS physical examinations and intelligence tests, then ordered to report early one Sunday morning to a location beside the old Christian Heurich brewery, not far from OSS headquarters itself. With eleven other officers I was loaded aboard a personnel carrier and the tarpaulin sides were lowered, adding a touch of mystery to the proceedings. An hour later the truck stopped, and we climbed out to find ourselves in the yard of a small white farmhouse, surrounded by what seemed to be acres of boxwood hedge. This was Area E—for evaluation—and the staff comprised several civilians who were either psychologists or psychiatrists. Each candidate was assigned a room in the farmhouse, after which we enjoyed an excellent Sunday dinner. Staff members were assigned to each table on a rotational basis, permitting them to scrutinize us in our more relaxed moments. Toward midafternoon the head of Area E addressed us, telling us that for a week we would be given intensive examinations and tests to determine our suitability for unorthodox warfare. He added that among us was one officer who was already a member of OSS—a plant, in other words. We were cautioned to use only our aliases and never to reveal our true identities either to our fellow candidates or to any member of the staff. My alias was simply

"William," an easy name to remember, for it had been the name of my Grandfather Totterdale and my brother who had died only a few days after his birth.

After dinner that night we were taken to the farmhouse basement and shown a simulated hotel room. On the bed were miscellaneous items, one of which I remember was a railway ticket between Vienna and Belgrade, Yugoslavia. There was money of different nations and in different denominations. There were some keys, part of an address book, clothing in a closet and an overturned chair. The impression given by the room was that a prior inhabitant had emptied his pockets on the bed and exited hastily, overturning the chair.

We were told that each of us would be allowed to examine the contents of the room for three minutes, after which we were to go to another room and write down our inferences from the circumstantial evidence we had seen. In turn, we entered the room, which was semidarkened, glanced around it, examined the closet and bureau drawers, catalogued the items on the bed and exited to write a series of wildly varying conclusions.

Mine suggested that a man, possibly a foreign agent, who had been traveling from Belgrade to Vienna, had reached the sanctuary of the hotel room, where he had begun to divest himself of all pocket litter. Interrupted by a sound at the window, he had fled. There were a number of inconsistencies in the story but I felt it was the best I could do in the allotted three minutes. After all papers were turned in to the staff and a suitable interval passed, we were told that there was no proper answer, that the scene had built-in inconsistencies in order to confuse us. What was really wanted was a test of our powers of observation—principally, how many of the items on the bed had we been able to remember and weave into our conclusions?

This was an early brush with the deviousness of clandestine work, and I never forgot it.

Next day we ran an obstacle course similar to those I had encountered in the Air Force, then we were taken down to a meandering creek. It was about seven feet wide and partly frozen over, seemingly about a foot deep. A staff member told us to devise a means of crossing the stream, which we were to consider as a bottomless chasm. The use of wood was not permitted. Having established the rules, he dropped a length of rope in front of us and sat down against a tree a few yards away. Among our number was Navy Lieutenant

Jay Rutherfurd, a former Princeton and Golden Gloves boxer. A massive man, Jay was eyeing the chasm as though considering a possible leap. I picked up the rope and suggested that Jay lift me on his shoulders so I could tie the rope around an overhanging branch. This done, we were able to swing across the stream—chasm—and land safely on the other side with several feet to spare.

The purpose of this test, I was to learn, was not to appraise our inventive faculties, but rather to determine who among us would take the initiative leading toward group success.

On another occasion we were taken to the empty barn. In it were two surly-looking Army privates—at least they wore Army fatigues—and a pile of poles about as thick as broomsticks. Holes had been drilled through some of the poles, and the staff man told us that properly assembled, the poles would make a miniature house frame. We were to come into the barn individually, examine the poles and decide what had to be done. Then without touching the poles ourselves, we were to instruct the privates how to assemble the house. The time limit for the exercise was five minutes.

When my turn came, I entered the barn and found the two privates sitting dejectedly on the floor, not even looking up when I came in. I took a look at the poles and told the men to lay certain of them in a rectangle and to raise uprights at the corners. With maddening slowness the privates got to their feet and shuffled about their work. Often I had to repeat instructions and countermand independent actions they seemed to be taking. The uprights finally were raised when one of the men stumbled against the frame and down it came. This they regarded as a great joke. I declined to join in the levity and told them to reassemble the structure. One of the privates said he had forgotten how, so obligingly I repeated my earlier instructions. One of them muttered that he hated all officers. I said that as a class officers were not my favorite people and suggested strongly that he get about his work.

By now four of the five minutes had vanished. And as one of the men was placing the fourth upright, he seemed overcome by a better idea. Instead of fitting it into the hole, he broke the pole across his knee, laughing hysterically. The buzzer sounded and the door at the far end opened. I filed out and found a grinning staff supervisor, who was shortly joined by the two truculent "privates." From him I learned that the test's purpose had not been to deter-

mine our command abilities, but rather to evaluate our capacity to
remain cool under trying and provocative circumstances. In a year's
operation, I was told, no one had managed to foil the two privates
and erect the structure. The privates, of course, were staff
psychologists. Jay Rutherfurd followed me, and after a couple of
minutes the barn door burst open and two privates ran off, pursued
by a yelling Rutherfurd brandishing a pole. It took our combined
efforts to convince Jay that the "privates" were merely following
instructions, but he was hardly mollified.

Finally Friday night came and with it a fine steak dinner. Afterward we pushed together the dining-room tables, and a bar was
fashioned in one corner of the room. Cases of liquor were brought in
and a staff member volunteered as bartender for the night. There
was nothing further to do, we were told, and all of us were to return
to Washington in the morning. This announcement was greeted
with glee and gratitude and there was a general rush for the bar.

All of us had been denied alcohol for at least a week, and I decided
to pace myself, not wanting a hangover when I returned to Washington in the morning. So after two highballs I nursed an empty glass
and reflected on the efficiency of the farmhouse heating unit, for the
dining room was suddenly filled with superheated air. I began
feeling groggy and had decided to turn in when the chief of Area E
appeared and announced that he had forgotten one little item: Our
final task was to carry on a debate. Half of us were to debate the
negative and the other half the affirmative of the proposition: President Roosevelt had no right to get us into this war.

Unobtrusively, I went to a bathroom, filled the basin with ice cold
water and submerged my face in it. The shock cleared my brain and I
returned to the room to find that I had been assigned to the negative
team, although I would have preferred the affirmative.

As my team began to apportion sections of the debate, it became
apparent that the alcohol was interfering with my teammates' ability
not only to speak articulately but also to reason. The ensuing debate
was ludicrous; only a few of us were sober enough to stay on our feet
and argue points back and forth.

While we were debating, I noticed that the cases of liquor were
hastily removed and the bar closed down. The debate, like so many
other OSS tests, ended in utter confusion, for the evening had
proceeded entirely according to prior plan. Some of the instructors

had been able to worm true names from drunken candidates, and the behavior of all of us following our alcoholic indulgence was noted in detail.

Next morning, before leaving, we were told to write on a small slip of paper the name of the candidate believed to be the OSS penetration of the group. After we turned in the slips, it was announced to my astonishment that the consensus favored me. However, I interpreted this vote as a tribute to my talents that were later to be more fully realized in CIA. We were driven back to Washington in a sealed truck and dropped off at the brewery. We said good-bye among ourselves, and of the dozen who spent that week with me at Area E, I was to see only three again. Eight of our group had been eliminated from further processing.

A few days later General Donovan summoned me to his office. There he confirmed that I had been accepted for duty in OSS and was henceforth relieved of further Air Force duties. He asked me which combat theater I wanted to go to, remarking that although the war in Europe was winding down, there was a need for personnel in the Far East. He told me that already a number of OSS teams had been withdrawn from Europe for duty in the Far East and seemed to imply that the China-Burma-India theater would be the place for me. I told him that I would be glad to go wherever the need was greatest, and Donovan suggested China. China was remote but romantic, so I agreed. Donovan said that a training class would be starting in a few weeks, and in the meantime he would like me to work around his office. He told me that each day his office prepared for President Roosevelt a situation report compiled from intelligence material gathered by OSS around the world. After editing, the reports were typed on a special typewriter with "Presidential" size type and sent by messenger to Grace Tully, Roosevelt's confidential secretary. It was these daily reports that Donovan wanted me to examine before he signed the note of transmittal. So for a couple of weeks I was a quasi-editor of the first national intelligence summary ever compiled and sent to a U.S. President.

Many of the uniformed officers around OSS headquarters had been attorneys in private life. Among those I came to know were Navy Lieutenant James Donovan, who was later to defend GRU Colonel Rudolf Abel, the Soviet spy, and who was instrumental in exchanging him for U-2 pilot Gary Powers. Another was Lawrence Houston, who was to become CIA's first general counsel.

After a couple of weeks at headquarters I was ordered to the West Coast with Lieutenant Ed Welch. We traveled to Los Angeles on the Super Chief and reported to the OSS office at Balboa. Among our training group were veterans of partisan warfare in France, Italy, Scandinavia and Yugoslavia. Two had even served in Greece. Now all of us were bound for China.

First, though, a rugged six weeks faced us on Catalina Island.

A speedboat took us across the channel and pulled into White's Cove, where we filed into buildings once occupied by a boys' school. The property belonged to William Wrigley, who had lent it to OSS for the duration of the war. Ed Welch and I roomed together, and he, having served previously with OSS in France, knew many of our comrades. Among them were Jack Singlaub, now an Army general, and Walt Kuzmuk, a CIA case officer.

Each morning before dawn we were rousted for calisthenics on a small parade ground. There the commanding officer, a young colonel, read the orders of the day, and we repaired to a dining hall for a fine breakfast. I was told that the chefs formerly had worked in the Waldorf Astoria and that General Donovan drew double ration money for every man in OSS. As a result, our food was superb.

Among disciplines we were taught were unarmed combat, knife and bayonet fighting, dacoit strangulation, rapid fire with handguns, the operation of Japanese mortars, machine guns, rifles and pistols; lock picking, flaps and seals, cryptography, Morse code, mountain climbing, night amphibious operations, bridge and general demolitions, the use of dynamite and plastic C-3, industrial sabotage, vehicular sabotage, limpet mines and field expedients for weapons and poison.

During the latter half of the course we were turned loose in groups of four on the island. This was a survival problem, before which we were weighed to check our weight loss. We were given no food, a few matches and an old Springfield rifle with a clip of shells.

Previously we had been given instructions in archery and laying animal snares. We had also been advised that large abalones were to be found below the low-tide mark on the rocks just off the beach. Goats ran wild over the entire island. With these sources of food, our instructor said, none of us should lose anything like the allowable ten-pound limit.

When it came my group's turn to return to nature, we found the instructors had spooked most of the goats into distant hills. However, a Marine Raider officer was able to bag one goat, but while we were climbing the face of a cliff to recover it, two instructors carried it off. So we dove for abalone, prying them off the rocks with hunting knives and cutting our hands in the process. These we baked in front of an open fire, around which we huddled at night, cold and miserable. For two nights it rained, but we kept the fire going and the abalones baking. We were unable to locate any of the edible tubers previously recommended to us by our instructor, and the abalones were so tough as to be nearly inedible, but we survived the ordeal, none of us losing more than five pounds of body weight.

Next we were divided into teams, issued civilian clothing and told to get into Mexico with a suitcase radio and transmit a coded message back to Catalina headquarters. Except for a five-dollar bill issued us, that was it. No identification or documents of any kind.

Getting into Mexico was no problem, none of the Mexican immigration guards looking twice at the motley groups coming across the border with no baggage other than a black fiber (radio) suitcase. We rented a room in a wretched Tijuana hotel, plugged the transmitter into room current, stood the bedspring by the window and sent an impolite message to Catalina. That done, the grittier problem remained: how to return to the United States without being arrested.

Documentation was the foremost need, and money would be useful. We decided to make a combined effort. Accordingly, each of us placed collect phone calls to reliable friends in the United States and asked them to cable ten dollars to the name under which we had registered at the hotel. Some friends were more responsive than others, and it was just as well, for as each man's cable arrived, he checked out of the hotel and started across the border into the United States. Getting the radio back proved less of a problem than we had anticipated. The customs inspector opened the black fiber case and passed our radioman on; the inspector had seen those black cases before.

Before reporting back to Catalina, I called on the mother and sister of Tony Jackson in Los Angeles, learning that my Naval Academy classmate was now flying multiengine patrol bombers in the Pacific, and as I took the coastal bus down to Newport Beach, I wondered if I might see him in China or on some Pacific island.

Earlier trainees for the European Theater had taken instruction at the Congressional Country Club outside Washington. From there trainees had been dispatched into the Baltimore area, rather than across the Mexican border, their goal employment in a defense plant and theft of a classified document or blueprint. The Martin Aircraft Company was the principal target, and most of the trainees were able to get brief jobs on the bomber assembly line and access to a page or more of a classified aircraft drawing.

Although many of my fellow Catalina trainees decided to take a transport from the West Coast to Calcutta, India, Ed Welch and I were ordered back to Washington. He left almost at once for Kunming, while I was given a few days' leave to see my parents in Albany and put my affairs in order.

From New York an Air Transport Command plane took me to Newfoundland, the Azores and Dakar, then east across the Mediterranean littoral to Karachi, where we were billeted in the vast hangar that once had housed the German dirigible *Hindenburg*.

At Calcutta I was dumped off at Dum-Dum Airport after dark. Finding transport to the OSS Calcutta office took another couple of hours, and when I arrived, an office party was in full swing. Staff officers and secretaries were dancing, drinking and having an unfettered time. Into this scene of general merriment trudged the dirty, unshaved, tired intruder, looking for a bed. No attention was paid me: I was only a second lieutenant and a transient officer besides.

Finally the billeting officer emerged from an upstairs room and became coherent enough to supply an address where, he said, I would lodge with other transient officers. It wasn't easy to find a taxi along Chowringhee at midnight, but eventually I got to the safehouse and found a bed.

Early in the morning I was awakened by the sound of sitar music from the house next door, blended with the wails of a muezzin from a nearby minaret. Chickens were kept next door, and the stench of their guano filled my hot room. I stumbled down to breakfast and settled for hot coffee, Indian bread and an egg fried in sour-smelling *ghee*. Soon other officers descended, and I was made to feel more welcome.

Among those waiting for onward transportation at our safehouse was a hunch-backed Indian, a so-called Morale Operations (psychological warfare) expert who had received a certain amount of education in the United States, toward which he felt undying hatred. He also loathed anything capitalistic or bourgeois, and during the following days we engaged in a number of sharp exchanges.

Poking around an unused room while scrounging for another mattress, I came across a pile of papers. I saw secret and top-secret classification stamps on them and began going through them to determine what they might be.

They were lists of OSS agents in Burma, India and China. I put them in my musette bag and caught a taxi for OSS headquarters downtown, where I turned them over to the detachment's commanding officer. During the ensuing investigation, it developed that our Indian companion had taken the papers from the downtown office without authorization. But because he was a civilian as well as a foreign national, he received no more punishment than the loss of a few days' pay and an administrative rebuke in his record. Worse, he was allowed to continue living with us at the safehouse.

One night when we Western officers had been drinking at the safehouse, the Indian made the mistake of upbraiding us for being a) white, b) officers, and c) bourgeois capitalists. In return we threatened to kill him and toss his body into the Hooghly River if he uttered another sound. The next day he attempted to justify his outlook by remarking to me that whereas in the West everyone sat on chairs, in his country most people sat on carpets. This was the basic difference between our two societies, he said, and the West must always bear this in mind.

To relieve the monotony of waiting for passage over The Hump to Kunming, we joined the Calcutta Swimming Club and dined at Firpo's and the Great Eastern Hotel. Then a cholera plague swept Calcutta and downtown eating establishments were placed off limits. So it was with a sense of relief that I boarded a C-47 for the dangerous high-altitude flight across the Himalayas into China.

Ed Welch was waiting for me at Kunming Airport and took me to the OSS compound within which everyone lived and worked. He showed me to the BOQ, after which we went to downtown Kunming for my first authentic Chinese meal. This was topped off, on the way back to Detachment 202's compound, with a bottle of "Tiger Jack's

Home Brew." This pestilential local product was guaranteed to produce immediate diarrhea, which in my case it did. A local mulberry wine produced the same effect, but there was nothing else to drink.

The commanding officer of Detachment 202 was Colonel Dick Heppner. A Princeton alumnus, Heppner was also a peacetime member of General Donovan's law firm. In the field heading a team was Captain Walter Mansfield, also a Donovan law firm alumnus, and after the war a New York judge.

I began the parachute-instruction course and completed the required three qualifying jumps, landing twice in muck-filled rice paddies. Briefings in the situation room completed my introduction to OSS/China. Our province, Yunnan, was ruled by Nationalist warlord Tu Li-ming. Under Chiang Kai-shek's system near autonomy was granted such regional warlords as General Tu, whose common characteristic seemed to be reluctance to fight the Japanese.

Under Mao Tse-tung the Chinese Communists had gathered at Yenan in Northern China. Occasionally they would sally from their redoubt to collect arms from an abandoned battlefield, but I never heard of their challenging the Japanese in open combat.

Japanese strategy in China was not to occupy the whole of that vast country, but rather to occupy and control strong points, i.e., cities and towns. OSS teams were able to operate outside and around these strong points, knocking off supply convoys, dynamiting bridges and sending Chinese agents into the coastal cities for intelligence gathering.

Administratively, OSS/China was divided into Secret Intelligence—collection, Special Operations—sabotage, Morale Operations—psychological warfare, and the Operational Groups—commando units. In Chungking OSS staffed a liaison office with the Nationalist Army, and OSS maintained forward bases in Chengtu, Hsian and Chihkiang.

Our problem, like that of every other operational unit in China, was logistics. Kunming was also the headquarters for General Chennault's Fourteenth Air Force, which had top priority in the China Theater. The arrival of B-29 bombers at Chengtu multiplied the already critical across-The-Hump supply problem, for all China gasoline had to be flown across The Hump in tanker aircraft.

Such supplies as OSS received came over the Burma Road, where trucks were often hijacked, abandoned by their drivers or lost to landslides or crumbling roadbeds.

As yet the group I had trained with on Catalina had not arrived. They were on their way by sea, and when they arrived in Calcutta, they volunteered to drive trucks over the Burma Road from Bhamo to Kunming rather than wait indefinitely for air transport across The Hump. Their arrival was about a month after mine, and we made them welcome and comfortable in our operational compound. Among them was Captain Lucien Conein,* once of the French Foreign Legion, a bilingual parachutist, who was destined for Indochina.

Presently there returned from Washington a major whom I'll call simply Raul. As the result of exploits reported by himself and largely unsubstantiated, he had been decorated with the Silver Star. To his misfortune, he was billeted with Operational Group types who very nearly beat him to death before dawn. Thus I became aware of an already-established tradition of self-effacement within our intelligence structure.

Other Detachment 202 figures, who were later to become prominent both in their home state of Florida and nationally, were Colonel Paul Helliwell and Rhodes scholar Louis Hector.

Colonel Ray Peers, commanding officer of Detachment 101 in Burma, was then preparing to move his detachment to China. In 1971 Lieutenant General Peers was in charge of the My Lai investigation.

The chief of our small graphics unit was Paul Child and the secretary he was later to marry became internationally famous as TV's French Chef, Julia Child. And from her wartime experiences, Elizabeth MacDonald was to write her best-selling *Undercover Girl*.

So it was that a number of us who worked for OSS in the Far East were destined to have significant careers—including myself.

In Kunming our detachment worked with the French Army liaison group on Indochina problems, with the British on problems

---

*After the war Conein joined CIA and until his retirement in 1971 served almost uninterruptedly in Saigon. Perhaps the most knowledgeable American on Vietnamese affairs, Conein was used by Ambassador Lodge as liaison to the generals who revolted and killed President Diem.

in Malaya and Singapore, and with the Air Force and Navy to establish ratlines to return pilots downed on the mainland or in the offshore waters.

Colonel Helliwell dispatched me to Hsian to appraise the alleged work of Korean General Li Bum Suk, whom OSS was supporting, as I found, in rather handsome style. Although I found General Li a colorful figure, it soon became apparent to me that he was neither obtaining intelligence from Korea nor had any operational plans to infiltrate his followers into Korea. My negative report on our Korean asset enraged Colonel Helliwell, for he was a firm supporter of General Li. Accordingly, the colonel vented his spleen not on Li, but on me.

From Hsian I moved on to Chengtu and found our base commander to be Major David Longacre, who had recently completed a well-publicized mission to the Dalai Lama in Tibet. To the Lama he hand delivered a scroll and a personal message from President Roosevelt, who hoped to keep Asian Buddhists friendly to our cause.

On the night of my arrival at Chengtu a four-engined tanker aircraft exploded on landing, cartwheeling to the end of the runway in a huge globe of flame. It was an unnerving experience and illustrated the difficulties of fighting the enemy in or from China. Without the tanker's gasoline the B-29 squadron then at Chengtu could not fly its scheduled missions over the Japanese home islands.

During the day temperatures soared to 120° and no one moved. Insulation melted from aircraft wiring in this terrific heat. We shaved our heads and worked at night, taking advantage of the coolness, dozing through the day in a heat-induced stupor until nightfall.

I returned to Hsian and went north with a team headed by Captain Bob Rodenburg, who was later to own the Baltimore Colts football team. Together we tried to encourage the local warlord to fight the Japanese, but our efforts were unavailing. Spoiling for a fight ourselves, we took our small party farther north until we found half a dozen Japanese soldiers camped on a riverbank. From the top of a bluff we opened fire on them, killing all but one, who fled. The next afternoon we were summoned to the presence of the warlord, whose rage was such that he would have had us executed had he dared. We had, he told us, disturbed the uneasy cease-fire with the

Japanese, who might, at any moment, sweep down and destroy him and all the forces under his command. He was, I knew, conducting illicit trade with the Japanese, smuggling radios and electronic equipment into Japanese hands and collecting gold bars in return. Thus, our intrusion threatened his economic base.*

As the war's last summer wore on, I was sent to Chihkiang to join another team that was to be dropped behind Japanese lines in Southern China. Dysentery attacked me and for a week I lay on a bedframe crisscrossed with ropes, no medicine and no physician, until the seizure ended. By then my team had been dispatched, and I was told to wait for the formation of the next one.

Presently there arrived at our compound a young, recently commissioned doctor. His mission was to parachute behind Japanese lines into a village whose headman was a powerful underground resistance leader. The headman's son was seriously ill, and our OSS team in the area had called for medical assistance. Although we had no parachute-training facilities, we gave the doctor a general idea of how to pull a rip cord and maneuver the risers.

After he jumped, we learned, he landed in a well, dangling there supported by the canopy. When he was hauled out, the villagers gathered round and applauded loudly; they have never seen such incredible aim before. In return the doctor was able to cure the sick child and was helped back through Japanese lines to Chihkiang by the Chinese Nationalist underground.

While waiting for the next team, I volunteered to take part in an airdrop resupply mission to a team headed by Captain Rutherford T. "Pinky" Walsh. His team was on the ground a few miles from Changsha and had not been supplied in more than a month. After our C-47 had been loaded with cargo containers, under the supervision of OSS Captain Blackwell, we were about to take off when a jeep drove up and we were joined by a lieutenant from the Fourteenth Air Force whose mission was to photograph the airdrop. Our pilot was also from the Fourteenth Air Force, but the copilot-navigator was an OSS officer.

---

*Nationalist currency was nearly valueless except in such urban centers as Kunming and Chungking. In the field OSS teams were supplied with gum opium and gold bars as mediums of exchange. Teams operating in Indochina were issued gold louis d'or coins newly minted by the U.S. Treasury. The bags of gold coins were so heavy that, carried by parachuting personnel, they often split from the landing impact, scattering treasure over the landscape.

To avoid Japanese radar, we flew at low level to the team area until we saw the markers spread by the team. Blackwell wore a parachute, as did the photographer, but there was none for me. So I held onto the static line while the plane circled low and we kicked cargo out of the open door. We stayed over the area long enough to see the team claim the cargo containers, then the OSS navigator came back and suggested to Captain Blackwell that we buzz Changsha. The navigator had a tommy gun and wanted the thrill of pumping a magazine at the enemy. The pilot agreed that it might be a fun thing to do, and so he climbed several thousand feet before beginning our run on the Japanese stronghold. Almost at once flak opened up on us, and I could see gray and black puffs through the open door. The dive steepened, and I sat down on the deck, my back against the forward bulkhead. Blackwell and the photographer stood in the open doorway, when a nearby burst rocked the plane. Hit, the photographer staggered out of the doorway and pulled his rip cord. Another burst, and Blackwell was struck in the head. He dropped to the deck but grabbed the doorsill and pulled his body out of the plane. By now I could see rooftops as the plane leveled off. The pilot flew low until we were out of antiaircraft range, then gained altitude, and the navigator came aft with his tommy gun. I saw the startled look on his face when he realized I was alone and at once began to ply me with questions. I answered in monosyllables, for I could barely stand the sight of him, attributing as I did the loss of our comrades to his irresponsible prank.

Back at the base I was ordered to write a detailed account of the incident, which with the pilot's report was used in a court-martial of the OSS navigator.

Later we were to learn that our comrades' chutes had only partly opened and they had struck the streets suffering serious injuries. Captured, they had been flayed alive, and their skinned bodies roped to bamboo poles like butchered pigs, and paraded through the Changsha streets by the Japanese occupiers. Thus ended an episode both tragic and needless, and one that could have cost me my life had I been wearing a parachute that afternoon. For, convinced as I was that the plane was going to crash, I would have followed the two men out of the open door.

4 SHANGHAI, ACAPULCO, PARIS AND VIENNA

UNDER the Army's point system, I was overdue for return to the United States and discharge. Then, when the first atom bomb obliterated Hiroshima, I volunteered to enter one of the occupied cities with a team whose purpose was to save the lives of Allied prisoners of war. We drew lots and I went with a team that flew into Nanking. Aboard the C-46 cargo carrier we had personal weapons, a bedroll, water, a few rations and an abundance of heretofore scarce C rations for the prisoners of war and civilian internees.

Not knowing what to expect, since the Japanese had not yet surrendered, we landed at Nanking Airfield between rows of shotup or burned Japanese aircraft. At the end of the runway was a tented structure in front of which we could see, stiffly drawn at attention, the Japanese commanding officer and his staff.

While we unloaded the aircraft, a Japanese interpreter approached and invited us to share cold beer with the Japanese officers. It was a boiling August day, but to a man we declined and sent back the message that the Japanese were to provide us transportation into the city and an escort to guarantee that we were not molested. Happily, our bluff succeeded.

Our team commander, Colonel Al Cox, demanded housing from the Japanese commander and we were driven to an old, deserted Japanese army barracks not far from the airfield. There we deposited our gear except for our personal weapons and continued on into the

46

city. We established headquarters in a hotel, then fanned out toward the POW camps. When the gates opened for the first time, the prisoners were incredulous. Cut off from outside news for almost the duration of the war, they could not believe that the Japanese had capitulated. Emotional scenes took place as we distributed rations and assured them they were no longer prisoners, but free men and women—and children, many of whom had been born in the camps during the war. A day or so later I was ordered to return to Kunming to join a team that was scheduled for Shanghai.

Shanghai, with its prewar polyglot foreign community, had more POW camps than any other city in China. For this mission our team, Sparrow II, filled two C-46 aircraft. Arriving at Shanghai Airport, we went through a duplicate of the scene I had witnessed at Nanking, then we were driven into the city proper, where we took over the American Club, ousting the Japanese occupants. On the roof we erected a radio antenna, and our senior officer sought out the Swiss consul, who was nominally in charge of protecting Allied prisoners.

This little man had long before come to terms with the Japanese power structure in Shanghai and was reluctant to give us any aid. Bowing to threats, however, he furnished us with lists of prisoners in the half-dozen camps in and around Shanghai. As a safeguard, we forced him to accompany us to Ash Camp, where we opened the gates and began distributing rations to the prisoners and their families. We repeated this at camp after camp, then began requisitioning Japanese Army stores and supplies to feed our new dependents. Many of the children had never tasted milk other than their mothers' and so were not reluctant to drink our powdered variety.

Within a week elements of General Wedemeyer's China command entered Shanghai—now that OSS had proved it safe—and the cruiser *Nashville* anchored off the Bund. Having been relieved by the Regular Army, Sparrow II turned to the recreational delights of postwar Shanghai and found them overwhelming.

In the basement of the American Club someone came across a dozen cases of prewar scotch whisky. These were brought up to the bar, but the first drinker of that scotch died in agony beside the American Club bar: The Japanese had doctored random bottles of whisky with cyanide before leaving.

This was bad news for a pair of OSS senior officers who had set about cornering the Shanghai market on scotch. Their hotel rooms were filled to the ceiling with cases of it, and they had made large investments in the whisky, anticipating thirsty visitors from the fleet. Now no foreigners in Shanghai dared drink scotch whisky, and the enterprising black marketers went bankrupt, to the general satisfaction of those of us who had been excluded from the promising transaction.

I was visited at my room in the American Club by an elderly White Russian lady who wanted to thank me for my part in releasing her from the concentration camp. With her was her daughter, a lissome blond named Marusha, who also expressed appreciation to me. Marusha was married, she confessed, to a young Soviet employee of Tass named Chernikov, but she assured me that it was a wartime *mariage de convenance*, and nothing of the heart. Marusha and I began meeting in tearooms, the back rooms of antique shops, bookstores, and of course at the American Club. Her husband, Valentin, I learned, was a junior officer of the NKVD who used the Tass news agency as cover for his intelligence assignment.

Our affair apparently reached his ears, for one rainy afternoon when Marusha and I were riding in a covered rickshaw down Bubbling Well Road, I heard shouting behind us, glanced around and saw Valentin brandishing his fist at me. Marusha, who spoke Shanghaiese, ordered the rickshaw man to turn into a street crowded with stores and sidewalk shops, then down an alley where she left the rickshaw and disappeared in the crowd. My rickshaw continued at top speed, but was finally overtaken, not without design, by Chernikov's. He leaped out, stared incredulously at the empty seat beside me, flushed and handed me his business card. Awkwardly, he explained he had heard of me through his mother-in-law and was anxious to express his appreciation for my intervention in her case. He suggested we might have a vodka one day in a café. I agreed and we parted. But from then on, Marusha and I met much more circumspectly.

Then one morning I read in the reopened Shanghai *Post* that President Truman had disbanded OSS. Within the hour Wedemeyer's headquarters was calling to tell our group to report to the Regular Army for duty. Determined not to become part of any garrison, we radioed Kunming and requested aircraft to fly us west. Two planes arrived the next day, and we flew back the width of China to our headquarters base at Kunming.

By now OSS teams that had been out of touch for months were straggling in, some on foot, others by plane or requisitioned Japanese transportation. Among these arrivals was Captain Robert G. North, whom I had not previously known, but with whose exploits in North China I was familiar.

Before leaving our detachment compound for the flight back over The Hump to India, we passed through the main courtyard and tossed our weapons on a growing pile. These weapons, we were told, were to be turned over to Chiang Kai-shek's Nationalist forces. However, they were appropriated by General Tu Li-ming, who soon made them available to the Chinese Communists, now stirring from their safe haven in Yenan.

In India we were put up at an abandoned British barracks outside Calcutta: Camp Kanchrapara. The thatched roofs rustled with rats and cobras, the heat was unbearable and water was in scarce supply. We were allowed to visit Calcutta on a rotation basis, and I was surprised to find how different now was the attitude of the Indians: Saved from the Japanese by the Allies, they eagerly resumed their longtime fight to rid themselves of the British raj. Street riots erupted in Calcutta, small-scale at first, then growing in size and ferocity. Eventually the Officers' Club was bombed and several officers killed, so none of us was reluctant to board the transport *M. B. Wheeler* and begin our long return voyage to New York.

The transport was overcrowded and innocent of air conditioning. Many of us slept on deck in order to avoid the oppressive heat below. Though the days were boring, our nights were enlivened by the presence of some Red Cross women and Wacs. Although officers and men were forbidden to debark at Port Said, the women were allowed ashore and brought back hampers of whiskey and wine. From then on, shipboard conditions became more tolerable, and our placid voyage through the Mediterranean to Gibraltar a thing of joy.

It was November now, and the North Atlantic was filled with violent storms. They slowed our passage, and we did not reach Hoboken until Thanksgiving Day. By command of the captain we were fed a turkey dinner for breakfast, then disembarked and force-fed a second turkey dinner at Fort Hamilton.

A special OSS train took us nonstop from New York to Washington, then a relay of buses drove us to temporary quarters at the

Congressional Country Club in Potomac.* Reporting in pro forma,
we broke for Washington and began a group celebration of the war's
end and our safe return that, like a floating crap game, moved from
hotel to hotel and lasted several days.

Before leaving China, I had been asked if I cared to join the newly
formed Central Intelligence Group as a civilian. Having witnessed
the demolition of OSS with the stroke of a Presidential pen, I had
little faith in the durability of a successor intelligence agency, so I
declined politely and firmly. Besides, I had received notification
that I had been awarded a Guggenheim fellowship in creative
writing for the succeeding year. On the trip home from China a
young officer had told me about a place in Mexico called Acapulco,
which he recommended as a deserted yet hospitable area where I
would be able to write without interruption.

We were officially discharged at the Congressional Country Club,
and I went at once to Albany to be with my parents. While I was
making plans to spend my Guggenheim year in Mexico, my father
suffered a near-fatal heart attack. For the next six weeks my mother
and I cared for him, and when he was up and around, I left for
Mexico with the doctor's assurance that my father's chances of a
recurrent cardiac embolism were slim.

There were few new automobiles of any kind to be had, but
through my next-door Albany neighbor, the superintendent of state
police, I was able to acquire a new Ford and proceeded at a leisurely
pace toward Mexico, stopping along the way in Memphis and New
Orleans to renew old acquaintances and make new friends. Eventually I crossed the border at Laredo and headed south for Mexico
City. There I took a room at the new Reforma Hotel and was
promptly bedridden with a recurrence of dysentery. When that was
behind me, I headed south through Cuernavaca and Taxco, narrowly missing execution or at least imprisonment:

As I drove through a small town, I saw at the end of the street a
line of soldiers, about six of them, rifles pointed at me. Slowing, I
stopped. An officer came over, yanked open my car door and ordered me out. In Spanish I asked him what the problem was, but he
thrust me into the jailhouse before he would reply. His detachment
had received a telephone report from the village just to the north: A

*Near my present home.

car with U.S. license plates traveling at a high rate of speed had struck and killed a little girl, then sped on. So notified, the captain said, he had been waiting for me to appear. Now I would be taken back to the town where I had killed the little girl and promptly tried and either shot or hanged. Mexican justice, he assured me, was prompt.

After an hour's fruitless conversation with the officer I asked him if he had been favored with any description of the fatal vehicle. He said he had not, but as I was the next car to pass through, he was entirely confident that I was the guilty party. In any case, he told me, witnesses to the crime were en route; they would identify my car and me.

After a lengthy wait the party arrived: the father and mother of the dead child and a shopkeeper who had witnessed the death. The shopkeeper stated that the killer car was black, whereas mine was green. Moreover, the black car had four doors and mine two. The child's parents were less sure. But while the debate was still going on, a telephone call notified the army officer who was holding me that the hit-and-run driver had been arrested two towns to the north. After the accident he had simply driven around the town and doubled back toward Mexico City.

I was released—with no apology.

For the next five months I lived in Acapulco at a pension, above the old airfield and with a fine view of the bay. I was the sole guest in a pension whose owner was a lady from the Yucatán. Her cooking was excellent, and though I was never able to accustom myself to highly spiced Mexican dishes, I enjoyed fried plantains and the daily offering of fresh-caught fish, fried, baked or broiled. And there was always an abundance of fruits from the nearby jungle. Occasionally the manservant would advise me that there were dwarf deer on the hilltop, and if the larder was low, I would take my Luger pistol and bring one down.

Mornings I would laze at Caleta beach and after lunch and siesta go to the afternoon beach. The waterfront drive that today serves Acapulco was then only beginning to be built. Downtown Acapulco, then a small and shabby area, was heavily covered with dust from road construction. Only a few hotels were active and catered almost entirely to Mexicans. In the months I was there I saw only one American couple—an airlines pilot honeymooning with his bride.

On subsequent visits to Acapulco over the years I have often reflected on the peace and tranquillity of those early days.

Working without distractions or interruptions, I finished my third novel, *Stranger in Town*, and sent it off to the publisher. Meanwhile, Bob North had been writing me from Los Angeles, urging me to visit him and perhaps form a screenwriting team. He was then turning out B pictures, working for a producer named Sol Wurtzel, and Bob was sure we would find a ready market for original screenplays.

I lingered in Acapulco long enough to relax and clear my mind, then drove in a few days to North Hollywood, where Bob North had rented a small house near the Lakeside Country Club.

A superb golfer, Bob won almost as much from golf bets as he earned at the studios. He was Old California, with relatives in Pasadena and the surrounding area. He had gone to Stanford, where, after a year's suspension for a prank, he was graduated. By coincidence we belonged to the same national fraternity.

I enjoyed every aspect of the screenwriter's life: meeting agents, actors and actresses and bit players, attending parties in Beverly Hills and becoming familiar with such fine restaurants as Chasen's and the Brown Derby. I renewed my friendship with Tony Jackson, who was now attending law school on the GI Bill. He had left the Navy as a full commander, whereas my promotion to first lieutenant had reached me only when I was in Shanghai. I introduced Bob and Tony and they became good friends. Everything was perfect except for one thing: The screenplays Bob and I were turning out had no market. Several originals were optioned and down payments made, but when the option period ended, the full sale price was not forthcoming and the options were dropped. Meanwhile, Bob's producer, Sol Wurtzel, became involved in a dispute with Twentieth Century-Fox Films, his releasing channel. Production stopped on those films on which Bob North was working, and it became apparent that under the impact of television Hollywood was entering a new and ominous phase.

For some time my expenses had been exceeding my income, so I reluctantly left Bob, Tony and Hollywood and drove back to Albany, New York.

Turning to the only trade I knew, I began writing a book that was accepted by Farrar, Straus & Co. It was a short, action-packed novel set in the Caribbean and titled *Bimini Run*. I was able to live well on the advance, joined the Fort Orange and Albany country clubs, where I played tennis, squash and golf, and frequently weekended with friends at Lake George. During the autumn I shot pheasant and quail and in the winter skied in northern New York, Vermont, Massachusetts and at Mt. Tremblant Lodge in the Canadian Laurentians. There I came across a number of Smith women I had known, as well as a honeymooning lass from Honolulu, whom I had last seen sharing Artie Shaw's bed in our Halekulani duplex. Understandably, she was not pleased to encounter me, and we avoided each other during our stay at the lodge.

When the snows melted in the spring of 1948, I decided that I wanted to return to Europe, Paris in particular. Through my father, I met Paul Hoffman, who had been appointed by President Truman to head the European recovery program known as the Marshall Plan. Hoffman agreed to take me on and suggested that I join the staff of the European administrator in Paris, Ambassador Averell Harriman. I met Harriman at the Washington headquarters of the new Economic Cooperation Administration, was hired by him and took note of one of his secretaries, an unusually attractive and intelligent lady named Dorothy de Goutière. On our lone Washington date she told me that she had spent the war years in Bern, Switzerland, working for the Treasury Department's Hidden Assets Division, the section that sought concealed Nazi assets abroad. At the end of the war she had been sent to Shanghai to open the Treasury Office there and had served as technical adviser on a Dick Powell film, *To the Ends of the Earth*, a story of Treasury's involvement in the international narcotics traffic. She resigned from Treasury to marry the Marquis Peter de Goutière, a civilian pilot for the China National Airways Corporation. With him she maintained homes in Shanghai and in the French concession of Chandernagore, the de Goutière family seat outside Calcutta. She had begun divorce proceedings in Florida, she told me, but was anxious to be in Paris long enough to receive a French divorce as well. We agreed to see each other in Paris, but I arrived there several weeks before she did.

At the Paris embassy I found my immediate superior to be Alfred Friendly, an enthusiastic Democrat who had been seconded to the

Marshall Plan by the Washington *Post*. His deputy, Waldemar Nielsen, after a stint with the Ford Foundation, was later to head the CIA-sponsored Africa Foundation. Among my close embassy friends were Perry and Harriet Culley and Glen Moorhouse, an officer of the CIA Paris station. Kingman Brewster, now president of Yale, was a member of Harriman's legal staff.

Chief of the ECA mission to France was David K. E. Bruce, whom I had known by reputation as chief of OSS operations in wartime Europe. From time to time we were visited by Paul Hoffman's deputy, Richard Bissell,* an economist from MIT.

Although Friendly had a competent press staff, Harriman occasionally brought over Arthur Schlesinger, Jr., to write or polish a particularly important speech. I had known Schlesinger's younger brother at Brown, but other than that chance circumstance we had nothing in common. Harriman, it was known, wanted to be Secretary of State if Truman was reelected.

The charges against Alger Hiss and William Remington were much discussed in ECA, particularly by those—and there were many—who had known both Hiss and Remington. Their innocence was loudly trumpeted by their partisans, and when I was asked why I did not share the general enthusiasm for their innocence, I replied that I had a profound belief in American justice and was content to await the verdict of their trials.

Although I did not immediately realize it, this drew the ideological line between myself and ninety-five percent of Harriman's staff. Later I became aware that I had landed in a briar patch of liberalism and found it inconsistent that those ECA officials who were charged with distributing billions of American recovery dollars to Europe —an effort in which the Soviet Union stoutly refused to join —showed ambivalent feelings toward the USSR. Some of this was tempered, though, when the Soviets isolated Berlin and the United States was forced to begin a costly and dangerous airlift of coal, food and supplies into that beleaguered city.

At the beginning of the famous airlift I flew into Berlin with Harriman, who was making an on-the-spot inspection to determine Berlin's present and future needs. Soviet planes buzzed the air

*Joining CIA, Bissell developed the U-2 aircraft and was deputy director for plans in charge of the Bay of Pigs invasion of Cuba.

corridors, and on the ground the Soviets refused to permit Allied truck convoys to enter Berlin. Thus the Soviet Union's true attitude toward the West became obvious, and I found it difficult to remain silent when, within the embassy, I heard the United States role in postwar Europe criticized and even denounced.

After President Truman had been renominated by the Democrats and the Republicans had chosen New York Governor Thomas Dewey to oppose him in the fall election, it was widely believed that Dewey would win and appoint former Senator John Foster Dulles as his Secretary of State. Dulles, who had played a leading diplomatic role in the postwar rapprochement between Japan and the United States, was scheduled to visit Europe for the drafting of an Austrian peace treaty with the Western Powers. When Dulles' ETA in Paris had been announced to Ambassador Harriman, he summoned me and said he would like me to accompany John Foster Dulles to Vienna and such other European cities as Dulles might visit. When I asked the ambassador why he had selected me, he replied with a wry smile that I was the only Republican he knew.

But before that trip I visited Athens and Vienna with Ambassador and Mrs. Harriman and came to know the high commissioner and his staff, as well as officials of the American Legation with whom I was later to work for a number of months in Vienna.

During the Vienna trip I met General Albert Wedemeyer, who had been American commander in China, introduced myself to him as a former subordinate in that far-off theater and was in turn introduced by him to a member of his party, a deputy assistant secretary of war named Frank Wisner.

During the war Wisner had served in OSS in, among other places, Turkey and seemed to me to be a hard-line anti-Communist. In any case, Wisner's approach to the problems of postwar Europe was heard by me in refreshing contrast to the ambivalent attitudes I had so often heard expressed in Paris by my ECA colleagues. A junior member of our party was Mike Forrestal, son of the then Secretary of Defense and a godchild of the Harrimans. Just out of Princeton, Mike was heading for Harvard Law School, but was so often in the company of Glen Moorhouse that I began to wonder whether Mike was a member of the Central Intelligence Agency.

As Thanksgiving (1948) approached, Dorothy told me she wanted to prepare Thanksgiving dinner at her apartment for myself and two other couples. The embassy commissary had announced the arrival of a shipment of turkeys from the United States, so I said, "Fine. I'll buy the turkey, and you take care of the trimmings."

"The only problem is, Howard, my oven isn't really big enough to roast a good-sized turkey."

"Well, I'll have Victor [my chauffeur] have it done at a rotisserie and deliver it at the appointed time. Uh—I have to go over to the Foreign Ministry this morning. Why don't you pick up the turkey at the commissary and I'll turn it over to Victor?" Without waiting for her reply, I left the embassy, returning after a lengthy lunch on the Ile St. Louis.

As I walked toward my office, I heard muffled laughter, and when I reached my desk, I saw the reason.

There, mounted on my blotter, was a turkey, plucked but otherwise intact. Propped against its ample chest was a large sign in Dorothy's lettering: EMPLOYEES ARE STRICTLY FORBIDDEN TO SLEEP AT THEIR DESKS.

Not particularly amused, I bagged the turkey, got it out of sight and strode to Harriman's office, where I found Dorothy at work. "What the hell's the idea of the turkey on my desk?" I thundered. "Everyone in the place thinks it's—"

"That's what you get for being inconsiderate, you SOB. I had to spend an hour waiting in the commissary line for your turkey and—"

"*Our* turkey."

"Well, *our* turkey, then. But I had plenty of other things to do and it was just damn inconsiderate of you. The more I thought about it, the angrier I got. So—*you've* got the turkey."

"And the funny sign?"

She dissolved in laughter. "I couldn't *help* it. The bird looked *so* funny there. . . ."

I kissed her lightly. "Let's hope it tastes better than it looks, *chérie*."

I instructed Victor to get the bird to a rotisserie, have head and legs chopped off, roasted on Thanksgiving morning, then delivered to Dorothy's apartment at three o'clock.

While the six of us were enjoying cocktails Thanksgiving afternoon, Victor arrived with an immense platter holding a handsomely browned turkey. "*Voici la dinde, M'sieu* Hunt," he announced proudly and carried the platter to the table.

While the maid added other cooked dishes to the table, I sharpened the carving knife, and when everyone was seated, I flourished knife and fork and made a fast incision into the golden breast.

Hissing vapor jetted toward the ceiling and we were assailed by a noxious odor. Undismayed, I laid open the other breast and, again, the steamy stench. As guests fled the table, Dorothy said, "What on earth—?"

"I don't know," I said, "but an autopsy's in order."

Carrying the turkey into the kitchen, I cut into the abdominal cavity—only to find the cavity full.

The rotisserie had indeed divested the turkey of head and legs, but—lacking specific instructions—had not gutted the bird. The flesh was permeated with bile and so inedible that even Dorothy's dachshund slunk away when offered a portion.

Dorothy's refrigerator held a single slice of baked ham, which I divided into six minute segments. So, with ample wine and recurrent laughter, the incident of the turkey passed into family history, a tale whose repetition our children always enjoyed.

Not long after returning from Vienna, I was told by Al Friendly that he wanted me to go on detached service in Vienna and do what I could to counter a situation which was interfering with full utilization of American relief supplies. The Austrian Communist party had spread a false rumor that tons of canned hake, a fish commonly eaten in Europe, was spoiled. As a result, this needed protein was sitting in warehouses or on store shelves, ignored by the Austrian populace.

After making my peace with Dorothy, I left for Vienna and began conferring with members of the legation, the office of the high commissioner, and the staff of the small ECA mission headed by Wendell Willcox. The consensus was that I should produce a documentary film highlighting the positive side of Marshall Plan aid to Austria without mentioning the allegedly poisoned seafood as such. I was given a budget in counterpart Austrian funds, wrote a script, had it translated into German and hired an Austrian director, who in turn hired camera crews. Because of the postwar shortage of raw film, I had quantities sent to me from Paris. Actual shooting took about ten days, and though the film was baldly propagandistic, it was well received by Austrian and American officials and by most of the

Austrian populace, the Communists excepted. The following year it even won a documentary film award.

Through the ECA mission I had come to know a man whom I'll call Jordan, recently transferred from UNRRA in Belgrade to the ECA mission in Vienna. At parties I had met his Yugoslav girlfriend and learned that he had brought her illegally into Austria using his diplomatic passport and automobile license plates.

Early one Sunday morning Wendell Willcox, chief of the ECA mission in Austria, telephoned me at the Bristol Hotel, where I was staying, and asked me to go to Vienna's central morgue and identify a body believed to be that of Jordan. Willcox said he regarded me as a representative of Harriman's office, which would have to be notified if the dead man was, in fact, Jordan.

My driver, a former Rommel tanker who had been captured in the western desert and interned in New Jersey for the rest of the war, drove me to the morgue—my first visit to such an establishment —and after displaying my diplomatic credentials, I was shown the almost unrecognizable body of Jordan. His face and skull were jellied from battering by heavy objects. There were no bullet holes in his body, but several bayonet thrusts. I identified the body and claimed it for the legation, then reported my findings to the ECA mission chief.

During the course of the day Jordan's final movements were reconstructed. Together he and the Yugoslav girl had left their apartment and driven into the Russian zone for dinner. While dining in a beer hall, both were collared by Russian soldiers and taken outside. They were forced into Jordan's car, and he was ordered to drive deeper into the Russian zone. After a few blocks the car stopped and the girl got out, the three Russian soldiers remaining. In a deserted area Jordan's head was struck by a rifle butt, knocking him unconscious. He was then dragged out of the car, and his face and skull were pounded to a pulp. The car was stripped of its tires and set afire. The blaze of the burning automobile attracted civilian attention; Austrian police arrived and were permitted to take the body to Vienna's central morgue, where I had identified it.

From the office of the high commissioner came the civilian chief of the Army's counterintelligence corps. The Vienna CIA chief, John Richardson, was not present, so for some reason the CIC man assumed I was representing CIA. He told me that Jordan's girlfriend was actually a Soviet double agent who had been targeted at Jordan in order to marry him and acquire U.S. citizenship. Recently Jordan had told the girl that he had no intention of divorcing his wife, who was on the verge of sailing from New York to join him. Whether Jordan's execution was the girl's idea or had been ordered by her Soviet masters I never learned. The Soviets, however, would not be likely to have ordered Jordan's death merely because the girl was piqued at Jordan's refusal to marry her. Her KGB masters, however, may well have decided to terminate in this bloody fashion an operation which for them was going nowhere.

The sight of Jordan's cadaver, the vicious cruelty of his death and the duplicity of Jordan's mistress, whom he had befriended and brought to Vienna at the risk of his own job, impressed me and heightened the hostility I already felt toward the Soviets.

On another occasion the American minister invited me to a large Austrian-American party on the Kahlenberg. The guests of honor were to be an Austrian cabinet minister and a lady deputy cabinet minister. We waited seemingly hours for their arrival, then came a message from the Army: While driving through the Soviet zone toward the Kahlenberg, their car had been stopped by a Soviet patrol and driven away. Of the two officials, nothing further was ever heard.

Not long afterward my driver, Fritz, was proceeding along the Ringstrasse near the grim Soviet Kommandatura. Nearly in front of the Kommandatura a body lay smashed on the sidewalk. Later I learned the victim was a man who had been picked up the day before for questioning by the Soviets. Evidently he had preferred suicide to Soviet interrogation.

Another international tragedy whose victim I knew was the to-this-day-unexplained murder of the American naval attaché in Bucharest, Captain Eugene Karpe. Gene Karpe would occasionally abandon joyless Bucharest for a few days in Vienna, where he stayed at the Bristol Hotel. I met him at the officers' mess and was occasionally able to obtain flights to Paris for him on military aircraft. Once he took a present from me to Dorothy.

In Budapest the preceding year American businessman Robert A. Vogeler had been arrested on trumped-up "spy" charges and imprisoned. During Vogeler's brief trial Karpe had visited him and his wife and so fell under Communist suspicion. What the Communists did not know was that Vogeler and Karpe had been classmates and friends at the Naval Academy, and Karpe's visits were of a personal, not a clandestine professional nature.

One winter evening I saw Karpe in the Bristol lobby. He was on his way to the opera and told me he was taking the midnight Arlberg-Orient express to Paris en route to Washington for reassignment. He was glad to be leaving three years of Iron Curtain duty, he said, and hoped to get a sea command. We shook hands and parted.

Next morning his body, smashed beyond recognition, was found in a tunnel near Salzburg, identifiable only through the passport and other papers found in his clothing. Karpe's murder, I felt, was as vicious as Jordan's, and I took both personally. From these and related circumstances developed my conviction that Soviet Communism was a bloody and implacable enemy, ready to kill and destroy on the slightest provocation—or even on mere suspicion.

One afternoon I had accompanied the American minister to a meeting with the high commissioner, General Geoffrey Keyes, when Keyes was notified that a Soviet plane had landed at Horsching airfield near Linz and its occupants were requesting political asylum. Other business was set aside, and the room rapidly filled with Keyes' senior aides. The general hope was that the incident could be hushed up and the flyers returned to the Soviets, but the information had been passed over land telephone lines from Linz to Vienna, and the lines were known to be tapped by the Soviets.

Reluctantly, the office of the high commissioner assented to the asylum request, and the minister (who had gone to law school with my Uncle Norris) enthusiastically concurred. The two Soviet Air Force defectors were Captain Peter Pirogov and a mechanic whose name I've forgotten, but will call Antonov. The mechanic had been half forced to accompany Pirogov on the life-or-death flight, and his intelligence was much lower than the captain's. John Richardson and other members of CIA's Vienna station arranged to have the two defectors flown to the United States, where they were interrogated.

Life magazine agreed to pay Antonov $50,000 for the story of his escape, but Antonov, after being surfaced by CIA, unwisely gave a press conference in which he ingenuously told the world the very things that *Life* had planned to publish. *Life* withdrew its offer, and

Antonov became morose, drinking heavily. Pirogov, meanwhile, was composing an "as told to" book and readily adjusting to life in the United States. He, at least, had no regrets over his defection.

Antonov, however, maudlin with liquor and love for Mother Russia, telephoned the Soviet Embassy in Washington and asked to be repatriated. He met Soviet officials at the Three Musketeers restaurant, a few blocks from the Soviet Embassy, and discussed his return with them. The area was thick with FBI surveillants, alerted by their interception of Antonov's telephone call, and they watched helplessly while Antonov, apparently of his own volition, walked with his Soviet escorts into a waiting embassy car and was driven away.

Months later the West received word of Antonov's trial and execution in the USSR. Thus, the disillusioned mechanic was reunited for all time with the soil of Mother Russia.

Pirogov, however, was given a new identity and funds to start a business. He acquired an American wife and settled easily into the life of a capitalist entrepreneur.

From this episode CIA learned something about defector management, the necessity of safehouses and ever-present "handholder" agency personnel until the defector's intelligence potential was thoroughly exploited and he was freed for resettlement.

Adjacent to the Bristol was a hotel occupied by Soviet officers. It was a noisy place, and from it at all hours issued sounds of music, dancing and smashing bottles. One Saturday night an Army private from the Appalachians strolled toward the guarded entrance, went berserk, snatched a submachine gun from the nearest guard, shot the other guard and ran into the lobby, where he machine-gunned men and women until the magazine was empty. By then he himself was dying from return fire.

The hotel was scheduled for demolition and when the Soviets moved out of it, I heard that it had been stripped by its Soviet occupants, who customarily used its grand pianos as latrines.

That Christmas Dorothy met me in the Tyrol for skiing and other winter sports. We stayed at the Zürserhof, with several married couples from Paris and Vienna, and had a memorable holiday. The only thing marring it was breaking my thumb while skiing.

I had made the mistake of leaving the trail and slanting down across the mountainside. A fresh layer of snow concealed a brook, and it gave way under my weight, my ski tips slamming into the bank on the far side. I was hurtled forward and my thumb bent backward until it snapped. At Zürs I found an Austrian physician who treated my fracture casually, but managed to get a small cast around my thumb and hand so that I could continue to ski. When I remarked to friends on his casual treatment, I was told that the doctor had served in the Afrika Korps and loathed Americans. It was some weeks before my thumb joint finally healed and I could remove the final cast. Because of indifferent orthopedic treatment, the fractured joint was not properly realigned and healed improperly, remaining partly separated to this day.

Although I was enjoying Vienna life and had more friends there than in Paris, I missed Dorothy increasingly. From Vienna it was difficult to telephone her in Paris because of the power drainage that occurred as taps were applied at what must have been dozens of points halfway across Europe. Consequently we could make ourselves heard for only the first few words, then power would be lost and our voices became inaudible. During our Zürs holiday we had reached a tacit understanding and I was anxious to rejoin her in Paris. Despite the offer of a substantial promotion if I stayed in Vienna, I made arrangements to leave on the unarguable grounds that my mission was completed.

When I got back to my former office, I found that Friendly's staff had multiplied enormously, and the work I had been doing was parceled out among half a dozen new arrivals. My secretary, Barbara Rurup, had been assigned elsewhere, and with the reelection of Truman, it seemed that ECA no longer wanted even a house Republican.

From Glen Moorhouse I learned that Pinky Walsh, whom I had last seen in China, was en route France, and a letter from Pinky confirmed this. He asked me to meet him at Le Havre, which I did, both of us being driven back to Paris by my chauffeur, Victor, a wartime French resistance railway saboteur. After staying overnight at my apartment, Pinky came to my office, where I introduced him to Barbara Rurup. They took an immediate liking to each other, and Dorothy and I began double-dating with them until I left France. Pinky, a Cornell graduate, had for apparently illogical reasons decided to take his doctorate at the Sorbonne. However, he seldom seemed to attend classes at the Sorbonne, and occasionally I saw him in the company of Glen Moorhouse. Finally I realized that Pinky, bilingual in French, was establishing cover in the French student milieu.

Around Eastertime Frank Wisner paid a visit in Paris and asked me to see him in his temporary office at the embassy.

He knew, he told me, that I had been with OSS and said I was well regarded by mutual friends. He was setting up within CIA an organization not designed for mere intelligence collection; that would still be handled by OSO, the Office of Special Operations, to which Moorhouse belonged.

Wisner's new organization, the Office of Policy Coordination (OPC), was to be America's action arm in the Cold War. Would I be interested in joining? I told him the idea was attractive but my taste of government service in ECA had not especially appealed to me. Wisner assured me I could work unfettered in OPC and mentioned the names of several OSS friends who had already joined.

I was tired of the Al Friendlys, the Wally Nielsens, the Arthur Schlesinger, Jrs., and ECA's ambivalent attitude toward Communism, of whose reality I had had a more immediate experience than anyone I knew. Wisner remarked that my field clearance would take perhaps as much as three months; meanwhile I would have to resign from ECA before I could officially file my application. I was already more than half persuaded and said I would give his proposal serious thought. On that note we parted.

Meanwhile, my Guggenheim fellowship novel, *Stranger in Town*, had become a paperback best seller. From its proceeds I thought I could sustain myself until I was cleared for OPC.

I gave Al Friendly my resignation and made plans to return to the States. At Orly Airport Dorothy said resentfully, "I don't know why you won't take me with you . . . or don't you love me?"

"Honey, you know I love you," I said, "but without a steady income I can't support a wife."

"If you loved me, you'd take me with you."

"It's not that simple. I don't have a job. I can't promise security when I can't even foresee it. Maybe after I—"

"Maybe 'after' could be too late. It's not just money, is it, Howard?"

"That's the *only* reason, darling."

"Then I'll take the first plane tomorrow. If you can't find a job, I'll keep on working."

I kissed her, then said softly, "We're both accustomed to luxuries—you know that. What would our life be like, jammed together in a one-room efficiency—with your dog?"

"I don't care about that," she said stubbornly. "I just want to be with you. If you loved me enough, you'd be willing to take a chance." She drew back and gazed at me. "*I* am."

Loudspeakers called my flight. I kissed Dorothy again. She said, "And you're willing to have it end like this?"

"No. I don't want it to end at all. But I don't know why you can't see things my way."

"Perhaps because I'm in love—and you're not."

I shook my head. "Maybe it's because I'm practical and you're not."

"You know that isn't so," she said in a low voice, clung to me for a moment and walked away.

"Will you write?" I called, but there was no answer. I boarded the New York plane.

In Washington I completed my final processing out of ECA and joined my parents in Albany. I was at work on another book when a call from my Hollywood agent, Ned Brown, informed me that Warner Brothers had bought *Bimini Run*. To me the sale price of $35,000 seemed like a fortune, and I cabled Dorothy, asking her to be my wife, then flew to Los Angeles to see my agent and Warner Brothers and to stay with Bob North and his new bride, Maxine.

This time the motion-picture colony was far more receptive to me than it had been on my first approach. At Warner Brothers I worked on a couple of nonmemorable films while waiting for Dorothy to leave Paris and join me. I had told Bob North of Frank Wisner's new organization, a concept that interested him at once. We agreed that if I could recommend the organization to him he would join it, and Maxine agreed. Between Paris and Los Angeles Dorothy and I exchanged phone calls on almost a daily basis. Finally she gave me her arrival date at Idlewild International Airport via Air France. I knew she must be bringing her dachshund, Coffee, with her, for in that era Air France was the only transatlantic airline permitting dogs aboard.

My parents were not enthusiastic about my marriage: They did not know Dorothy, and she was a divorcée and, worse, a Catholic. From previous experiences as an only son I knew that my parents would never wholeheartedly approve any bride I might bring home, so I took that into consideration, confident they would accept the inevitable, as eventually they did.

But after Dorothy's arrival friction with my parents developed, and instead of being married in Albany, we were married in Millbrook, New York, spent our first night at the Sherry-Netherland Hotel in New York, and drove my recently acquired white Cadillac convertible to Sea Island, Georgia, for our honeymoon.

It was there that I received a telegram instructing me to report at once to CIA headquarters in Washington, D.C.

So, on CIA orders, I interrupted my honeymoon and reported with my new wife to Washington, where I began a career in intelligence that was to occupy me for the next twenty-one years.

5 THE CENTRAL INTELLIGENCE AGENCY

UNLIKE CIA's Office of Special Operations, the covert collector of intelligence, Frank Wisner's Office of Policy Coordination had been designed, largely by Secretary of Defense Forrestal, to be our government's clandestine action arm. Its initial cadre was composed largely of OSS European veterans who had attended Ivy League colleges. Functionally, OPC was organized much like OSO, with geographic area divisions in the chain of command. The then CIA director was Admiral Roscoe Hillenkoetter, whom I had met during one of the admiral's inspection trips to Vienna. He was Frank Wisner's nominal superior, but lacked Frank Wisner's political power base, which included such men as John J. McCloy, Averell Harriman, William Draper, Secretary of Defense Forrestal, and Secretary of State Marshall. At headquarters, alongside the reflecting pool, OPC established functional staffs for Paramilitary Operations, Political and Psychological Warfare and Economic Warfare. The Political and Psychological Warfare staff, to which I was assigned, was headed by Joseph Bryan III, Navy veteran and writer. To assist him he had brought in writer Finis Farr; Gates Lloyd, Philadelphia investment banker; Lewis "Pinky" Thompson, a New York and New Jersey financier and a man of many parts; and Carlton Alsop, late a motion-picture producer and once a well-known Hollywood agent. All except Alsop and myself were Princeton alumni.

Artist-illustrator Hugh Troy joined Bryan's staff and formed a highly competent group of political cartoonists and polemicists.

The Office of Special Operations resisted the growth and expansion of OPC, which it saw, quite rightly, as encroaching on its worldwide operations. In simple terms, OSO was mandated to supply covert intelligence and OPC was created to utilize it against the enemy. The enemy, of course, was international Communism in all of its worldwide manifestations.

Wisner at once began establishing overseas stations, paralleling those which OSO had since the war maintained in our embassies abroad. The embassies resisted our unwelcome additions, but Wisner's political clout was sufficient to quell the complaints, and overseas staffing went on smoothly.

A top priority was getting an OPC chief to Rome, where his initial mission was to reverse Italy's leftward political trend and defeat the Communists at the polls in the imminent Italian elections.

Al Cox, once of Kunming, was dispatched to Taiwan to bolster the shaken Nationalist government, newly arrived from the conquered mainland. After his initial work Cox was to become president of Civil Air Transport, the CIA-owned and operated Nationalist airline.

To London went Merritt Ruddock, to work with ORD, the small British equivalent of OPC. By high-level agreement with the British, CIA was to conduct no operations, whether by OSO or OPC, in any part of the empire. With the French we had no such limiting arrangement.

Soon after our marriage Dorothy became pregnant and over our first Christmas miscarried, to our deep grief. Her French maid did not like the isolation of Alexandria so we took a house on Dent Place in Georgetown and acquired a mate for her dachshund, named Kuchen.

Dorothy's ancestors had settled around Dayton, Ohio. In addition to being descended from the Presidential Adams and Harrison families, my wife was one-eighth Oglala Sioux and brought to our home numerous Sioux artifacts handed down from her mother's family.

In Europe OPC efforts were aimed at destroying Communist influence in labor organizations, the press and among youth and students. The electoral campaigns of high-level pro-West officials were aided by OPC funding. Within organized labor anti-

Communist union candidates were helped with OPC funds. Front organizations were established to provide alternatives to Communist organizations of long standing. For these and other major expenditures Marshall Plan counterpart funds were used. These local-currency equivalents of dollar loans and contributions made by the United States were held in escrow accounts to reduce the quantity of local currency in circulation and in theory reduce inflation. Nevertheless, Candy, as the counterpart funds were known, was freely available to OPC.

Radio Free Europe was founded, with a distinguished board of directors, and funded by OPC, although annual appeals for public funds were made to provide a credible explanation of the funds' source.

The founder of United World Federalists, Cord Myer, Jr., though lacking prior intelligence experience, was made head of the International Organizations Division within OPC. His deputy, Tom Braden, was a California publisher and OSS veteran. Their division, as its name implied, controlled international labor unions, womens' and veterans' organizations and student movements abroad. But IOD eventually financed the U.S. National Student Association.

By now Admiral Hillenkoetter had been replaced by Eisenhower's former Chief of Staff, General Walter Bedell Smith. As his deputy, Smith brought in Allen W. Dulles, who, while chief of the OSS station in wartime Bern, played a prominent role in the withdrawal of Italy from the war.

Early in World War II Latin America had become an FBI protectorate by Presidential edict. South from the Rio Grande, CIA station chiefs were almost entirely former FBI agents who had served in Latin America during the war. Basically law enforcers in outlook, these FBI retreads collected information through liaison with local police departments and were unaccustomed to the concept of covert action as spelled out in the OPC charter. In most cases they were hostile to it. While OSO men were generally satisfied to forward intelligence to Washington, where it would be filed, OPC was eager for that same intelligence so that we might put it to work. Although OPC had a skeletal Latin American Division, as yet no OPC stations in Latin America had been opened.

Because of my OSS background I was excused from the routine CIA courses required of all new employees, taking more advanced courses, such as counterintelligence and agent handling. At Joe Bryan's request, I set up the first OPC-type training courses in covert political and psychological warfare and gave an introductory series of lectures at our training areas.

For a time in the spring of 1950 I shared an office with a Marine colonel who had been assigned to CIA. He was Bob Cushman, later to become Commandant of the Marine Corps and a peripheral figure in the Watergate scandals.

I also met and frequently conferred with Dr. James Burnham, a Princeton classmate of Joe Bryan's and onetime professor of philosophy. Burnham was a consultant to OPC on virtually every subject of interest to our organization. He had extensive contacts in Europe and, by virtue of his Trotskyite background, was something of an authority on domestic and foreign Communist parties and front organizations. Through him I was to meet a young Yale graduate, William F. Buckley, Jr., whose *God and Man at Yale* was stirring great controversy within the Eastern academic establishment.

Like myself, Buckley was recently married and reportedly a committed and articulate anti-Communist. He was, Burnham told me, looking for the optimum way of working against the Stalinists. Moreover, Buckley was trilingual: in English, Spanish and French. I was impressed by Bill and decided to find a means of using his demonstrated and potential talents.

About this time the Fawcett Publishing Corporation began publishing paperback originals under the Gold Medal imprint. Jim Bishop, the editor, signed me to do several paperback originals, offering what was then an unheard-of guarantee. I turned out the books quickly, was well paid for my work and asked for further books.

I knew that OPC was planning to break the OSO stranglehold on Latin America and volunteered to open the OPC station in Mexico City. Because I spoke Spanish and had actually lived in Mexico, my suggestion was accepted. So, beginning in the late summer of 1950, I began laying operational plans for Mexico, processing into the Department of State as a Foreign Service Reserve Officer and interviewing candidates to work for me as agents outside the embassy. First on my list was Bill Buckley, who readily agreed and set about working out details of his cover, as did several other agents, including a woman. As my secretary, I was assigned a bilingual

Puerto Rican lady, Isabel Cintrón, whose previous background was
with Naval Intelligence.

My wife was again pregnant, and all signs pointed to a successful
delivery. Meanwhile the French maid's behavior was becoming
increasingly eccentric, and Dorothy and I decided to dispense with
her services, offering her return passage to Paris. Instead, she
joined the household of Hugh D. Auchincloss* across the Potomac
in McLean, Virginia, and I wrote to the Immigration and Naturaliza-
tion Service disclaiming further responsibility for her.

As my departure time neared, Frank Wisner warned me that the
FBI maintained a large and active station at the Mexico City embassy, covered, as is the FBI abroad, under the title of Office of the
Legal Attaché. The Bureau would be jealous of its prerogatives in
Mexico and unlikely to be helpful to me. Moreover, the OSO station
chief in Mexico was a former Bureau agent in Latin America who was
thoroughly disliked by the Office of the Legal Attaché. In due course
a letter of instruction was prepared for me which codified in both
general and specific terms my mission in Mexico.

Finis Farr and Carlton Alsop were now beginning initial negotiations with the widow of George Orwell. From this was to come the
animated cartoon film of Orwell's *Animal Farm*, which CIA financed
and distributed throughout the world. But production was delayed
by the leaden weight of a bureaucracy which began spreading within
OPC. Accountants, budgeteers and administrators proliferated,
most of them from such comparatively pedestrian government
bureaus as the departments of Agriculture and Commerce and the
Bureau of the Budget. Few if any could claim prior intelligence
experience, much less any comprehension of what OPC had been
formed to do.

A brilliant writer and creative thinker, Joe Bryan became increasingly impatient with the dilatory attitude of OPC's nonoperational
personnel and was eventually to leave in disgust.

During the autumn I was given courses in station administration
and fiscal management, report writing and current studies of the
international Communist government.

Because of Dorothy's previous miscarriage, her physician had set
a date after which she was not to travel. I made this known to the

*Stepfather of Jacqueline Kennedy Onassis.

Latin American Division, and we found a renter for our house coincident with the date of our departure. Even so, it was not until within a few hours of flight time that I was able to secure our diplomatic passports, and while we were sitting in our empty house waiting for the taxi to take us to National Airport, two men came to the door, announced themselves as insurance investigators and asked if we would be willing to comment on the mental health of our former French maid. According to them, the maid developed change-of-life paranoia while employed at Merrywood and threw herself from a balcony in an apparent suicide attempt. She was in Georgetown Hospital, and the investigators were attempting to determine wherein responsibility lay. We were barely able to provide what little information we had when our taxi arrived and we departed for National Airport.

After a change of planes in Dallas we flew south to Mexico City, arriving next morning in the city where my two daughters were to be born and where we were to spend the next three years.

6 MEXICO OPERATIONS

AFTER some uncomfortable nights in a ratty hotel chosen for us by the embassy, Dorothy and I rented a small furnished apartment on Villalongin, not far from the location of the old embassy. In the meantime, I had made myself known to the OSO station chief and to Chargé d'Affaires Paul Culbertson. When I mentioned to him that because of my wife's advanced pregnancy she would not be able to make the expected calls on those embassy wives whose husbands outranked me, Culbertson said, "That's all right, Howard. Marie [his wife] and I are as easy to get along with as a pair of old shoes."

I left Culbertson's office and at once telephoned my wife. I repeated my exchange with Culbertson and she agreed with me that regardless of how badly she felt, she must comply with protocol. From that time on, in embassy wives' meetings, Mrs. Culbertson always cited Dorothy as an example for other wives to follow, and we were included among the Culbertson's select circle of friends. For us it was an unforgettable example of embassy politics.

The OSO station chief found an old storage room which he permitted my secretary and myself to use. We had it cleaned and borrowed old furniture, for the embassy was soon to occupy several floors of a just-completed office building downtown, along the Paseo de la Reforma.

Within a few days the New American ambassador arrived. He was

William O'Dwyer, who had left the New York mayoralty under something of a cloud. However, his Irish extroversion and his attractive new wife were well received by Mexicans and embassy staff alike.

During my bachelor days in New York I had come to know the ambassador's wife, then Elizabeth Sloan Hipp Simpson, as one of several Powers models I had been dating. Her arrival posed no particular problem, although my wife often found reasons not to accept the hospitality of Bill and Sloan O'Dwyer.

A few days after O'Dwyer's arrival, when he had not summoned me to his office, I asked for and was granted an appointment. The ambassador greeted me cordially and asked the purpose of my visit. I told him that General Walter Bedell Smith, CIA director, had written O'Dwyer a personal letter outlining my mission. O'Dwyer frowned, then said, "I received a personal letter from Beetle Smith, but he didn't mention you."

"Whom did he mention, Mr. Ambassador?"

"He spoke about someone named 'John F. Rittenhouse.' " He eyed me. "Could that possibly be you?"

"Yes," I said resignedly, "that's me."

It was an embarrassing error, for whoever had drafted the letter for the director's signature had used not my true name, but my Agency-assigned pseudonym, which, of course, had to be changed. I often wondered how O'Dwyer regarded this unprofessional lapse, but he never referred to it and in many ways was extraordinarily helpful to me, within the limits of ambassadorial flexibility.

One by one, my outside agents were arriving in Mexico, Bill Buckley among the first, with his pregnant wife, Pat. She and Dorothy quickly became friends, as did Bill and I, frequently lunching at what was then the only good French restaurant in Mexico City: La Normandia.

At embassy functions I became acquainted with leading American businessmen in Mexico. Those whom I regarded as being potentially useful I had name-checked in Washington. If they were clean, I asked permission to contact and recruit as informants. Once recruited, they, in turn, suggested other Americans or Mexicans who would not only be useful, but were believed susceptible of approach. So, within a comparatively short time I acquired a large number of external assets in Mexico, including a popular young

Catholic priest active in the anti-Communist movement at one of the universities.

Dorothy's time was fast approaching, and we had located a comfortable house in Lomas de Chapultepec, overlooking the city from the west. Our household effects had reached Veracruz, whence they had been trucked to Mexico City, but of our Cadillac nothing was known.

At my urging, the consul general telephoned the American Consulate in Veracruz for information about the car and reported to me that the vehicle had indeed been landed. It was merely waiting to be picked up. So my office chauffeur drove me to the port of Veracruz, where I called on the consul. He took me to lunch in his tropical-style home, told me more about Veracruz than I wanted to know and drove me for a leisurely tour of the waterfront. However, though we drove up and down among the warehouses, we were unable to see what should have been a distinctive sight—my white Cadillac convertible. Finally the consul conferred with the Mexican customs chief, who searched his records and led us around the corner of a customs shed. There, parked near the seawall, half buried under sand, stood an automobile. Apparently it had once been a convertible, for strips of tattered canvas played in the sea breeze, but of the white paint, nothing remained. A storm lasting several days had sandblasted the paint from my car, and I could hardly believe that it was the same vehicle we had turned over to the movers in Washington only a few weeks before. But with a new battery and a few gallons of Pemex gas the engine started, and slowly and apprehensively I began driving my car back to Mexico City. The sun was hot enough to make me wish for the nonexistent top, and I paused frequently at roadside stands for refreshment, confining myself to bottled beer in memory of my brush with Mexican belly bugs four years before.

I reached Mexico City after dark and left the car in a commercial garage next door to our apartment. To Dorothy I reported the dismal findings and the even worse news that insurance coverage for the damage was so debatable that I anticipated having to litigate my claim. Next morning I went to the garage to take out the car so that I could drive Dorothy to visit our newly rented house, but I had barely turned the corner when I saw a car half blocking the street, nose smashed into a lamppost. It was, of course, my car and when I entered the garage, the attendant was nowhere to be found.

It developed that the night attendant, both entranced by and unfamiliar with an automatic shift, had decided to experiment during the small hours of the morning. Unable to stop the car inside the garage without ramming other vehicles, he had headed for the exit and come to rest against the lamppost.

As it turned out, his misfortune gave me a needed break: The garage insurers had my car towed to the Cadillac dealership, where it was repaired and painted to my satisfaction; even a new top was thrown in.

Dorothy and I now had to decide whether to move to the new house or to stay in the temporary apartment. If we moved, we were concerned lest the arrival of the baby catch us only half unpacked, but staying in the apartment had its disadvantages too.

Below us was a street-floor nightclub. Through the thin floors penetrated the music of mariachis and the jukebox beat of samba, rumba, fox-trot and bolero. Unaccountably, cars arrived and departed from dusk until dawn, making sleep difficult. Finally it dawned on us that we were the unsuspecting upstairs neighbors of a joy house whose staff and clientele were highly mobile.

After a particularly riotous night below we decided to move away. That evening, after a long day of unpacking, we were sitting exhaustedly in the one bedroom we had managed to assemble when labor pains began. Like any expectant father, I drove my wife at breakneck speed to the hospital—the British Cowdray—and waited anxiously in the anteroom until a pink light signified that we had a daughter.

Our firstborn child was named Lisa Tiffany Hunt, and her birth was inscribed jointly in the civil register of Mexico City and in the consular lists of Americans born abroad.

Although on the surface relations between the OSO station chief and myself were correct and occasionally even amiable, he was generally less than helpful in easing my operational path. By chance I learned that his communicator was showing him my dispatches and radio messages before transmitting them. This practice countered my letter of instruction, which had guaranteed me unhindered access to station communications, and was typical of the type of bureaucratic sabotage indulged in by OSO until the eventual merger of OSO and OPC.

I was visited by my division chief, who complained that I was sending too many plans and requests for name checks for his staff to handle. I remarked that it was much easier for him to acquire additional personnel in Washington than for me to attempt to extract more personnel slots from the embassy. I also pointed out that my OPC station and its projects were breaking new ground; accordingly, both of us should try to learn from the experience.

My relations with the local FBI office, cool at first, then cautious, became friendly and cooperative when the Bureau agents realized that I shared their enthusiasm for hunting and fishing. This cordiality was cemented when I helped finance and form a largely FBI duck-hunting club only forty-five minutes from the embassy, and this cordiality brought me FBI cooperation that the OSO station chief had never been able to gain.

One day an FBI agent asked me if by chance I knew the whereabouts of the former Spanish Republican guerrilla General "El Campesino," whose true name was Valentin Gonzalez. I asked the reason for the Bureau's interest in El Campesino and was told that a Congressional committee desired him to testify in Washington concerning the worldwide Communist movement. Although I denied knowledge of his whereabouts to the Bureau agent, in fact El Campesino was concealed in a Cuernavaca safehouse, where he was telling his life story to a biographer. I knew the glare of Washington publicity would diminish the credibility of El Campesino's book and give the Communists a golden opportunity to accuse and defame him as an American capitalist lackey. A rough, untutored peasant, El Campesino was notorious during the Spanish Civil War for his brutality, as much as he was famed for his brilliant guerrilla tactics.*
When the Communist side capitulated and the Spanish Civil War came to an end, El Campesino and many thousands of refugees were taken to the Soviet Union along with literally all of Spain's gold bullion reserves in consequence of their wartime control of Madrid. There El Campesino was sent to Frunze Military Academy, but with the outbreak of World War II, El Campesino fell under suspicion of bourgeois tendencies. When he declined to sign a prepared confession, he was sentenced to a forced-labor camp in Siberia. A tough man, physically and mentally, El Campesino survived two Arctic

*El Campesino appears in the pages of Ernest Hemingway's *For Whom the Bell Tolls*.

winters before being shipped to Moscow as a laborer to dig Moscow's underground subway. He managed to escape from the Soviet Union to Iran and at the end of World War II surfaced in Paris. There a Marxist writer-intellectual brought him to the attention of the Paris station, with the suggestion that El Campesino's life story be recorded in book form. Soon he and his biographer were brought to Mexico and became my responsibility. The book, *Life and Death in the USSR* was one of the first personal revelations of Soviet and Stalinist terror and barbarity and enjoyed translation into many languages, particularly Spanish, and was sold throughout Latin America.*

Another client was Eudocio Ravines, the Chilean Marxist intellectual. A sometime disciple of Mao Tse-tung, Ravines successfully conspired to install in Chile the first Popular Front (Communist) government in the Western Hemisphere. But like many Communist intellectuals, he became disaffected by the Hitler-Stalin pact and fled Chile to wander from country to country until he was contacted by CIA. Living under an alias in Mexico City, Ravines was finishing his book. I assigned Bill Buckley to help him complete *The Yenan Way* and translate it into English for American and British audiences. For several months this project occupied most of Buckley's time; and when the English translation had been accepted in New York by Scribner's, Buckley decided to leave Mexico and CIA. He was, he told me, thinking either of purchasing the *American Mercury* magazine, which had been on the downgrade for several years, or founding a magazine of his own. But his mind was made up, and in any case Pat was not enthusiastic about living indefinitely in Mexico. So, reluctantly, I saw them go.**

Meanwhile, my station agents had established anti-Communist organizations that embraced many sectors of Mexican life: youth, students, women, church and labor. Through recruited journalists, I had access to the pages of Mexico's most respected newspapers, penetrations of the Communist Party of Mexico and the Trotskyite

---

*Soon after Castro took over Cuba I noticed *La Vida y La Muerte en la URSS* in Havana bookstores, but copies were quickly confiscated and destroyed.

**Drawing our wills, Dorothy and I asked Bill Buckley to become guardian of our children and executor of our estate in the event of our death. Already the children's godfather, Bill agreed.

offshoot and two organizations that could accomplish medium-size public demonstrations on call.

From time to time our Mexican agents disrupted Communist meetings held indoors with CIA-manufactured stink bombs and itching powder. One such disturbance took place during the well-attended recantation speech of Communist artist Diego Rivera.

At my request Joe Bryan lent me an artist who spent a month at the station and turned out enough poster designs so that for several months a different anti-Communist poster appeared on the walls of Mexico City each week. These poster campaigns did much to awaken Mexican public consciousness to the menace of international Communism and appeared under the aegis of an organization headed by a Mexican of unimpeachable reputation.

A long letter from Bob and Maxine North in Bangkok informed me that Bob's cover work was to establish a Thai film industry, erect a modern studio and produce a lengthy film reenactment of an epic Thai legend. For her part, Maxine was learning Thai and improving her already first-rate golf game. En route Washington for consultation, Bob spent a few days with me in Mexico City, where we planned a complicated operation designed to discredit a prominent Mexican Communist. The operation required critical timing and a good deal of work by the printing services section of CIA's Technical Services Division.

The Mexican Communist leader was then visiting Peking. On the day of his departure Bob North airmailed me a copy of a Chinese newspaper announcing his departure, sending a duplicate copy to CIA headquarters. To replace the departure announcement I fabricated a story in which the Mexican Communist was quoted as deprecating fellow Mexicans and saying, among other things, that Mexican peasants could never hope to achieve the cultural level of the superior Chinese. I cabled the fabrication to headquarters, where a special type font had been made by reproducing samples from the local paper. My fabricated story was set in this duplicate type and the entire front page of the local paper re-created by technical means. A dozen copies were pouched to me and were received before the target Communist returned to Mexico.

The fabricated newspapers were made available to local journalists who published facsimiles of the offensive interview together with a translation into Spanish. The target's protestations of innocence gained no credence whatever, for technical tests conducted on the duplicated Chinese paper affirmed that the type in which the story was printed perfectly matched other type samples in the same newspaper and so had to be authentic.*

*It was this sort of technical assistance from CIA that I lacked when I undertook to fabricate two State Department cables in 1971.

7 A DEFECTOR ARRIVES

within every American embassy there is an Interagency Defector Committee (IADC). Generally it comprises the ambassador, the United States Information Service head, the senior Department of Defense attaché, and is chaired by the senior CIA representative. Abroad our embassies are guarded by Marines who are supposed to be familiar with standard operating procedures in the event that an apparent defector seeks asylum at an embassy.

These standard instructions are promulgated by the senior defector committee in Washington, and embassy officials abroad are supposed to be familiar with their contents.

In Mexico City the CIA station was running technical penetrations of several Iron Curtain embassies. ("Technical penetration" means either that the target embassy was bugged with microphones or that its phone lines were being tapped.) During a periodic review of local technical operations, which I participated in, the subject of an embassy which I'll call the Hungarian Embassy—but which was not—came up.

After months of listening to that embassy's incoming and outgoing telephone calls and receiving surveillance reports on the senior embassy personnel, the OSO chief of station declared that while there were two or three defector possibilities within the Hungarian Embassy, the one man who would *not* defect was the political counselor, whom he described as an old, hard-line Communist. Not long after this meeting I noticed a general rush of American Embassy personnel in the direction of the main reception room. Inquiring the reason for the mass gathering, I was told that the USIS chief was arranging a press conference featuring the Hungarian Embassy political counselor, who, a few minutes before, had walked into the American Embassy and asked for political asylum. I sprinted into the room, found the USIS chief and demanded to know what he proposed to do. All smiles, he said that he was going to publicize the defection of the Hungarian diplomat. Heatedly, I asked if he recalled his obligation in the event of a walk-in. My question jarred his memory, but before he could reply, I told him that all that was required of him was silence.

In the meantime we had been joined by the OSO station chief, and together we told the now-flustered USIS man to cancel the press conference without explanation. In an anteroom we found the Hungarian political counselor and asked him to leave the embassy at once. Hungarians were a drug on the market, we told him, and his only chance of obtaining U.S. asylum was to return to his embassy, bring out as many records and code books as he could and submit to extended debriefing. There was one alternative, we told him: Return to his normal duties, but as an agent for American intelligence.

He replied that he believed he had come under suspicion for pro-Western leanings and did not believe he would be allowed to remain long as counselor. As to the first alternative, he was clearly nervous. We asked if his wife and children were safe and he said they were: He had taken them to a hotel and registered them under a false name. If we insisted, he would attempt to enter the main embassy safe and bring back the documents we requested. However, by now, he felt, his absence must have been noticed and he feared that if he returned, he would be walking into a trap. Nevertheless, he would make the effort. We told him, frankly, that he would be surveilled during his return to the Hungarian Embassy and that once inside he was on his own. We gave our word, however, that if he were held at the embassy, we would be responsible for the safety and resettlement of his wife and children. Then we alerted a surveillance team and had the counselor leave our embassy by a back door. By now, Ambassador O'Dwyer had been alerted to the defection attempt and wanted to know what was going on. When he was given details, he harshly rebuked the USIS officer, whom the OSO station chief and I could cheerfully have killed for his stupidity.

Half an hour passed, then an hour. The surveillance team called in to report that the counselor was still in the Hungarian Embassy. A station officer went over to the hotel to stay with his wife and children pending the outcome of the counselor's burglary attempt. Finally, the team called in: The counselor had exited the Hungarian Embassy carrying a thick briefcase and was headed toward Chapultepec Park. They would keep him in sight and continue reporting.

We recontacted the counselor in Chapultepec Park and he turned over his bulging briefcase to CIA. He had been lucky to leave the embassy, he told us, for while he was rifling the safe, word reached his ambassador that he, the counselor, had defected and was even then at the American Embassy. But the counselor's presence in the Hungarian Embassy gave the lie to the otherwise unsubstantiated rumor.

Although his codes and documents were of substantial value, we would much have preferred to run him as a penetration agent within the Hungarian Embassy, but this rare and golden intelligence opportunity had been denied us by the asinine behavior of the USIS chief.

We called the IADC into session, and a series of flash messages between Mexico and Washington resulted in the counselor and his family being granted asylum and resettlement in the United States.

This episode was an early demonstration to me of the fallibility of embassy personnel and the likelihood that during a critical incident they were likely to react according to instinct rather than to previously established rules, procedures and regulations.

8 SURREPTITIOUS ENTRY

IN the fall of 1952 our second daughter, Kevan, was born. My mother-in-law was with us for that event, and after her departure the arrival of my mother in Mexico to see her two granddaughters signaled family reconciliation.

The leaders of some of my student organizations began to bring in alarming reports from neighboring Guatemala. A delegation of Mexican anti-Communist students had been visiting their counterparts in Guatemala City when they were seized and roughly treated by the police of left-leaning Jacobo Arbenz. A man of modest intellect, Colonel Arbenz had married the daughter of a prominent San Salvador family, and she, a doctrinaire Communist, had guided his career from army ranks to the presidency of Guatemala.

Three of the Mexican students had been tortured on Arbenz's orders: their testicles burned with electric wires and water forced into their mouths and rectums. I reported these disturbing occurrences to headquarters and for a while heard nothing.

In Guatemala City a new American ambassador had effectively silenced the CIA station by insisting that only messages personally approved by him could be sent to CIA headquarters in Washington. The preceding ambassador had been embarrassed when a technical installation in the headquarters of the Guatemalan Communist Party had been discovered and traced back to the CIA station. So it was that at a time when our Guatemala City station should have been supplying intelligence to Washington that would have established the Communist trend in Guatemala, it remained almost entirely silent.

I now made a concerted effort to obtain intelligence on the internal Guatemalan situation, using Mexican border crossers, most of whom were students. As my reports began receiving more attention in Washington, I was summoned to headquarters for an audience with the director of Central Intelligence.

Beetle Smith,* a few members of his staff and my division chief heard me out, and when I left the meeting, I was optimistic that something was going to be done.

But before returning to Mexico, I visited old friends on the PP staff: Bryan, Farr, Alsop, Thompson and Lloyd, then stopped at the security office for a periodic polygraph test, a standard lie-detection routine covering sex, money and foreign contacts. Failure to pass this CIA test meant immediate dismissal from the service. When that unpleasant ordeal was completed, I stopped at the desk of the security officer whose task it was, among other things, to review materials written by Agency employees prior to publication. In Mexico it had been my custom to forward one copy of a finished book to the Department of State for review and simultaneously a copy to CIA security. State customarily assented by return pouch, but some six weeks had passed and I had not yet heard from my own security office. I asked the officer if there was any problem with the manuscript, and he admitted that there was none. I said that as long as I was there I might as well pick up the manuscript and take it back with me. At this his face reddened, and he said that he was having difficulty locating the manuscript. As my questions became more pointed, he confessed that his secretary had taken my manuscript to her apartment to read at leisure and unaccountably had lost a large section of it. I was welcome to the remainder, he said, and he would redouble his efforts to locate the missing portion.

I told him that I was not writing for the amusement of his staff and that if the Office of Security took the review procedure so lightly, then I proposed to treat the requirement in equal terms: Henceforth, I would publish what I chose, and the Office of Security was at liberty to lodge complaints against me after the fact.

---

*In reference to the large number of retired military officers for whom Eisenhower had found sinecures in CIA, Beetle Smith is reliably reported to have said, "Every time I sound reveille around here they think it's a call to stack arms."

Almost without exception I followed that formula until my retirement in 1970.

On returning to Mexico City, I was visited by the Guatemala chief of station, an old and uninspiring FBI retread. He was totally subservient to his ambassador and quite content to exercise no operational responsibilities. Apologetically, he suggested that I not rock the Central American boat and wondered aloud what, if anything, could be done to alter the ominous trend in Guatemalan politics.

To him I outlined in general my exposition to the director after extracting a promise that he would not inform his ambassador of my Washington meeting. My revelations shocked him, and mentally looking down the road, I felt that he would have to be replaced before any serious action could be undertaken in Guatemala.

As the days and weeks went on, my original optimism began to fade and finally I learned from a visiting branch chief that as concerned Guatemala, no initiatives were being planned.* Word-of-mouth reports reaching me indicated that Beetle Smith was considering merging OPC and OSO stations around the world. The reports had the dismal ring of authenticity, and I was told that Wisner and the headquarters OSO chief were even then deciding those stations in which the OPC chief would take over the merged station and those in which the OSO chief would become the senior CIA representative. In Mexico the OSO chief of station, by virtue of his many years with the FBI, was already my senior in terms of grade. He, however, had received orders to take charge of a station in Europe, and so I felt (rightly, as it turned out) that the relative seniority of his successor would be the determining local factor.

The Fuchs-Rosenberg-Gold atom spy ring had been much in the news. One morning Ambassador O'Dwyer summoned me to an early meeting, attended by only the OSO chief, the Legal Attaché and myself. Angrily he denounced the FBI special agent in charge of the Mexico City office for having brought about the arrest of Morton Sobell the preceding night and his expulsion from Mexico to

---

*Had the President authorized intervention even at that late stage, overthrowing Arbenz would have proved much simpler than it did in 1954. The Nixon Administration did not authorize covert activity in Chile until it had been presented with a fait accompli, in the form of Allende's Marxist government. I have never fully understood whether these delays were the result of reluctance to engage in covert political action or top-level misperception of events which, to us in the field, were abundantly clear.

the United States. The FBI chief took the rebuke but offered no excuses. In the exchanges that followed it became apparent that the FBI had advance knowledge that Sobell, a fugitive, was hiding in Mexico and that the Soviets had provided him with contact instructions. On a fixed date Sobell was to have stood by the Christopher Columbus statue near the American Embassy and wait to be approached by a man carrying a folded newspaper under his arm. Recognition signals were to have been exchanged, after which Sobell would have been spirited out of Mexico, presumably to the Soviet Union. Through informants, the Office of the Legal Attaché had located Sobell in a motel just outside Mexico City. At Bureau request the federal police arrested Sobell and put him in a car driven by FBI agents, a Mexican policeman riding as passenger to give the peremptory expulsion the thin aura of legality.

Driving in relays, the Bureau agents had reached the border not long before our meeting with the ambassador and delivered Sobell to FBI agents on the American side. Had there been a road accident, the ambassador kept repeating, the whole affair would have become known and he would have had to make difficult and embarrassing explanations to the Mexican Foreign Ministry. Moreover, he said pointedly to the Legal Attaché, the Bureau had no arrest power in a foreign country and really very little business being in the embassy at all. According to O'Dwyer's view, Sobell, while in Mexico, should have been a CIA responsibility and not a Bureau target. I agreed in principle, but reminded the ambassador that CIA had no arrest powers whatever, foreign or domestic. I was embarrassed, of course, that CIA had not known of Sobell's presence, much less the instructions given him by Soviet Intelligence.

Twenty years later I was to learn that what the Bureau had done to Sobell, they did routinely to fugitives they were able to locate abroad.

I had not taken part in a surreptitious-entry operation since Sparrow II burglarized the office of the Italian consul in Shanghai and photographed his lists of Nazi and Soviet agents in China. That entry had been hardly surreptitious, with uniformed men piling out of jeeps and bursting into the consulate, where we set up a Recordak camera and photographed records for many hours, hardly caring whether the consul appeared or not.

One Communist Embassy in Mexico City was located two blocks from the American Embassy in an apartment building. From our CIA offices we had a direct line of sight to the front windows of the embassy, which were on the third floor of the apartment building. According to prescribed form, we cased the target office and mounted round-the-clock surveillance on the principal embassy officers. With the concurrence of the National Security Agency a date was fixed for surreptitious entry, and a week or so before that date a team of CIA safecrackers arrived in town. These highly skilled men were part of a small cadre of specialists that traveled, and perhaps still travel, for entry operations in different parts of the world.

We recruited the charwoman who cleaned the Communist Embassy offices and placed a microphone in the ambassador's office from which could be heard conversations relayed to an apartment—the Listening Post—we had rented one floor above. The microphone installation supplemented telephone taps which had been active for some time. Several station cars were equipped with mobile transceivers that operated on frequencies not normally utilized in Mexico. We had a floor plan of the offices, a description of the safe, and a putty imprint of its keyhole. The charwoman provided us with a key to the embassy service door, and we duplicated it. Now we were ready to move.

A Friday night had been selected for the first entry attempt, for, according to their pattern, the Communists left their offices early Friday afternoon and did not return until Monday at midmorning. With the aid of binoculars, the interior of the ambassador's office could be seen from my office, the planted microphone would inform us of any movement within the target, and as each staff member left the offices that Friday afternoon, they were followed to their homes or apartments and continuing surveillance established. By about eleven that night surveillance reported most of the staff members asleep and the remaining few accounted for. A precautionary telephone call was placed to the Embassy; through the pickup mike we could hear it ring repeatedly, but no one answered. The word was Go.

Using the duplicate key, the entry team gained access to the target premises and reported the location dark and quiet. Through the microphone we could hear them moving quietly around. They did not really need to transmit to us on their walkie-talkies, for we could hear their conversations perfectly well.

The operating procedure followed in this and all other entry operations I participated in was to cover all windows with opaque black muslin, to eliminate the possibility of team flashlights being seen outside the embassy, then the team went to work on the safe.

Meanwhile, in the basement below, the night watchman was drinking tequila and playing cards with one of our agents who had begun his cultivation a month earlier.

Above, the entry team forced a soft metal compound into the safe keyhole and, when the compound hardened, used it to make a sturdy duplicate key. Before opening the safe, an amplifying listening device was applied to the keyhole to detect such sounds as, for example, the ticking of a time lock or a booby-trap bomb.

As soon as the safe door was open, a Polaroid photograph was taken of the contents and developed on the spot. Later, by referring to the photograph, everything in the safe could be replaced in its original position. In a small room off the ambassador's office the team set up a camera specially designed by CIA for document photography. Floodlights were plugged into the embassy's electrical system, and for the next three hours the entire contents of the safe were photographed.

Inside an inner drawer the team found more than $30,000 in American currency but were ordered to leave it there. Photography completed, the team packed up and withdrew from the target area in reverse order, removing the blackout drapes just before they left.

Before dawn the entry team had flown from Mexico to Dallas, where they changed identities and flew to Washington. Pouched separately was the photographic record of their night-long work. The code-book film was sent at once to NSA, and the rest of the filmed documents were examined at leisure by interested sections of CIA. Soon the Mexico City station received lists of Mexicans whom the Guatemalan Embassy had subverted, as well as the names of prominent Mexicans still on their target lists. Of equal importance were ambassadorial notes covering his efforts to purchase arms and munitions in Mexico, a physical description of the ambassador's Soviet Embassy contact and a number of profiles in which the ambassador appraised senior officials of the American Embassy.

If we were able to burglarize at will, we were also vulnerable to Mexican burglars.

An FBI agent and his wife, asleep in their bed, were chloroformed and their dog killed while burglars removed everything from their home with a moving van. My own home had been entered twice and looted. We lost my wife's jewelry, my typewriter, assorted sterling silver, a radio and other valuables. All these effects were insured, but Dorothy and I preferred to wait, hoping the Mexican police would produce, at least, her jewelry.

A distinctive sapphire earring of my wife's had been dropped by the second set of burglars, and with it to go on, its mate was located in the Thieves Market downtown. Spurred on by the urgings of the Legal Attaché and myself, Mexican detectives called daily at my home, assuring me they were following all leads intensively. Moreover, the insurance company had offered a large reward for the return of our stolen valuables.

Presently I was summoned to Mexican police headquarters and a strongbox opened for my inspection. In it was most of my wife's missing jewelry. I identified it as such, but to my surprise saw the strongbox closed, locked and removed. The jewels were needed for evidence, the detective told me; otherwise the thieves would go unprosecuted.

I was much less interested in a thief's prosecution than in the recovery of my wife's valuables, many of which were family heirlooms. I consulted with the insurers, who indicated that the jewels would be released to me as soon as the reward was paid. After this was done, I was again summoned to police headquarters and again permitted to see my wife's possessions. This time I expected to take them with me, but no, not just yet. The detective dilated upon the number of men and man-hours the investigation had consumed and suggested an additional reward should be forthcoming. I named the sum already paid him by the insurance company and suggested that it was quite enough. He closed the lid of the strongbox. I asked him what figure he had in mind. He raised the strongbox lid. Five cases of scotch would do nicely, he told me with a vulpine grin. I felt like shooting him, but bargained him down to three. True at last to his word, the detective came to my home the following day, turned over the strongbox to me and carted off three cases of Scotch, which, I knew, he would be able to sell for three or four hundred dollars on the black market.

I had been slow to learn the traditional way of dealing with Latin American policemen, but it was an object lesson I never forgot.

There now arrived from Washington a long dispatch from Beetle Smith addressed jointly to the OSO station chief and to myself. The two stations were to be merged and the overall station chief would succeed the OSO incumbent. I was named deputy. I accepted the change with what good grace I could muster, but asked that I be reassigned. Not long thereafter the new station chief arrived and within three months my replacement reported to the embassy.

Before departing, Dorothy and I were remarried in her Catholic faith and our daughters baptized as Catholics. For as long as I could I kept this intelligence from my parents, for I knew that it would inevitably produce ill feeling. Then, after a month of farewell parties and making last-minute purchases and packing, we saw our lift van trucked away and were driven by friends to the airport.

From there we flew to Florida, where we vacationed in a cottage given us by Dorothy's mother. Toward the end of my leave I went to Washington to find a house and receive word of my next assignment. I was to spend a year or so at headquarters, I was told, as chief of covert operations for an area of the world with which I had had no prior experience whatever: the Balkans.

COVERT ACTION IN THE BALKANS AND GUATEMALA

CIA's Southeast Europe (the Balkan) Division was responsible for Albania, Yugoslavia, Greece, Bulgaria and Rumania. In addition, to service the intricate web of Balkan politics and intrigues, SE had small bases in Frankfurt, Paris and Rome. With the exception of Greece, all of the target countries were Communist, and Greece itself had had a near escape from Communist domination. In the wake of the Greek Civil War, thousands of children from northern Greece had been taken into Bulgaria, and their fate was a continuing source of sorrow and concern to Greeks and their government alike.

Under Josip Broz, Tito, Yugoslavia had chosen a course divergent from the Kremlin's, yet as a Communist country was seeking no rapprochement with the West.

The ancient city of Trieste, at the head of the Adriatic Sea, was also a concern of my new division and a source of sharpening controversy between Italy and Yugoslavia. Though it is not essential to detail Triestine history, suffice it to say that after a saber-rattling Yugoslav attempt to take over the entire city it was eventually divided between the two contesting nations into Zones A and B.

In Athens we had a sizable station whose chief was close to the royal family and enjoyed close working relations with the chief of Greek Intelligence. From Greece's northern borders CIA agents crossed into Bulgaria, and air operations were run from an airfield near Athens into all Balkan countries with the exception of Yugoslavia and Albania. From Bari, Italy, airdrops of leaflets, needles, flour and halvah were made into Albania.

Because Albania had long been considered within the British zone of influence, all agent operations into Albania were conducted jointly by CIA and MI-6. Our initial cadre of Albanian agents had been drawn almost entirely from the bodyguard of exiled King Zog. These men were trained and equipped in West Germany and launched by air from Bari, but losses were extraordinarily, if not suspiciously, high. On one occasion an Albanian team signaled for the snatch ("skyhook") pickup of an allegedly injured team member. It was decided to combine this hazardous mission with a leaflet overflight, with the snatch pickup to come first.

The site signaled by the team was a valley between two parallel ranges of low mountains. Our C-47 made its approach down the valley, flying only fifty to sixty feet above the ground, its skyhook trailing. The pickup rig was not discernible on the ground, but the occupants of the plane suddenly found that they were being fired upon from the mountains on either side. So low was their altitude that antiaircraft guns were actually firing *down* upon the plane. Although struck several times, the C-47 managed to escape and half glide back across the Adriatic to a crash landing at Bari. Impact caused the release into the air of hundreds of thousands of leaflets that had been destined for Albanian patriots. The Italian Army was cooperative, however, and was able to recover most of the leaflets, although mention of the strange occurrence appeared in the Italian press.

Somewhat later the malfunctioning of a leaflet-drop device caused Bulgarian leaflets to be released prematurely over the Aegean Sea. The winds unfortunately carried the leaflets over the Greek mainland, and both Athens and Piraeus were showered with propaganda leaflets in the Bulgarian language.

By now Allen Dulles had become director of Central Intelligence, and his deputy, Air Force General Charles P. Cabell. Cabell's final clearance was required on all air operations over Communist countries, and the problem of securing these clearances for Balkan overflights fell to me.

A short, rather aggressive man, Cabell* came to CIA with no prior background in covert intelligence, much less in propaganda or political-action operations. I recall making an overflight clearance request to Cabell which included items in scarce supply in Albania that were to be air-dropped in the name of the Albanian National Liberation Front. In each bag was a pound of flour, some razor blades, needles and the Middle East delicacy, halvah. Cabell seemed uninterested in the flight track of the aircraft, its altitude and the location of enemy antiaircraft and airfields. Halvah puzzled him until it was explained, then he began interrogating me about the flour:

"Sure it ain't moldy?"

"I'm sure, sir."

"Got maggots in it?"

"I'm sure it doesn't, sir."

"Well, where did it come from?"

"Army surplus stores."

"Army, huh? I know all about that Army stuff. Better make damn sure there's no maggots in it, eh?"

"Yes, sir."

"What about the razor blades? Rusty?"

"No, sir."

"Where did the blades come from?"

"The Army, sir."

"Well, just make damn sure that stuff is OK, see?"

"Yes, sir. Is the mission approved?"

"It's approved."

Cabell scrawled his signature on the operational proposal and I departed to cable Athens his OK.

The Greek royal family permitted CIA to erect a large radio transmitter on royal property. For several years the transmitter beamed clandestine broadcasts into the Balkan countries.

During one visit to Athens I was guest at a luncheon hosted by the Greek colonel in charge of military intelligence. He was a gutsy little officer who had fought both Nazis and Communists on his native

---

*In April, 1961, Cabell suspended a scheduled air strike against remaining aircraft on Cuban airfields. His intervention cost the cancellation of the strike and deprived the CIA-trained Cuban invasion brigade of any chance for victory.

soil. The meal offered, among other Ottoman dishes, sheeps' eyes and testicles and copious drafts of *retsina* wine. Liking neither the eyes nor the resin wine, I opted for the wine as the lesser of the two evils and was nearly immobilized for the next twenty-four hours. On another occasion I attended a diplomatic ball and found myself dancing with a charming young lady. Rapport established, we were conspiring to abandon the ballroom in favor of a quiet *taverna* when the Athens chief of station beckoned me aside. She was, he told me, an Egyptian princess and sister to Faruk. Although she was separated from her husband, our ambassador hoped I would do nothing that could lead to a situation susceptible of misinterpretation and possible unfavorable publicity.

On the basis of these and other incidents I decided that while Athens might be a great place to live, I found it a difficult city for visitors.

Near Frankfurt, CIA housed and continued training the steadily diminishing remnants of King Zog's bodyguard. Intelligence from their predecessors had been nil, and the near loss of our C-47 had caused the entire operation to be viewed with deep suspicion. Because the anti-Communist Albanian political leaders had settled in Rome, it was there that both we and the British maintained contact with them. So it was to Rome that Division Chief John Richardson and I went to break the news to CIA and British case officers.

There we informed Rome station and its SE Division component that because of unacceptable losses, we were canceling further Albanian operations. By prearrangement we met the British representative at a sidewalk cafe not far from the American Embassy, on the Via Veneto.

I have forgotten his name, but let us call him Pointdexter. He could have been a prototype for one of Graham Greene's burnt-out cases: With rheumy eyes, trembling hands and a capillary-flecked face that had not been shaved in several days, Pointdexter presented neither a professional nor a reassuring appearance.

While waiting our arrival, he had been drinking, and now as we sat down, he ordered a round of double "martoonis" for all of us.

Richardson came quickly to the point, and when Pointdexter had tossed off his drink, he stared unbelievingly at us, eyes welling, tears trickling slowly through the stubble on his face.

"Then it's all over," he said faintly.

"All over," Richardson replied.

"I don't know what they'll say about it in London," Pointdexter said, twirling his empty martini glass.

"London already knows,"* Richardson told him.

"They *know*?"

"They know," Richardson repeated, and after some sterile amenities we left, wondering how MI-6 would absorb its alcoholic derelict.

King Zog of Albania, whose retainers we had fed into the maw of the KGB, had been granted asylum in Egypt by then King Faruk. The two kings shared more than a common bond of royalty, for Faruk was descended from an Albanian pasha. However, with Faruk's overthrow and the brief accession of Mohammed Naguib, Zog's sanctuary was threatened. Moreover, Naguib had been deposed by another army officer, Gamal Abdel Nasser, whose minions had begun systematically harassing Zog, his sisters and retainers.

Anticipating eventual asylum in the United States, Zog had purchased a large estate on Long Island where he intended to house his retinue and maintain them from crops grown on the lush acreage. Zog, however, had never been able to occupy the estate, and though local police occasionally patrolled the area, it became the target of vandals. Every month or so a CIA security officer from the New York office would travel out to the estate and look it over. He now reported it to be in deplorable condition, with windows broken and destruction from fires lighted on the ballroom floor from visiting vandals. Through the Cairo station came a plea for help from Zog. Egyptian customs officials refused to permit him to gain possession of a large refrigerator he had begun importing before Faruk's downfall. Worse, royal jewels and currency in a safe-deposit box had been blocked and he and his followers were in financial straits. Having unwittingly killed off a large portion of his exiled followers, CIA recognized a certain responsibility for King Zog's welfare.

To that end I was dispatched to Cairo, where I encountered

---

*MI-6 not only knew, but as was later revealed, the MI-6 liaison officer in Washington, Kim Philby, had for years been giving the Soviets advance information on all joint CIA-MI-6 operations. In Washington Philby was a popular figure with CIA contacts who were awed by his Cambridge University background, and Philby was never suspected of playing a double-agent role.

Kermit "Kim" Roosevelt, then chief of CIA's Middle East Division, who was in Cairo on business with President Nasser unrelated to the fortunes of King Zog. During a meeting at the Semiramis Hotel Roosevelt introduced me to Nasser, who was clearly enjoying his first flush of power. A tall, handsome man with flashing white teeth, Nasser exuded the charisma so typical of other popular leaders around the world who rose from anonymity to unexpected power. In my brief conversation with Nasser I was careful not to mention the purpose of my visit to Cairo, but on the following day Roosevelt told me that Nasser was disposed to reconsider Egypt's attitude toward the unwelcome royal exile.

When I returned to Washington, and after an exchange of cables with the Cairo station, it was decided that the simplest way to free Zog's prized refrigerator was to bribe a customs guard, and as to the problem of Zog's blocked assets, we could do no more than await the outcome of Nasser's good offices.

As for the royal family itself, we activated a plan whereby Egyptian authorities would wink at the departure of Zog's yacht, which would then head for Marseilles, and negotiations with the French government for Zog's asylum were put in the hands of the Paris station.

Meanwhile, despite increased police surveillance, Zog's Long Island estate was suffering rapid deterioration, and with Zog's annoyed consent CIA concluded arrangements for its sale.

By now Dorothy was expecting our third child and was experiencing a difficult pregnancy. Tony Jackson was in Bangkok working for Bob North, and my work at headquarters had settled into predictable routine. Then to my welcome surprise I was summoned to the office of C. Tracy Barnes, a wartime associate of Allen Dulles, Wall Street lawyer and brother-in-law of Joe Bryan. Barnes swore me to special secrecy and revealed that the National Security Council under Eisenhower and Vice President Nixon had ordered the overthrow of Guatemala's Communist regime. If I accepted the proposed assignment, Barnes told me, it would be as head of the project's propaganda and political action staff, and he added that nationally no clandestine project had higher priority than this.

I expressed concern over what I anticipated as a lengthy separation from my pregnant wife, and Barnes said that while he sympathized with my family situation, he nevertheless felt confident that I would be able to arrive at an accommodation which would meet both Agency and my personal requirements.

My transfer out of Southeast Europe Division coincided with the initially unexplained departure of two of my principal assistants, one a bachelor, the other a young father of two. I was later to learn that routine Agency polygraph tests detected their homosexuality and they had been allowed to resign.

The Guatemala project was set up as a semiautonomous unit within the Western Hemisphere Division. With its own funds, communications center and chain of command, it was able to operate without the customary smothering attentions of proliferating advisory staffs within the conventional CIA structure.

On joining the Guatemalan project, I was turned over to Central Cover Division, which provided me with documentation in an alias name, authentic but nonfunctional credit cards, bank references and the like, then began a series of concentrated sessions with the project's senior officers. During the first of these meetings I asked why it was that after my unproductive presentation to General Smith a year and a half before the climate was suddenly right for a political-action effort in Guatemala. In reply I was told that the difference had to do with domestic politics. Washington lawyer Thomas G. Corcoran ("Tommy the Cork" of New Deal days) had, among his clients, the United Fruit Company. United Fruit, like many American corporations in Guatemala, had watched with growing dismay nationalization, confiscation and other strong measures affecting their foreign holdings. Finally a land-reform edict issued by Arbenz proved the final straw, and Tommy the Cork had begun lobbying in behalf of United Fruit and against Arbenz. Following this special impetus our project had been approved by the National Security Council and was already under way.

There were, I was told, three Guatemalans around whom the nucleus of a provisional government might be formed: Colonel Castillo Armas, Colonel Idigoras Fuentes, and Juan Córdova Cerna. The two military men were unknown to me, but I had met Juan Córdova Cerna not long before leaving Mexico.

In a YMCA room the Guatemalan jurist had told me what Communism was doing to Guatemala and accurately predicted what Arbenz would do in the future. At the time I reported our conversation to headquarters, but its contents aroused no detectable in-

terest. Now Córdova Cerna was a figure of prime importance to the
Agency, and there was a consensus that it would be far better if
Guatemala were to be headed by a distinguished civilian rather than
continue under military rule, even if a strong man were resolutely
anti-Communist.

Our field headquarters occupied a two-story barracks on the
partly closed-down Marine air base at Opa-Locka, Florida. We slept
and worked in the same building and ate at the base mess hall not far
away. Several project officers with military reserve status wore
uniforms in order to lessen interest in our building. However, the
presence of our female secretaries was enough to arouse base speculation concerning our activities, and the previous installation of
heavy cables, telexes and other communications equipment sparked
interest in our building even before it was occupied.

A highly competent young officer whom I'll call Knight was in
charge of my propaganda unit, and we soon decided to prerecord a
series of terror broadcasts for D-day use over the Guatemalan
national radio frequency. In a safehouse Knight maintained a cadre
of Guatemalan newspapermen whom he turned into propagandists.
They prepared newspaper articles, pamphlets and leaflets and
served as sounding boards for propaganda ideas.

After a few weeks their enforced and unaccustomed celibacy
became the motive for a threatened strike. They wanted female
companionship and they wanted it fast. So, without the customary
immigration formalities, we flew girlfriends to Opa-Locka and installed them in the safehouse. The strike threat was averted, and
production resumed as before.

But if the Guatemalans were now all smiles, our security officer
was morose and reacted violently whenever he was jokingly charged
with pimping. Aside from maintaining the security of our operations
building, he was responsible for such collateral duties as fixing traffic
tickets for CIA and Guatemalan personnel and bailing out of jail
stray Guatemalans who had been arrested for lacking formal immigration documents.

A senior Guatemalan churchman had come to our notice through
his anti-Communist pronouncements. Cardinal Spellman arranged
clandestine contact between him and one of our agents so that we
could coordinate our parallel efforts. Anti-Arbenz and anti-
Communist pastoral letters were given wide publicity in the Latin

American press, and we air-dropped many thousands of leaflets carrying the pastoral messages into remote areas of Guatemala where they otherwise might have escaped notice.

Meanwhile in Honduras a small force of Guatemalan patriots was being assembled under the leadership of Colonel Castillo Armas, it having been decided in Washington that Colonel Idígoras Fuentes was a right-wing reactionary.*

Reluctantly Juan Córdova Cerna had left Guatemala for New Orleans. There it was discovered that he suffered throat cancer and treatment was begun at the Oeschner Clinic. There was available no other Guatemalan civilian of comparable prestige, so rather than our being able freely to choose Arbenz's successor, the nomination was made for us by circumstance: Colonel Castillo Armas.

Arbenz's emissaries had been busy behind the Iron Curtain procuring large quantities of Czech arms and munitions. This development was watched with apprehension, for if the armaments reached Arbenz before we were able to mount the invasion, the odds would be even more heavily weighted against Castillo and his men.

From time to time I was called to Washington on consultation and took advantage of these trips to stay overnight with my family and console my wife. Because my whereabouts at any given moment were unpredictable, my mother-in-law joined Dorothy, and through fortunate circumstances, I was in Washington when my first son, Howard St. John, was born in late March, 1954.

From Opa-Locka we were running airlifts to Honduras, where Castillo Armas' small band—never more than 140 men—was being trained. In one respect we planned to duplicate the technique through which, under Kim Roosevelt's direction, CIA had managed the nearly bloodless overthrow of Iranian Premier Mohammed Mossadegh: psychologically preparing the minds of the target government and population, then a sudden show of apparently massive force.

From Opa-Locka a CIA staff officer, documented and disguised as a European businessman, entered Guatemala and achieved the defection of a senior officer on Arbenz's staff. Through him we were able to gain up-to-the-minute situation intelligence concerning

---

*By a strange turn of fate, it was President Idígoras Fuentes who in 1960 and 1961 provided CIA with facilities for training and launching the Cuban invasion brigade. His clandestine cooperation with the United States, when exposed, caused his overthrow and expulsion.

Arbenz's intentions and the disposition of his troops. It was this officer who confirmed for us the expected arrival of the Czech munitions ship, and this date now became paramount in all our planning.

For the operation's final phase Tracy Barnes joined us in Opa-Locka and took charge. From him I learned that my next assignment would be in Tokyo as chief of covert operations for the North Asia Command. The news was not well received by my wife, whose stepfather had been killed on the Bataan Death March. Nor was I happy at the prospect of serving in a country whose soldiers, seamen and pilots had killed so many of my friends in World War II. Nevertheless, Barnes told me, the die was cast, the job was extraordinarily important and the CIA senior representative, a retired admiral, was demanding my prompt dispatch.

This meant I would not have the satisfaction of being in Opa-Locka during the actual invasion of Guatemala, but with all political and psychological-warfare plans now firmly made, I had to concede that the success of our project would not be determined, in the final analysis, by my geographic location.

I had barely reached Tokyo with my family when the overthrow of Colonel Arbenz was made known to the world.

After warning the civil population, our fighter aircraft made low-level strafing runs on Guatemala City and dropped some relatively harmless smoke bombs. From neighboring Honduras our powerful transmitter overrode the Guatemalan national radio, broadcasting messages to confuse and divide the population from its military overlords. A British ship unloading at Puerto Barrios was mistaken for the Czech arms-carrying freighter, bombed and sunk.*

Marching overland, the troops of Castillo Armas seized control of the capital and captured Arbenz and all his followers—including an asthmatic Argentine medical student and Communist camp follower named Ernesto Ché Guevara.

Among the Guatemalan victors there was much sentiment for dealing summary justice to them all, but a CIA man on the spot dissuaded Castillo from initiating what might well have turned into a nationwide blood bath. Stripped and searched at the airport, Ar-

---

*For many years reparations negotiations dragged on between CIA and MI-6; eventually the British were fully reimbursed for their loss.

benz, Guevara and their followers were allowed to board planes into exile. Guevara was granted political asylum in Mexico, where he soon joined the partisans of Cuban rabble-rouser Fidel Castro. Arbenz disappeared in Czechoslovakia but emerged several years later in Uruguay.

Nearly all personnel associated with the successful project received awards or commendations, and I felt a great sense of personal satisfaction over the outcome and the role I had played, beginning with my earliest warnings sent from Mexico. For the first time since the Spanish Civil War a Communist government had been overthrown—and in "Good Neighbor" Central America, at that.

In Guatemala the political transition was unexpectedly smooth, and Castillo Armas became a popular elected president until his untimely assassination by a member of his personal bodyguard.*

So ended my first field operation in international political action. Five years later they were to recommend me for a similar role in the far more massive United States effort to rid Cuba of its Communist dictator. Then through friendships and associations I formed on the Cuban project, I was able in 1971 and 1972 to recruit Cuban Americans to assist me in a series of White House-directed operations that came to be known as Watergate.

But all that was undreamed of as Dorothy and our three young children began life in postwar Japan, where I was covered and documented as a Department of the Army civilian adviser to General Matthew Ridgway's Far East Command.

---

*Among the bodyguard's possessions were documents showing he had been a constant listener to Radio Moscow's Spanish-language broadcasts.

10 NORTH ASIA COMMAND

IN Tokyo we were assigned quarters in the Ochanomizu (Teawater) District, across from the small Russian Orthodox church, Nikolaidomu. The house had been built by Frank Lloyd Wright while he was in Tokyo designing the old Imperial Hotel. Half the house was in traditional Japanese style, and the other half, which we occupied, was a European-style dwelling, though scaled down in size for its former Japanese occupants. The grounds had a moon gate, a courtyard, a garden with granite shrines and, most important, a large, deep lily pond which we converted into a swimming pool adequate for our children's use.

We acquired an excellent staff of Japanese servants, including a nursemaid for my infant son, and my daughters began attending classes at a small school run by a group of French nuns.

My office was in the CIA building at Pershing Heights, seat of the Far East Command and only about a ten-minute drive from our home. The North Asia Command's area of responsibility was immense: the Chinese mainland, North and South Korea, all of Japan, the islands of Taiwan and Okinawa, Hong Kong, and a forward base at Subic Bay in the Philippines. As I got to know the hundreds of CIA personnel in and around Tokyo who were working in one way or another for the North Asia Command, I was first startled, then amused, to find that our China operations group contained not one man who had had operational experience on the China mainland, although many of my former OSS comrades from wartime China

102

were scattered elsewhere throughout CIA. I felt this situation unfortunate, for in the Far East Red China was our principal enemy; the North Koreans were mere puppets of the Red Chinese.

While with the SE Division I had begun to sense what was confirmed in the Far East: CIA lacked the esprit de corps that was the binding cement of OSS. in its place was intense, backbiting competition among units and personnel. There was no longer that essential feeling of group elitism with its comforting assurance that you could trust your fellow officer with your life.

In the decade since the war our national intelligence organization had become peopled with bureaucrats and administrators, paper processors and analysts. Personal courage and resourcefulness were no longer prized; emphasis was on form, not substance; on conformity rather than individual daring and enterprise. This was perhaps due to a "democratization" of CIA, the need to rapidly absorb large numbers of "adequate" personnel, train them and hope for the best. As a result, CIA was soon faced with the problem of disposing of inadequate personnel lodged tightly within the interstices of the organization. A kindly man, Allen Dulles did little to confront the problem, but when Dick Helms became director, he moved affirmatively to rid the Agency of deadwood.

Although actual fighting in Korea had ended, we maintained a large unit in Seoul, presided over by CIA quasi-military personnel. On Taiwan we had a large station under Navy cover whose activities comprised mainland overflights, leaflet drops, agent infiltrations and massive radio propaganda broadcasts.

On Okinawa the CIA support base provided logistical support for CIA throughout the Far East. In Hong Kong we maintained a joint refugee-interrogation unit with the British, but ran no independent operations, Hong Kong being within the purview of Scotland Yard's Special Branch.

Every six weeks or so I would have to visit each of these bases, flying from Tokyo to Seoul and spending a day or two at each base as I continued south, skirting the Chinese mainland and ending my tour at Manila or Subic Bay. At CIA headquarters in Tokyo there was under way a more or less continuous counterintelligence review of the Fecteau-Downey case. These two young CIA men had been captured by the Chinese when their aircraft crashed on the mainland. Sentenced to long terms in prison, they were victims of a

Chinese double-agent penetration of a team whose launching had been overseen by Fecteau and Downey.

Of immediate concern to us was the capture by the Chinese of a B-29 bomber, piloted by a Far East Air Force colonel whose normal duties placed him in liaison with CIA in Tokyo. Evidently the aircraft had wandered over the mainland and had been forced down by Chinese MIG fighters. It was soon made known that the colonel possessed a number of high-level and sensitive clearances which gave him access to special information the Chinese would have been delighted to obtain. In such a case the operational assumption is that the captive has talked, told everything. This assumption had been made in the earlier case of Fecteau and Downey, and when they were released many years later, the assumption proved to have been correct.

After a few months the Chinese returned the colonel and his crew members through Hong Kong. Following a final damage assessment, orders were established throughout the Far East Command curtailing travel into potentially hazardous areas by anyone possessing sensitive clearances. Although I was permitted to visit Kowloon on the mainland side of Hong Kong, I was not permitted to drive within several miles of the New Territories, from which the armed border with mainland China could be observed.

As a member of the Tokyo Lawn Tennis Club I played there occasionally when duty permitted. Although I was unaware of it at the time, a GRU lieutenant colonel from the Soviet Embassy was also a member of the tennis club, having joined specifically to attempt to recruit an American. After several fruitless months passed, the colonel learned that he was to be recalled to the Soviet Union; he interpreted the recall in the worst possible light and set about making plans to defect.

On a cold winter Sunday morning the colonel left his lodgings and, because he knew no American Embassy personnel, headed for the British Embassy. There he was welcomed, and MI-6 began planning his evacuation. MI-6 officers escorted him to a British aircraft at Haneda Airport and sat with him in the plane, hoping the snow would cease and the plane could take off. However, a blizzard developed and the colonel now had second thoughts. He asked for and was given his personal-identification documents by his British escorts, who drove him back to downtown Tokyo. Walking the city streets, gripped by indecision, the colonel felt himself between two worlds, both of them dangerous. He had not been impressed by British handling of him, and the only American he knew was a secretary who worked for the Army's Counterintelligence Corps (CIC). He telephoned her, explained his plight and asked for her recommendations. She told him to remain where he was, then called a CIA officer for whom she had formerly worked when he had been a member of CIC. Her call alerted the CIA station, and a car was sent out to bring the colonel in. However, during the interval the colonel wandered away from the phone booth to get warm and was drinking hot *sake* in a bar. More cars were added to the search, and finally when the colonel emerged from the bar, he was spotted, picked up and flown out of Japan that night. For months thereafter he was interrogated by teams of skilled Russian-speaking specialists who elicited every possible scrap of information from him. Meanwhile, the Soviets complained to the Japanese Foreign Ministry about the disappearance of their colonel. Foul play was suspected, the Soviets claimed, and the *Gaimusho* (Foreign Ministry) was urged to spare no efforts in locating him. The American Embassy was questioned as a matter of course and reluctantly admitted to the Japanese that the Soviet was in American hands. Japan's left-wingers were many in number and extraordinarily vocal. They made much of this (slight) infringement of Japanese sovereignty, as they did later when it became known that U-2 aircraft based in Japan had for years been overflying the China mainland and the Soviet Union. Nevertheless, the Soviet colonel was a rich prize and well worth the comparatively small embarrassment occasioned by his impromptu exfiltration.

The British, although initially bitter at having lost "their" defector to us, shared in the intelligence take and were spared the expense of interrogating and maintaining him—always a matter of keen concern to our British colleagues.

As had happened previously in Albania, many of our intelligence teams dispatched into North Korea were captured on arrival or rolled up subsequently. Prospects for the successful infiltration of more Korean teams to gather high-grade intelligence were bleak, so we decided to attempt to attract defectors instead.

Although leaflet overflights were forbidden, balloon airdrops of leaflets were not. This method had been pioneered by the Radio

Free Europe staff in Germany, and the technology was already available. Because of prevailing winds, sea launchings were essential, and a corvette-size ship was brought to Yokosuka, where it was altered for our special needs. To head the project I hired as a contract agent Colonel Luke, a former OSS/China colonel and professional parachutist. Luke took charge of the project; scores of helium-filled gas cylinders were acquired and loaded aboard the main deck of the balloon ship. A mixed American-Korean crew inflated the balloons, attached their leaflet payloads and launched them at sea for later timed release over North Korea.

There was nothing subtle about the leaflets: They offered a reward of $5,000 to any North Korean pilot who would deliver a MIG-15 to the West. The balloon project continued through the summer months while weather was fair, but with autumn and its deteriorating weather, a tentative decision was reached to close down the project, particularly since it had failed to produce defectors. Then, to everyone's astonishment, a Soviet-made aircraft landed in South Korea, and the North Korean pilot and copilot emerged, each clutching a balloon-borne leaflet. True, the Soviet plane was not a MIG-15, but an old propeller-driven Yak trainer. Nevertheless, the pilot customarily flew MIGs, had flown them against the American Air Force during the Korean War and had even flown advanced models of the MIG fighter. He and his copilot were given asylum, debriefed extensively and later allowed to fly American jet fighters so that comparative studies of Soviet and American combat aircraft could be made.

With that, the balloon project was closed down, and Colonel Luke returned to the United States. I was next to see him in the early part of 1961 at a secret airfield in Guatemala where Luke was training the parachute battalion of the Cuban invasion brigade.

When news of the Yak's arrival was flashed to us in Tokyo, I thought back over the years to the gripping news that a Soviet aircraft had landed near Linz, with Peter Pirogov and his luckless companion. Our North Korean defectors were handled in a far more productive way.

To the great sorrow of Dorothy and myself, Maxine North cabled us that Bob had died. Taken to a Bangkok hospital for treatment of meningitis, he had been placed in an iron lung. A power failure immobilized the mechanical respirator and he died of suffocation in the dark.

Although his widow went on to become Thailand's leading businesswoman, she was never able to reconcile herself to his loss.

Neither was I, and during some of my darkest days I tried to extract from my memories of him the advice and counsel Bob North would have given me had he then been at my side.

The Chinese Communist (ChiCom) regime now announced the opening of their first trade fair in Japan. Commercial and intelligence interest in their products was high, for the exposition was to show samples of "advanced" ChiCom heavy machinery, both industrial and agricultural. CIA readied a special team of analysts to examine the display machinery. From it they would be able to learn a great deal not only about current ChiCom technology, but such recherché matters as ChiCom production of coal, iron, steel and other metals.

An invitation-only preview of the trade fair told us what CIA had long suspected: that most of the display machinery was copied from Western models, many long outdated, and the machinery itself at least partly handcrafted for the trade fair. However, it was our purpose to discourage ChiCom trade with Free World nations so we set about disrupting the exhibition. This now seems ironic, since it was during my service in the White House that President Nixon effected détente with China.

One night, at my suggestion, hundreds of thousands of leaflets floated down on Tokyo, dropped by a blacked-out plane. The leaflets were public invitations to every Tokyo resident to visit the ChiCom trade fair. On the back of the leaflet was printed an admission ticket and other coupons which, when presented inside the hall —according to the legend—would guarantee as much free beer, rice and *sashimi* as the bearer could consume or carry away.*

As anticipated, the exhibition hall was stormed by thousands of Japanese who became increasingly angry over the failure of the trade fair's ChiCom managers to honor the leaflet promises and admit them to the bountiful feast inside. There were minor clashes between Chinese and Japanese, and the Chinese retreated behind

---

*This technique is known as "the monster rally."

the closed doors of the exhibition hall, whence they demanded police protection. This defiance only added to the fury of the hungry and thirsty crowd, and had it not been for the arrival of police reinforcements, the ChiCom trade fair would certainly have been sacked and burned. This loss of face by the ChiComs was recognized on both sides, and to add to ChiCom discomfiture, we planted stories in the major Japanese newspapers deriding as unreliable antiques the products the ChiComs had chosen for their display.

Several years prior to my arrival in Tokyo a multimillion-dollar political and psychological-warfare project had been under way. When the project came up for annual renewal, I examined it with care and interviewed the half-dozen case officers who were charged with its administration. Basically, the project was the brainchild of an old and respected Tokyo samurai and his son. Through Occupation contacts they had come to the attention of CIA, and their proposal was appealingly simple: Give us the money and we, by virtue of our position and many useful contacts, will provide access to the press, political intelligence, student demonstrators, a propaganda shop, anti-Communist labor unions and so on.

To my astonishment I learned that neither father nor son had ever signed a receipt for moneys that were funded them, and when I suggested this be promptly done, the CIA nisei case officers professed themselves abashed to make such a request of so distinguished a pair of Japanese gentlemen. This nonreceipt procedure was at wide variance from normal CIA fiscal requirements and suggested that other aspects of the project needed further examination. Accordingly, I plunged into background files and determined that, over the years, there was little correlation between the claims of the samurai and what they had provably accomplished. During the next meeting of the project-review committee I suggested either cancellation of the project or notification to the samurai that they would have to produce certifiable results within six months or that would be the end of the sleigh ride.

To my surprise the admiral—the CIA senior representative in Tokyo—was extremely reluctant to force a confrontation with the two "agents." The senior project case officer defended it glowingly, and after a series of cable exchanges with Washington a decision was made to replace the project's present case officers and bring in a new team for a hard and continuing look at the project. In due course the new team of case officers arrived, but soon became so enamored of the samurai, father and son, that professional skepticism soon went out the window.

Despite the opposition of both my seniors and my juniors, I continued to register complaints and suspicions about the project to the point that during a Tokyo visit Frank Wisner lectured me on the desirability of maintaining an open mind. After his departure I began hearing rumors that the project was a pet of Allen Dulles and therefore untouchable. From my own estimate of the director I felt this to be unlikely, and during the director's next visit to Tokyo I put the question to him bluntly.

He was familiar with the project, yes, but he had no special interest in it and was certainly not protecting it from the normal project-evaluation process.

So armed, I was able to cite the project's long record of abysmal failure, and eventually it was wound down and terminated.

At the final meeting with the Japanese father and son our case officer almost begged their forgiveness for what he was forced to do, the old samurai smiled wryly, said everything had to come to an end, and he had been wondering for months, if not years, how long it would take CIA to catch on.

In other covert action, however, the North Asia Command was more successful. From an immense field on Okinawa (as well as from Taiwan itself) propaganda broadcasts were beamed across the Chinese mainland, occasionally with signals so powerful that they overrode the broadcast beams in Peking, Shanghai and Tientsin. North Korea and the Soviet Union were also prime targets, and our radio engineers, through a special technical legerdemain, were able to transmit powerfully into the Soviet Union by bouncing radio signals from the Heavyside layer and through other electronic means. Those who listened to the broadcasts were asked to drop a card to post-office boxes in Seoul, Paris or Hong Kong. Periodic analyses of these listener-response cards persuaded us that our clandestine broadcasts were indeed reaching their intended target audiences.

For relaxation I shot duck in Tokyo Bay, upland game on Honshu and ring-necked pheasants on the Korean island of Cheju. From the

air the island looked like a decapitated volcano rising from the
Yellow Sea. Used as a POW camp during the Korean War, Cheju
was now abandoned except for a few miserable Koreans who existed
there, and the still-usable airstrip would take our recreational C-47.
The Korean peasants we encountered seemed to exist solely on
crocks of odoriferous *kimchee*, whose presence we were always
aware of due to the strong prevailing winds. Pheasants were literally
as thick as sparrows, but the Korean inhabitants were uninterested
in them, despite the obvious shortage of meat protein in their diets.
Pheasant shooting in Cheju was the sportiest I had encountered
anywhere in the world. Pheasants, startled by our approach, would
leap into the air and fly away, their natural speed accelerated by an
average forty-mile-an-hour wind, making them challenging targets
indeed. In the summer I could troll off the beach of our summer
home at Hayama, not far from the summer palace of the Emperor
and Empress. Dolphin were the usual catch, though occasionally
larger game fish such as tuna could be caught.

For my children life in Japan was a never-ending delight. Given
the equivalent of twenty-five cents, a maid could take the children to
a nearby toy store and return arms laden with every imaginable type
of children's toy. There was the Ueno Park Zoo, the Imperial Castle
in downtown Tokyo with swans in the moat, and excursions with
Dorothy and me to Nikko, Nara and Kyoto.

We entertained a good deal and were entertained in turn. Although for the first time in our married life we had Army rather than
diplomatic cover, we developed a rapport with the Tokyo diplomatic
colony, particularly the Latin American representation, and in due
course Dorothy began working for the Argentine ambassador as a
part-time speech writer. Perón was then dictator of Argentina, and
relations between the United States and Argentina were strained.
Despite this, the Argentine ambassador began using Dorothy to
code and decode his confidential cables to the Foreign Ministry, and
one day, when the embassy was closed for midday siesta, she
brought out the embassy's entire stock of code books, which were
quickly photographed, then returned.

Despite our initial resistance to the Tokyo assignment, my wife
and I came to realize that it was by far the most pleasant and
interesting city in which we had ever lived. We accepted the

Japanese as a matter of course, but it was not until one night when Dorothy and I returned early from a party that our war wounds finally healed.

In our darkened living room sat our entire staff of servants watching a television program. The women were sobbing uncontrollably, and even the houseboy's cheeks were wet. I was about to reprimand them for unauthorized use of the television when I realized that the program was the long-awaited release of wartime films taken by Japanese photographers and sealed in the Imperial War Museum. For the first time the Japanese public was being shown how their country, their army, navy, air force, husbands, sons, fathers and entire families had been systematically destroyed by the insanity of the ruling militarist clique. The screen showed kamikaze planes diving to a watery destruction, the death agonies of Japanese carriers and capital ships, the bloated corpses of Japanese soldiers at Buna Beach and Guadalcanal, Tarawa, Okinawa and Iwo Jima. Now our servants were seeing this for the first time. Three of the four women had been widowed by the war, and the family of the fourth had been incinerated at Hiroshima. Silently, we knelt beside them and watched the program to its end, then my wife embraced each of the women, attempting to console them for their loss, and sent them off to bed.

From that time on, I could not hate the Japanese people or carry with me the unchristian spirit of vengeance I had nurtured so long.

Dorothy began to frequent museums and Buddhist temples and gradually acquired some fine and ancient Orientalia. She learned the art of Japanese flower arrangement and found ways to blend in Japanese cuisine along with the Chinese cooking she knew so well.

My two young daughters were equally fluent in English, Japanese and French. Little St. John, spoiled beyond belief—as is every firstborn son in Japan—spoke only Japanese to his adoring nurse-maid. At home my daughters dressed in kimonos and zori, sang Japanese songs and played with the Shimizu daughters, who lived in the other half of our unique house.

One day the mother superior at the girls' school asked Dorothy if we might not be able to give lodging for a weekend to a Korean refugee girl who had recently reached Tokyo from Hong Kong. According to the mother superior, the girl's father had been killed in the war and the girl, Stella, brought up by English nuns in a convent near Shanghai. A group of refugee girls had been permitted out of China, and the mother superior's facilities were overtaxed. We at once agreed, but the initial weekend extended for the rest of our stay in Japan.*

By now our admiral/senior representative had been transferred to London, and his deputy, Lloyd George, moved up to fill the admiral's far-from-oversized shoes. During my first meeting with the admiral, two years before, I decided we were going to have communication problems. Soon after taking over my job as CA chief, I had written a four- or five-page cable, and because it dealt with policy matters, it required release by the admiral.

After a few days, when I had not noticed a comeback copy of the cable, I consulted Lloyd George, who suggested I see the admiral and determine what his objections were, if any. Admitted to the admiral's office, I noted on his desk my still-unsent cable. He played nervously with a pencil, glanced at the cable and said, "Suppose you tell me what it's all about."

Having dictated some 1,500 words that constituted the text of the cable, I felt it was self-explanatory. However, I recalled my Naval Academy classrooms where each midshipman recited beside his desk or at the blackboard, and there was comparatively little paperwork. So I began painstakingly to review the background of the cable for the admiral, then summarized the text for him. His face lighted and without further comment he signed the cable and sent it on its way.

His love for oral communication was demonstrated in other ways: Each day began with a small staff meeting of senior personnel, during which the special intelligence officer briefed us on overnight intercept developments. The SI briefing over, the door opened to admit other staff members who had no need for special intelligence. Another briefing was conducted at this level, then more officers joined us, including usually a visiting chief of station, until by noon

*Through the influence of Governor Lehman, Averell Harriman and Cardinal Spellman, plus the energetic activities of Albany friends, we were able to obtain an immigration visa for Stella, then thirteen. She finished high school in Albany, became a registered nurse and married a young man who, in 1973, befriended me at the Federal Prison Camp in Allenwood, Pennsylvania.

there was nothing further to be said, and the admiral, still not having seen a scrap of paper, released us for lunch at the Officers' Club.

Lloyd George was quite the opposite. A seasoned intelligence professional, Lloyd had worked with Thai resistance during the war and had been chief of OSO's Far East Division. Warm, intelligent and broad-gauged, Lloyd was a welcome replacement for the admiral, whose first concern on reaching London was to requisition a tinted windshield for his CIA official car. This request became a *casus belli* between Wisner and the admiral, and Frank was later to remark to me that though headquarters was losing a lot of the skirmishes, he did not anticipate losing the war.

With Lloyd in charge of the North Asia Command, relations with our military hosts quickly and lastingly improved, as did our relations with subordinate operating units in the Far East. Unlike the admiral, Lloyd George was able to delegate authority, and at all levels morale was good.

In the summer of 1956 I received surprise orders appointing me as chief of station in Montevideo, Uruguay. A quick look at the map reassured me that Uruguay was on the ocean, not inland, as is its neighbor Paraguay, whose capital, Asunción, was rightfully regarded as a hardship post, in contrast to comfortable Montevideo. So we set about packing to leave Japan even more reluctantly than we had prepared for the Tokyo assignment. A departure date was chosen and reservations made on a Pan American Stratocruiser, which offered the comfort of bunks for transpacific flying. But a day or so before our scheduled departure the Pan American office informed me that due to booking error, there were not sufficient bunks aboard our scheduled flight to accommodate us. By way of alternatives, Pan American suggested either an earlier or later departure: On other flights they could provide us with four bunks. We chose the later date and when we arrived in San Francisco learned that the plane we originally had planned to take had gone down in the Pacific with several lives lost.

Friends and relatives who had not known of our flight delay assumed that we had perished, for press accounts indicated that among the dead were a Foreign Service officer, his wife and children.

From San Francisco we flew to Sarasota and occupied our

seldom-visited home. While Dorothy and the children stayed in Florida, I flew to Washington and began processing back into the Foreign Service Reserve, reacquainting myself with the merged Western Hemisphere Division and its new chief, signed up for courses in station administration, wiretap management, mobile surveillance, surreptitious-entry operations and a seminar on KGB operations in Latin America. Those steps taken, I was granted a few weeks' leave and returned to Sarasota for a holiday with my family.

11 MONTEVIDEO, THE BAY OF PIGS AND SPAIN

AT headquarters I paid protocolary calls on Allen Dulles and General Cabell, Frank Wisner* and his principal assistant, Tracy Barnes. Freed from the parochialism of OSO, Dick Helms was now chief of operations for the entire Clandestine Services. In each other we discerned kindred spirits and formed a friendship which, though sporadic, due to my extended absences abroad, continued until the summer of 1972, when my name was first mentioned in connection with Watergate.

When my training courses were completed, I worked at the Uruguay-Argentina desk familiarizing myself with current operations and projects, reading dossiers on the principal political and Soviet intelligence figures in the area and otherwise making the professional transition from the Far East to Latin America.

The annual Latin American chiefs of station conference had been set for December in Havana, Cuba. And as Montevideo COS designate, I was invited by Division Chief J. C. King to take part in the meeting, which lasted several days and was held in the American Embassy in Havana.

While paying our farewell respects to Ambassador Gardner, we were interrupted by an aide who conferred briefly with the ambassador. Gardner told us that President Batista had just informed him

*A diminutive personal assistant to Frank Wisner was known as the Ozard of Wiz.

115

that a boatload of Cuban revolutionaries had been sunk off Oriente Province and the few survivors routed by the Cuban Army and Air Force. The ambassador remarked that the leader of the expeditionaries was a former Havana University agitator named Fidel Castro and was one of those killed.

Most of us recalled Castro as having been involved in the infamous *Bogotazo* (the coup attempt in Bogotá) of 1948, but Batista's information was fatally wrong. Of the boat's 83 occupants, 16 survived, among them Fidel and his brother Raul, and the peripatetic Ernesto Ché Guevara, who, along with Colonel Arbenz, had been allowed safe passage out of Guatemala two and a half years before.

Early in the new year we sailed on the Argentine liner *Río Tunuyan* and suffered Atlantic winter weather until well into the southern latitudes. Among my fellow passengers was an attractive Argentine diplomatic couple, their son and English maid, Mary, who was later to work for my family for many years. The Argentine diplomats had been stationed at one time in Rio de Janeiro and helped us see much of Rio during our ship's brief stopover. On to São Paulo, then Montevideo, our final destination.

As the ship pulled into the harbor, I was unimpressed by my first view. From the sea Montevideo looked as gray and dirty as Trieste, and the effect of the city's architectural hodgepodge was somber.

Until Dorothy found a house in suburban Carrasco, we stayed at the Victoria-Plaza Hotel a few blocks from the embassy. Remembering the fate of my convertible at Veracruz, I had brought our Cadillac with us aboard the *Río Tunuyan*. Thus, in addition to embassy and station transportation, Dorothy was able to use our personal vehicle for house and school hunting.

The French lycée, in which our children enrolled, was across the street from our newly rented home, and each day our Anglo-Argentine governess took the three children in their fresh white smocks and floppy black bow ties across the street to the lycée door, returning for them at noon.

Our house was only a block from an excellent ocean beach, and when they were not attending classes, the children customarily gamboled there. My MI-6 colleague lived only a half block from me, and he, his wife and children remain friends to this day.

Despite its small size, Uruguay was a country of considerable social, political and economic complexity. Modeled not altogether successfully on Swiss-style democracy, Uruguay had been governed by the same Colorado Party for more than ninety years. Urban-based and worker-oriented, the Colorados' administrative philosophy was: spend, spend, spend—elect, elect, elect. In contrast, the minority Blanco Party was made up of Uruguayans who owned and worked the land and exported the meat, wool and hides on which the economy of Uruguay was based. The Colorado government was socialist in orientation and the nation atheistic by constitution. My new ambassador, an Eisenhower political appointee, was a well-meaning—if ineffectual—man. Handicapped by an unfortunate stammer, he had great difficulty in making himself understood in English, much less Spanish, although he readily understood spoken Spanish.

His deputy, the counselor, was a wild-eyed, highly nervous career Foreign Service officer, whose wife was a hopeless lush. Pleasant enough when sober, after a drink or so it was her pleasure to kick off her shoes and execute pirouettes and jetés, regardless of her surroundings. As first secretary, I was next in protocolary descent, and because Dorothy and I neither stammered nor drank to excess, we found ourselves included in many diplomatic functions where the presence of an American Embassy official was desired —but not that of the ambassador or his deputy.

As might be imagined, the situation caused some intraembassy resentments, but with the departure of my CIA predecessor, I became immersed in a series of critical operations and was too busy to give much thought to what were, after all, embassy rather than CIA problems. Too, the ambassador's wife was the sister of a senior aide to Frank Wisner and a friend of Frank's as well. An active, creative and thoroughly sensible lady, she labored heroically to make up for the deficiencies of her husband and his deputy.

My COS predecessor was a career civil servant who, unfortunately, both looked and acted like one. Despite the vivacity of Montevideo society, he left me no contacts to take over except one retired American—his stockbroker. So, as in Mexico, I began the lengthy and burdensome task of identifying and cultivating the country's power elite. Nor did I inherit much in the way of police liaison. The chief of police, a favorite of President Luis Batlle's, had held my unfortunate predecessor in such low esteem that he declined to receive the CIA station chief at police headquarters or lunch with him, or if an appointment were made, the police chief would break it with little, if any, notice.

By chance I met the police chief at an Argentine Embassy reception. Though far from a Yankee admirer, the chief was surprised and pleased to find that the embassy's new first secretary spoke understandable Spanish. I mentioned to him that in addition to diplomatic duties, I had consular responsibilities which involved the protection of visiting Americans and suggested an appointment with him in order that I might benefit from his experience. We lunched at a secluded table in the Jockey Club—to which I belonged, but the chief did not—and over liqueurs, he said expansively, "Now tell me, Mr. Secretary, what can I do for you?"

"What you can do for me," I told him, "is tap some embassy telephone lines."

His eyes grew large. He put down his liqueur glass and stared. "You're"—he began—"you must be from CIA." Happiness had left his face.

"From CIA," I confirmed. "Chief, I can make the taps with or without your help, the difference being that if we do it together, we can share the take."

Frowning, he considered. "I'd have to tell Luis Batlle," he said unhappily.

"Why not? He's your President, and more than anyone, he should be interested in what's going on in Uruguay."

Actually, Luis Batlle was anti-American, and both the chief and I knew it. Moreover, Batlle was looking more and more to the Soviet Union as a market for Uruguayan exports of meat, wool, hides and rice, to boost his country's failing economy. Accordingly, my suggestion made the chief understandably uncomfortable.

We adjourned *sine die*, but with a promise to meet again and discuss our mutual interest in foreign efforts to subvert Uruguay. Meanwhile, said the chief, he would seek an appropriate moment to make known my request to the President and would get back to me.

Presently, on my instructions, the deputy chief of police was recruited by one of my station officers. This gave me an inside view of the federal police as well as daily reports of the chief's activities. The deputy would have tapped even the chief's private phones.

Meanwhile, I had added a pair of Russian-speaking Soviet experts to the station and brought in a Communist Party specialist who had served under me in Mexico. We established radio-controlled mobile surveillance teams, acquired penetrations of the Uruguayan Communist Party and became familiar with the faces and activities of the large KGB representation at the Soviet Embassy.

At that period Brazil did not maintain diplomatic relations with the Soviet Union, so all KGB and GRU operations in Brazil were run from the Montevideo embassy. The distances and communications problems involved made these Soviet cross-border operations unusually vulnerable. Moreover, the Soviets in Uruguay—as elsewhere in Latin America—were contemptuous of Latin American police. This disregard of local security services led many Soviets into careless practices which violated their own strict tradecraft rules. Such operational infractions, had they been known to the Kremlin, would have resulted in harsh reprisals against the guilty intelligence officers. However, we in CIA were content to benefit from Soviet lapses and hoped they would never find occasion to tighten their operational security.

During the preceding year the FBI in New York had noticed clandestine contacts between a member of the Uruguayan UN Delegation named Ramírez and a KGB case officer whose cover was that of a member of the Soviet Delegation to the United Nations. When Ramírez returned to Uruguay, his case was turned over to the Montevideo CIA station. Ramírez was surveilled by the station and found to be in contact with a local Soviet case officer. Further surveillance revealed that after the initial meeting between the two men, contact was maintained through a dead drop—a hole in an old brick wall—where messages were left. To signal that the dead drop was charged, the man leaving the message turned a nearby tin can upright. When the recipient of the message picked it up, he knocked over the tin can before leaving the area.

Somewhat ingenuously, my predecessor revealed the case to the federal police chief, who affected astonishment, outrage and a burning desire to catch Ramírez in the act. Joint surveillance of Ramírez, the Soviet case officer and the dead-drop site was established. But what my predecessor did not know, and what I learned in the interim, was that Ramírez was something of a protégé of the Uruguayan President. Like so many other Uruguayan diplomats and Uruguayan Embassy personnel, Ramírez had no particular qualifications for diplomatic work other than loyalty to the ruling Colorado Party, of which the President was the active head.

In anticipation of arresting Ramírez while he serviced the dead drop, CIA and the Uruguayan police staked out the area. Distant surveillors reported the two men converging on the dead-drop site. The Soviet charged the dead drop and was permitted to leave the area. But just as Ramírez came into view and was rapidly approaching the wall, up drove the chief of police, siren wailing, brakes screeching to a halt only a few yards from the dead drop. Understandably frightened—and warned—Ramírez took to his heels and disappeared.

When told what had happened, the chief of police apologized all around, blaming himself for a bumbling performance. He also had the gall to lament that, lacking hard proof, he would be unable to have Ramírez removed from the Foreign Ministry. So the case was put in the suspense file until I was able to review and reactivate it.

No serious cooperation could be expected from the chief of police, and it was unlikely that President Batlle cared whether Ramírez was a Soviet agent or not.

Among our agent assets was a smuggler who took gold bars from Uruguay into Argentina, Paraguay and Brazil, concealing them in the doors of his car. He was young, aggressive, successful and had a profitable working relationship not only with customs officials, but with important officers of the federal police. Through his station case officer I learned that he could obtain as many as fifty valid Uruguayan passports and wondered if the station might not want a few. Because obtaining authentic foreign documentation was a standing CIA requirement, I agreed to purchase five of the blank passports, but asked the case officer to determine from his agent the identity of the Foreign Ministry official who was prepared to make the sale.

To hardly anyone's surprise, the vendor turned out to be Ramírez.

Having been thwarted once in its effort to purge the Uruguayan Foreign Ministry of Ramírez, the station consensus was that the corruptness of Ramírez offered us a second chance to cause his dismissal.

We bugged our agent's car, and when Ramírez brought the

passports to conclude the sale, the agent had Ramírez read aloud the number of each passport he was selling while the agent wrote it down. Bargaining ensued, and a final price was arrived at.

Within a few days one of Montevideo's principal newspapers received a package containing the stolen passports and a tape recording. Anonymously, duplicate tape recordings were sent to the Foreign Minister and to the chief of police. When the story broke, Ramírez resigned, was arrested on a technical charge and later released, never again to traffic in passports or diplomacy.

The chief of police knew full well who had been responsible for the operation, and I suspected that the Foreign Minister did as well, for at diplomatic receptions I often noticed him staring at me thoughtfully.

Not long afterward the police chief was replaced, pensioned and assigned to an international organization. His successor was a tough, bulky cop of Italian descent. When I called on him, he referred laughingly to the first fiasco involving Ramírez and expressed his admiration for whoever had engineered the second. I was noncommittal, of course, but we took an immediate liking to each other, and he declared that he was dedicated to two things: fighting crime and thwarting Communism in Uruguay.

Through him I met the chief of army intelligence and found him also to be a hard-line anti-Communist. The three of us formed an operational triumvirate, and to the station's assets were added not only those of the federal police but of the Uruguayan Army as well.

Some of the younger intelligence officers at the Soviet Embassy were a new breed; in CIA we called them "joy boys." They were generally good-looking, reasonably well tailored, could speak a language or two, were able to play bridge or at least hearts, could dance to other than Slavic music and were able to move through their target countries with considerably more ease than their glowering, clodhopper predecessors. One, whose name was Vadim, was quite a charmer. At diplomatic parties on three successive evenings he appeared with three different Russian females and unblinkingly introduced each as his wife. This caused some merriment in the diplomatic colony, where Vadim quickly acquired a useful reputation as a lady-killer. If he had a wife, she was undoubtedly living in the Soviet Union, hostage to his good performance abroad, and the ladies who accompanied him as his wife had been designated for that particular role by the KGB *rezident*. This was one Samoilov, a glum, nervous and unhappy man, but an exception to the general rule that the KGB does not permit Jews to reach high positions in intelligence work. In social situations Samoilov was ill at ease and was also guilty of an apparent plurality of wives. Or perhaps he felt that our confusion would so increase station work load as to affect the health of his CIA enemies. In any case, there came a night when both Samoilov and I were guests at a diplomatic affair and found ourselves standing next to each other. He offered me a Russian cigarette, which I declined. Nervously lighting one and puffing it, he seemed to be searching for a conversational subject when he suddenly blurted, "You are a friend of the Chernikovs."

"I am?"

"Yes. You knew them in Shanghai."

Shanghai, I thought. Who? Then I remembered Valentin and Marusha. My memory might have been faulty, but not the KGB files. Pleasantly I asked, "How are they?"

"Fine, fine," Samoilov said. "They have three fine children now."

"Is he still with Tass?"

"No, oh, no. He is now a diplomat." He smiled almost mockingly. "Like ourselves."

"Where are they?"

"In Bangkok. They—he works in Bangkok."

"Then you must give them my regards," I said, smiled as affably as had Samoilov and left him in favor of the buffet.

Among the many prominent Uruguayan families I had met was one I will call Redondo. Amilcar was a shrewd and wealthy landowner who dabbled in national politics. When I first met him, he was one of the directors of the National Bank, and because his estate was only two blocks from my home in Carrasco, he occasionally invited me over for an evening of political discussion while servants roasted lamb or young beef in an open pit.

Through our political discussions, Amilcar gradually concluded that at the embassy I discharged more responsibilities than the usual first secretary, and he began to speak freely with me concerning the plans of his party for (an unprecedented) electoral triumph. He himself, he confessed, was more of a Ruralista than a dyed-in-the-wool Blanco, and he attributed Blanco electoral losses over the past half century to Blanco desire to emulate the Colorado Party in appealing for urban and labor votes. This he believed to be a fundamental mistake, for Uruguay had almost entirely an agricultural economy, and he believed that the Blancos should now begin to represent the country's agricultural sector. To that end, he was about to arrange a political fusion between the small Ruralista Party and the Blancos. He had in mind, he told me, something the Blanco Party had always lacked before—a man of the people.

Such a man was Benito Nardone.

Son of an immigrant Italian cobbler, Nardone was largely self-educated and had been a frequent contributor to Montevideo newspapers on questions of importance to Uruguay's rural population. If the city workers and bureaucrats were for the Colorados, the men and women who labored on Uruguay's *estancias* were solidly for the Ruralista Party, whose emergent leader was Nardone.

Redondo arranged a small informal barbecue as the occasion to introduce Nardone and myself. When he found I was an enthusiastic horseman, had hunted *perdiz* and fished for *dorado* over much of Uruguay and had visited most of the country's principal *estancias*, he warmed to me, and as with Amilcar Redondo, I soon became friendly with Nardone.

In the months before his candidacy was announced we saw each other two or three times a week, and I became increasingly convinced that of the opposition leaders I had met, Nardone was the one best suited to confront the Colorados and lead Uruguay from economic decline and emotional self-pity. Although Uruguay had stood steadfastly with the Allies during World War II, it, like neighboring Argentina, had profited hugely from the war. Latin America had been not only a granary for the Allies but for years —including the Korean War—had been able to export its wool, meat and agricultural products at artificially high prices. Uruguayans were still living in a wartime economic euphoria, and more than one political leader remarked unguardedly to me that the best thing that could happen to Uruguay would be to have another world war break out. There being no war in sight, Uruguay's products were forced to compete on the free international market. Uruguay could have lived comfortably well but for the smothering welfare-state bureaucracy which found more than half the population on one government payroll or another, with retirement at age fifty on full pay, and other cradle-to-grave benefits more appropriate to affluent manufacturing countries such as Sweden or Switzerland.

I became aware of occasional street demonstrations in favor of the Cuban guerrilla Fidel Castro, whose partisans, known as the 26th of July Movement, were collecting funds throughout the hemisphere. Uruguay, with its inbred fear of dictators, contributed freely to Castro's partisans and made his emissaries welcome. Still, my station received no indications of headquarters interest in the Castro movement, and having plenty of other things to keep us occupied, we ignored the Cuban militants.

At that time Uruguay maintained diplomatic relations with every Communist country save Albania and mainland China. This provided my station with an almost limitless number of targets, and in addition the Soviet Embassy was the largest one south of Mexico City. There was a small but influential Uruguayan Communist Party, a Trotskyite offshoot, and, of growing concern, an active group of Argentine exiles plotting feverishly for the return of ousted dictator Perón. Soon an émigré family from Czechoslovakia took a house two blocks from mine and moved in: They turned out to be Colonel Jacobo Arbenz, his fanatical wife and two lovely daughters.

By now President Castillo Armas of Guatemala had been assassinated by one of his bodyguards; in the ensuing election General Idigoras Fuentes was elected and from all accounts was doing a fine job governing Guatemala. For unrelated purposes I had some months previously recruited a Central American diplomat who now turned out to be a distant relative of Maria Arbenz, the colonel's wife. I encouraged the diplomat-agent to renew his boyhood friendship with her, and through his reports I was able to keep apprised of what went on not only in the household, but in the mind of the former Communist dictator. As fate would have it, Dorothy and I met the Arbenz family at a golf club to which they also belonged and found him to be a dullard almost completely dominated by his wife.

There now arrived in Montevideo a new ambassador, Robert Woodward, a career diplomat whose previous ambassadorial experience was confined, I believe, to the challenges of Costa Rica. With him he brought a new deputy chief of mission, and as Woodward and his deputy took over, I had correspondingly fewer protocolary functions to perform, a situation I met with gratitude.

In Washington Woodward had heard that I was in some fashion connected with the overthrow of Guatemala's Communist regime. In one of our first meetings he told me quite frankly that he disapproved of American intervention and hoped I was fomenting no plans for anything of the sort in Uruguay. I assured him that my mandate did not extend to overthrowing a friendly government, and he seemed satisfied with my reply.

During his first few months, however, Woodward frequently expressed astonishment at the breadth and depth of my contacts across the country, and as a straight Foreign Service type he resented my progress, feeling that CIA officers should, somehow, be relegated to the back room, with only legitimate FSOs allowed any personal contact in the host country. Although I could not have disagreed more, I did my best to maintain working relations with him, though I was not always successful.

Just before national elections the embassy predicted another Colorado win and officially discounted the challenge of Nardone and his Ruralista-Blanco supporters. But for the first time in nearly a century the Colorados were defeated, and at that night's victory party tendered Nardone by his enthusiasts, I was the lone American invited from the embassy. And it galled Woodward that though he was obliged to meet the incoming President before inauguration, he was forced to arrange the introduction through me, for no other embassy officer was on speaking, much less social, terms with the President-elect. After inauguration Nardone replaced the chief of police, but I persuaded him to maintain the chief of military intelligence as the best available man for the job.

The new police chief was an Army colonel who knew nothing about police work and less about intelligence. But he was loyal to Nardone, and because I was obviously a favorite of the new President's, he gave me full cooperation. When I took him on an inspection of our cladestine facilities, the new police chief was astounded to find what we could do in our coverage of local targets. Later he told me his predecessor had either carried off or destroyed the card files of all known subversives in Uruguay. (Actually, when I heard the files were to be destroyed, I asked permission to photocopy them before the cards were destroyed by the outgoing police chief. These photocopies had since been integrated into the files of my station.) Without violating his predecessor's confidence, I told the new police chief that from my own files I would be happy at any time to supply him with information on any individual of interest to his department.

While at a country club dance I learned from the embassy watch officer that my father had died, and I departed early next morning to join my mother in Albany and make funeral arrangements in Hamburg. He was buried in the Hunt cemetery plot beside my infant brother, and I was granted a week's leave to help my mother settle the estate and arrange the sale of our now too-large home.

All my life my father had been to me a singular figure of strength, rectitude and affection, and his passing was mourned not only by his relatives, but by hundreds of friends he made during his life and legal career. It was and remains a source of sorrow to me that I had not seen him for months before his death.

As it developed, death spared my parents and my wife the long anguish of my Watergate humiliation and imprisonment.

Meanwhile, over the months the station had been conducting technical penetrations of a number of embassies and the residences of key personnel. One entry operation remains in my mind because of its unexpected outcome.

Planning the operation had taken nearly two months. As in all such entry operations, extensive casing had been done, keys obtained, personnel located, guards and watchmen bribed, and finally the entry team arrived from headquarters. On a Friday night the team gained access to the target embassy and spent practically the next three days inside the embassy, trying to open the steel safe, which was about five feet tall, three feet wide and three feet deep and locked with a series of keys. The team was able to defeat the first two locks, but the third resisted all efforts. After X-raying the lock from three angles, the team decided that further attempts would be of no avail: The safe was more than a hundred years old, solidly built and manufactured by a European manufacturer who had gone out of business sometime in the 1890's.

As they repacked their tools, the team said they were heading for Europe to try to locate a replica of the safe in a junk or antique store. Only thus, they said, could the target safe be breached and forced to yield its secrets.

Shortly after his inauguration Nardone mentioned to me that he was considering reappointing the former Colorado Party Minister of the Interior. I demurred and next day delivered to Nardone photographs taken by our agents of the former Minister of the Interior meeting with a KGB case officer. The minister was known as a compulsive gambler and had lost large sums at the Carrasco Casino. It was this vulnerability, we agreed, that probably opened the door to the Soviets. The former minister's relationship with the Soviets was not publicized, however; Nardone eliminated him from consideration and instead appointed the son-in-law of Amilcar Redondo as Minister of the Interior. Prevention of the reappointment was, I felt, a notable blend of intelligence collection and the exploitation of the intelligence collected in positive political action.

I was visited by my division chief on what initially appeared to be a routine inspection; then he zeroed in on the real reason for his visit: Ambassador Woodward had complained that my home was too opulent for a first secretary, as were the entertainments held there for our wide circle of diplomatic and Uruguayan friends. For a couple of days we discussed the matter, once with the ambassador, whose evident motive for criticizing me was his resentment that I, rather than he, was Nardone's American confidant. And the ambassador's enmity was to pursue me for several more years.

When then Vice President Richard Nixon and Mrs. Nixon came to Montevideo on the first leg of their action-packed South American swing, I took occasion to recall to the Vice President an earlier meeting with the two of them at Harvey's Restaurant in Washington. Nixon had been addressing the Society of Former FBI Agents and was lingering over coffee in the restaurant when Dorothy and I arrived for aftertheater supper and found ourselves seated next to the Nixons. Impulsively, I went over to his table, introduced myself and congratulated him on his pursuit of Alger Hiss. They invited us to join them, and the four of us spent what was for me, at least, a pleasurable half hour discussing the foreign and domestic political scene. In Montevideo Nixon remembered the incident, as did his wife. Their interpreter was Colonel Vernon Walters, whom both Dorothy and I had known well in Paris.

Although in Uruguay there was a good deal of resentment toward the United States, the Nixon visit went off well, with only one untoward incident: A Secret Service helicopter overflying the motorcade accidentally released a small smoke grenade, which fell into a backyard. The Communist and leftist press, of course, inflated the incident into a *Yanqui* attempt on the lives of Uruguayan citizens, but by then the Nixons had departed for other South American cities where their lives were actually endangered.

During a previous visit by President Eisenhower I was hauled into service as his interpreter, pending the delayed arrival of Colonel Walters. And each morning during Ike's stay at the embassy I hand-delivered to his chief of staff the daily intelligence summary so it would reach him on schedule abroad, just as it did each morning at the White House.

From several early-morning contacts with the President I found there was considerable disparity between the public figure of a broadly grinning Ike and the private man, who struck me as petulant and autocratic toward his staff. This experience considerably dimmed my enthusiasm for the President, but convinced me that Vice President Nixon would be a more than worthy successor.

Some weeks before Ike's arrival I had been discussing with Nardone the special security measures required for a Presidential visit, as well as Ike's itinerary while in Uruguay. After exploring this area, Nardone informed me that he had decided to ask Ike to extend my normal two-year tour so that I could continue in Montevideo during Nardone's incumbency as President. I told Nardone that it was his prerogative as a chief of state, but that I felt obliged to notify Ambassador Woodward, even though I was sure Woodward would object. At the conclusion of Ike's visit Nardone did request my continued presence but Ike declined to alter plans which, he said, Ambassador Woodward had told him were well advanced.

Soon afterward a cable signed jointly by Richard Bissell and Tracy Barnes summoned me to headquarters. Bissell had succeeded Frank Wisner as chief of the Clandestine Services, and after hospitalization brought on by overwork Wisner had been assigned to the relatively relaxed post of London chief of station. As a special aide to Allen Dulles, Bissell had created the concept of the U-2 aircraft, then managed that successful program. I had held several perfunctory meetings with Bissell during consultation periods in Washington and a lengthier one during a Latin American chiefs of station conference in Lima, Peru.

As principal assistant to Bissell, Tracy Barnes told me, I was needed for a new project, much like the one on which I had worked for him in overthrowing Jacobo Arbenz. My job, Tracy told me, would be essentially the same as my earlier one—chief of political action for a project recommended by the National Security Council and just approved by President Eisenhower: to assist Cuban exiles in overthrowing Castro. Representative Cuban leaders were grouping in Florida and New York, and my responsibility would be to organize them into a broadly representative government-in-exile that would, once Castro was disposed of, form a provisional government in Cuba. He and Bissell told me that initial project organization was under way using the cadre of officers who had worked against Arbenz. This time, however, there must be no taint of U.S. involvement, and so the Cuban leadership and I were to be located not in the Miami area, but in Costa Rica, where ex-President José (Pepe) Figueres had offered us facilities. I was to resign from the Foreign Service and take my family to the Costa Rican capital, where I would stay with the Cuban government-in-exile for the duration of the project, which they estimated at from six months to a year.* Although it was spring in the United States, in Montevideo the autumn school term had begun, and Dorothy and I decided that she and the children would remain in Montevideo until the end of the first school semester while I was in Washington making arrangements for our presumed relocation in Costa Rica. But by the time my family joined me in July our destination had become Mexico City rather than Costa Rica, and so we spent the summer in Mexico with my group of Cuban exile political leaders, from which I was to fashion a government-in-exile.

Mexico, however, subjected these Cuban exiles to such harassment that with the consent of President Eisenhower, we moved to Miami, my family returning to Washington while Central Cover laundered me, i.e., a new name and consonant documentation, and assigned me a safehouse in Coconut Grove, not far from the project's forward base in Coral Gables. Opa-Locka was utilized, but only for project air operations. Thanks to President Idigoras Fuentes, a training base called Trax had been made available to CIA, and there in Guatemala the ill-fated Cuban Invasion Brigade 2506 was being trained by a combination of CIA and Green Beret officers.

As my principal assistant, a Cuban American named Bernard L.

---

*Full details of the Bay of Pigs operation are furnished in my book *Give Us This Day* (New Rochelle, New York, Arlington House, 1973). Dr. Mario Lazo's book, *Dagger in the Heart*, provides perhaps the definitive overview of the significance of this failure to Cuba—and to the world.

("Macho") Barker was assigned to me. For years in Havana Bernie had worked for the CIA station, and after he joined the Cuban federal police at the behest of the station, his citizenship became forfeit. Still, Bernie was a cheerful and tireless worker with broad contacts throughout the entire Cuban exile community. Through him I maintained daily contact with the dozen or so leading Cuban figures who had been selected to form the provisional government.

The most impressive of these was twenty-seven-year-old Dr. Manuel F. Artime, a Jesuit-trained psychiatrist who had joined Castro's forces in the Sierra Maestra and served as a regional agricultural official after Castro's victory. Shocked and disillusioned by the summary executions of anti-Communist friends who had followed Castro, Artime denounced the revolutionary leader and took refuge with Bernie Barker, who, with the aid of the Havana CIA station, managed to exfiltrate Artime to Florida.

Politically aware and personally courageous, Artime enjoyed a popularity among the growing Cuban-exile community that extended far beyond the membership of his university-founded Movement for Revolutionary Recovery. His anti-Batista credentials were impeccable, and his youth and leadership qualities recommended him to the early attention of the Eisenhower Administration.

Friendship between "Manolo" and myself was immediate, and when he was captured in the Bahia de Cochinos swamps after the invading brigade's defeat, I reproached myself bitterly for having authorized his participation in the invasion. My second son, David, was born while Manolo was enduring seventeen months of solitary confinement in Cuba's most degrading prisons. In absentia Artime became David's godfather and during my own later imprisonment he received David warmly into his household, caring for my son with the same warm affection he extended to his own children. Meanwhile Artime actively supported the legal defense and families of my four Miami Watergate colleagues. To this remarkable man and insatiable Cuban patriot I owe an unrepayable debt.

As to the military plans, the invasion was predicated upon a total wipeout of Castro air power by a series of strikes just prior to the invasion landing. And it was on this premise that all related military plans were made.

Meanwhile, the electoral contest between Vice President Nixon and John F. Kennedy was under way, with most Cubans enthusiastic over Kennedy, who was vociferous in his calls to aid the Cuban exiles in their effort to overthrow Fidel Castro. Nixon, however, had little to say on the subject in public. Secretly, however, he was White House action officer for our covert project, and some months before, his senior military aide, Marine General Robert Cushman, had urged me to inform him of any project difficulties the Vice President might be able to resolve. For Nixon was, Cushman told me, determined that the effort should not fail.

After the election the Kennedy Administration took a long, hard look at invasion plans before approving them. President Kennedy's sole reservation was that he be allowed to recall the invasion task force during a period of twelve hours following its embarkation from Puerto Cabezas, Nicaragua.

Once the brigade had cleared a perimeter around the airstrip at Playa de Cochinos, I was to fly there with the provisional Cuban government, which would then broadcast to the world a declaration that it was a government-in-arms and appeal for aid in overthrowing the Cuban despot. To provide prompt aid, a sizable task force of U.S. Navy ships had been assembled off Cuban waters; it included the aircraft carrier *Boxer* and several contingents of Marines. Following the provisional government's declaration, it could be aided under international law and American Marines and logistical supplies overtly put ashore.

None of this was to happen, of course, for the brigade and its landing vessels were pounded by Castro aircraft that had escaped the first strike by our B-26 bombers. Defeat of the brigade was ensured when, after the first strike, General Charles Cabell, then acting director of CIA in the unfortunate absence of Allen Dulles, entered our project war room on a Sunday morning and noticed the air officers ordering our aircraft in Guatemala to arm for a second and final strike against Castro planes that had been located through U-2 overflight photography.

Although President Kennedy had never limited the number of air strikes, Cabell gratuitously decided to seek approval, with the result that the strike was canceled and Castro's aircraft took off to assist Castro's ground forces in the destruction of the brigade.

In the wake of this fiasco, the New Frontier privately blamed CIA, as did the Joint Chiefs of Staff. Yet JFK's public assumption of responsibility for the disaster was well received by the nation, although in Latin America, and particularly in the Soviet Union, the President's indecisiveness was recognized for what it was. Having taken the measure of the American President, Khrushchev confidently erected the Berlin Wall and began arming Cuba with atomic missiles, concerning whose supposed removal we are still only able to speculate.

Within CIA those of us who had participated in the project —though not responsible for its failure—were made to feel like pariahs and were discriminated against with regard to subsequent assignments. Aware that I had an overview of the operation from inception to failure, Allen Dulles assigned me to his staff as an assistant charged principally with helping him respond to inquiries from various investigative bodies quickly activated by the New Frontier.

At the end of 1961 Dulles was forced to "retire," and Richard Bissell followed. He was succeeded, not by Tracy Barnes, but by Richard Helms, untainted by the Bay of Pigs.

After a considerable bureaucratic struggle Barnes established the Domestic Operations Division and appointed me its chief of covert action. The new division accepted both personnel and projects unwanted elsewhere within CIA, and those covert-action projects that came to me were almost entirely concerned with publishing and publications. We subsidized "significant" books, for example, *The New Class*, by Milovan Djilas, one of a number of Frederick A. Praeger, Inc., titles so supported; ran a couple of news services —one based in Washington's National Press Building—even subsidizing the printing and distribution of a well-known series of travel books. The work was not particularly demanding, and at the end of the day I still had sufficient energy to write fiction at home.

While I was away from home on the Cuban operation my mother-in-law had died. Now my work for Tracy Barnes required comparatively little foreign travel and I was able to spend much more time with my wife and family than had been the case in previous years.

It was proposed that I become deputy chief of station in Madrid. I had always wanted to live and work in Spain, and although the suggested appointment represented a demotion—I having previously been a chief of station—I assented and assumed the Department of State would agree. I had not counted, however, on the hostility of the American ambassador in Spain, Robert Woodward, who, it will be recalled, had been displeased with me in Montevideo. Woodward, as was his prerogative, declined to accept me, and though Helms told me he was willing to push my appointment, I decided that if I were forced on Woodward, my life in Madrid would be exceedingly uncomfortable.

During the summer of 1964, after both Republican and Democratic parties had made known their candidates, I received confidential orders from the division executive officer, Stanley Gaines, to have some of my "outside" personnel obtain information from the nearby headquarters of Republican candidate Barry Goldwater. This was a White House matter, I was told, President Johnson being keenly interested in the plans and utterances of Barry Goldwater. In response to these instructions, press material, position papers and advance speaking schedules were picked up frequently at Goldwater headquarters by CIA personnel on some pretext or another and taken from there to the White House, where the messenger was met by Chester Cooper, then the CIA officer attached to the White House staff. Although I was a vocal Goldwater partisan—a fact which gave me little popularity within the Agency—I allowed my subordinates to carry out this domestic political mission, seeing myself not as a partisan political appointee but rather as a career officer of the CIA whose professionalism required that he respond to the orders of whatever administration might be in power. This was my first exposure to White House use of Agency personnel against a "domestic enemy," and I found it disturbing. (Even after I retired from CIA in 1970, I remained predisposed by long professional service to accept without question orders which I believed to emanate from the White House.)

Soon Victor Weybright, editor in chief of the New American Library and one of the original leaders in the rise of paperback publishing, who had reprinted several of my novels, approached me with the suggestion that I write an American counterpart to the popular James Bond series, which his firm also published. I submitted the idea to Dick Helms, who agreed that certain public-relations advantages would accrue to CIA if such a series were well received. His sole proviso was that I clear each manuscript in advance with him or his deputy, Tom Karamessines.

On this basis I developed the "Peter Ward" series, of whose

fictional CIA adventures eight paperback books were published. The first book had barely been placed on the newsstands when the Agency librarian, Walter Pforzheimer, informed me that the Library of Congress copyright card gave my true name in addition to the pen name "David St. John,"* under which the series was appearing. Only Helms and Karamessines had known the true identity of Peter Ward's creator, and they were apprehensive lest the truth become public knowledge. The only solution that seemed feasible and was generally acceptable to all of us was to get me out of the United States for a period of time. So I resigned from CIA and was at once rehired as a contract agent, responsible only to Karamessines. These moves were cautionary in the event some Congressman might raise questions. A delicate but hardly time-consuming political-action assignment was found for me in Madrid, and in 1965, having sold our house, we sailed for Spain aboard the pride of the Spanish merchant fleet, the liner *Covadonga*.

Formerly used almost exclusively on the New York-Havana run, the *Covadonga* was by far the worst passenger vessel on which either my wife or I had ever sailed, World War II included. It offered neither bath nor laundry facilities even for first-class passengers, and the food consisted mostly of meat fried in olive oil. A day or so out of New York my infant son, David, who had been born in the fall of 1963, became ill. We attributed his intestinal upset to the unrelievedly oily Spanish food, but because there was no doctor aboard ship, we could do no more for him than experiment with the limited available menu. The *Covadonga* wallowed across the relatively calm North Atlantic and fourteen days later put us ashore at the port of Santander. As it was a Sunday morning, no customs officials were to be found, and there was some delay before my Buick could be hoisted from the hold and deposited on the pier. Finally we began driving south through Spain's verdant perimeter, pausing overnight in Burgos, where we visited the cathedral that held the remains of El Cid, and climbed the following day to the arid plateau of Castile and Madrid.

By prearrangement we moved into the apartment owned by Bill Buckley's brother Reid, who was summering on Spain's northern coast. The heat of summertime Madrid, however, proved unbear-

*The names of my two sons.

able, so we were forced to abandon Reid's uncomfortable apartment for the quasi-air-conditioned Hotel Castellana-Hilton.

On arrival in Madrid we immediately began seeking medical assistance for David, who, even with a less oleaginous diet, was not responding, and we began a round of medical research that was to last a year. From physician to hospital to clinic, then back to another physician, another clinic and another hospital, we took our ailing child.

We moved to the small suburb of Aravaca, and in September the three older children entered the American School of Madrid, whose instruction was of such poor quality as to make the year a total academic loss. Meanwhile David's illness had been tentatively diagnosed as cystic fibrosis, an almost inevitably fatal disease.

Just after New Year's I was notified that my mother had died in Albany, and when I returned for her funeral, I took David's medical reports with me. After my mother had been buried beside my father and brother, I went to Washington and told Helms my problem. Sympathetically, he agreed that the welfare of my son was paramount and left in my hands the decision whether to remain in Spain or return to the United States.

At Children's Hospital in Washington another diagnosis was made, and this one was more encouraging. On the basis of the Madrid tests, the staff concluded tentatively that David was suffering not from cystic fibrosis, but from celiac disease, which would respond to a nonfat diet and the addition of certain enzymes. Before returning to Madrid, I purchased a large quantity of rice flour and fat-free powdered milk, took along an ample supply of enzymes and was greatly relieved to find my t begin to improve almost at once. Nevertheless, return to the United States was inevitable; the cost of renting and heating our small house was about double the American average, and because as private citizens we had no access to the military's PX economy, the price of essential food items was prohibitively high. Accordingly, I signaled Helms my intention to return the following July and he agreed.

A letter from Frank Wisner (now retired) told us that he and Polly were coming to Spain for their annual quail shoot. He asked that I make reservations at Madrid's Ritz and meet them for cocktails and dinner the evening of their arrival.

Dorothy and I waited in the lobby for them to check in, finally

returning home and calling the Ritz the following two days. Finally a
Washington friend sent me an obituary notice: Frank Wisner had
died by his own hand. Years of dedicated overwork for the Agency,
including night after night of only four hours' sleep, had under-
mined his mental health.

The tragic news depressed me. If this extraordinarily able and
imaginative man had found life no longer worth living, I began to
wonder what promise life still held for me.

Although we admired and loved the Spanish people and found
their country a vast art and antiquarian museum, I eliminated Spain
from my list of possible countries in which I would be willing to
retire. Over the long haul, the problems of medical aid and education seemed insurmountable, as did the inflationary rise in the cost
of food and lodging. So, in the summer of 1966, only too familiar with
the Spanish steamship line, we flew from Madrid to Washington,
but not before Dorothy and I had taken our children for a visit to
Paris, where, to their delight, we pointed out places and scenes
related to our courtship.

My return from Spain marked the end of my service abroad for
CIA. It was also the beginning of a new and tragic period in the lives
of myself and my family.

12 FAREWELL TO CIA

IN suburban Maryland we bought what was to be our final family home. On its ample acreage were paddocks, a stable, outbuildings and woods. To CIA headquarters at Langley, Virginia, was no more than a twenty-minute drive.

Soon there appeared newspaper accounts involving CIA Director Helms and a former OSS and now retired CIA colleague, Hans Tofte. According to the story, Tofte had put up for sale his Georgetown house. A CIA-connected visitor poking through one of the closets came across an assortment of highly classified CIA documents. CIA Security was notified and sent security agents to repossess the documents. Tofte alleged that the agents not only entered his home illegally but stole a quantity of his wife's jewelry and sued Helms over the incident. Meanwhile the Agency was considering countercharges of its own, but Tofte's litigation dragged on and melted into obscurity.

The episode echoed the notorious World War II "Amerasia Case," which concerned the theft and publication of classified OSS documents whose originals were repossessed by an OSS entry team. The case surfaced and eventually brought about the discharge of several high-ranking Department of State China experts.

My reabsorption into the mainstream of Agency activity at Langley headquarters proved difficult. The Bay of Pigs stigma remained, and with a healthy Agency emphasis on promoting junior officers there was an increasing scarcity of slots for older and more senior officers like myself. Then toward the end of summer I was assigned to Western Europe Division, where I worked under Roger Goiran and in time became chief of covert action for Western Europe.

A former division chief, Roger had also been chief of station in Tehran and Brussels. A man of penetrating intelligence and intolerant of imperfection, Roger and I got along well. He was commencing an encyclopedic study of high-level Soviet political penetrations in Europe, identifying the local Soviet agents and their KGB case officers. To Roger Goiran must go credit for fleshing out the agent-of-influence hypothesis,* which provided CIA with yet another tool to measure the pervasiveness of Soviet subversive accomplishments.

Roger's imminent retirement plans caused me to focus for the first time on my own. Obviously I was never going to be director of Central Intelligence, nor did I particularly want to be. Though my salary was reasonably rewarding, I had never depended entirely on it and decided that if I could retire at age fifty, with the director's approval, I would be able to take up a second career and still write fiction for additional and necessary income.

Knowing I had four years ahead of me in which to make these plans a reality, I began for the first time to lead less the garrison-style life so typical of CIA and instead involved myself in normal community activities. The Brown University Club of Washington was a natural vehicle for renewing old contacts and meeting alumni of a younger generation. I interviewed applicants for university admission and otherwise became active in Brown Club affairs.

A classmate, Representative Bill Bates of Massachusetts, was principal speaker at a banquet held to introduce Brown's new president. The toastmaster was Charles W. Colson, whose poise and articulateness I admired and whom I was to meet that night for the first time. Drawn together through club activities, Colson and I became friends, and I was gratified to learn that he, like I, was a conservative Republican. Formerly administrative assistant to Senator Leverett Saltonstall, Colson was an active and leading partner in an established law firm and an acute analyst of the domestic political scene.

At our Potomac home we kept horses and rode regularly as a

*The basis of my recent novel, *The Berlin Ending*.

family, and my children were recovering from the Spanish misadventure in the area's private schools. Then, on Kevan's fourteenth birthday, tragedy struck.

My daughters had been weekending at the estate of friends in rural Virginia. Dorothy and I had planned to drive them back for Kevan's scheduled birthday party, but their hosts said they had to drive to Washington anyway and would bring our daughters with them. All that Sunday afternoon Dorothy, our two sons and I waited for word from Kevan and Lisa, then the telephone rang and a man identifying himself as a Virginia state trooper asked if I were the father of a girl named Lisa Hunt. There had been a multicar crash and the number of victims was unknown. Stunned and incredulous, I heard the name of the hospital where the victims had been taken, then Dorothy and I drove to the Front Royal Hospital, an hour and a half away.

The girls' hosts had decided not to drive to Washington, but instead had sent the girls in an old car belonging to and driven by their Ecuadorian houseman. Speeding over a country road, he had come to a highway intersection and ignored the stop sign. Cars coming from either side had smashed into his and driven it into a tree. The body buckled and Lisa was flung forty feet away. Trapped in the rear, Kevan had been hurtled forward, the force of the impact nearly tearing off one leg. When we arrived at the hospital, Lisa was unconscious and Kevan's compound fracture had been inexpertly set. But at least they were alive. The pelvises of both girls were broken and each suffered kidney damage, but Lisa's injuries were the worst: Her brain was damaged.

The girls returned to school after New Year's, hobbling on crutches, but gamely trying to make up their lost schoolwork. Then one of Lisa's teachers called Dorothy to say that Lisa's attendance was irregular, and the following morning Dorothy found Lisa wandering in a nearby field, crying.

We had not realized it, but she was suffering from amnesia so total that she could not remember whether she had just left a classroom or whether she was supposed to go there. Although we then sought psychological counseling for her, we were unprepared for attempts she made on her life.

After therapy at George Washington University Hospital for several weeks Lisa was admitted to the Sheppard and Enoch Pratt

Hospital in Towson, Maryland, where her life, at least, would no longer be threatened. We were permitted to accompany her to her room with its barred windows protected by heavy mesh wire. Our sixteen-year-old daughter sat unresponsive on the bed, pale and thin, wrists still bandaged, staring at Dorothy and me as though we were strangers. For us the agony was overwhelming.

A few weeks later we were permitted to visit her. Family therapy was recommended once each week and we agreed, although we tried to make the psychiatrist understand that Lisa had suffered organic brain damage and was not withdrawn as a result of schizophrenia, the hospital's diagnosis. Meeting each month's hospital bills was a challenge, and after only a few months our resources were exhausted.

Learning of my situation, Dick Helms made the Agency's resources freely available to me, and they included legal and psychiatric counseling, plus no-interest loans from a special employee fund. All these things kept the family afloat until the defendants in our civil suit settled out of court two years later—for less than the cost of Lisa's hospitalization.

During this troubled time I began setting down my recollections of the Bay of Pigs project. I did this to distract my mind from the unhappiness into which Lisa's near tragedy had plunged my family and to provide my children with an explanation of why I had been so frequently absent from them during their youth. (Until the following year, 1967, I did not reveal to them my CIA career. Uncomplainingly they had accepted our moving from place to place and our lack of permanent friends. Only then did they understand the reasons for our mobility and the artificial isolation in which we always lived abroad.)

At one point Lisa was released from Sheppard-Pratt to enter a nearby private girls' school and to continue treatment as an outpatient. But after a few days at the boarding school Lisa again was institutionalized. The effect of her hospitalization and our heavy burden of debt had a traumatic impact on the entire family. Finally, after two and a half years, there was simply no more money to continue Lisa at Sheppard-Pratt, so we brought her home against the advice of the institution. Nevertheless, reunited with her family, she began to improve and was even able to enter a nearby community college.

In the meantime I had continued my Brown alumni activities and became vice president of the club while Chuck Colson was president. During the fall of 1968 I became aware that Colson was active in the Nixon Presidential campaign. I mentioned my several contacts with Nixon, expressed my admiration for Nixon and my hope that this time he would succeed. To Colson I described my role in the Bay of Pigs and Nixon's special interest in the project. I also told Colson I was anxious to retire from CIA so that I could work in private industry and reestablish my family's financial security. In the fall of 1969 Colson joined the White House staff, and we lunched occasionally to mull over possible employment opportunities. At one point he suggested my joining the White House staff after retirement, but I explained that if I did so, I would be unable to draw my CIA annuity and that government salaries being what they were, I knew that the White House could not meet my salary requirements.

Then, in the spring of 1970, Helms formally agreed to my early retirement and not only stood as reference for future employers, but personally recommended me to the heads of several large corporations where, he thought, I might work in public relations, my chosen field.

Through CIA's placement service I was introduced to Robert Mullen, head of a small public relations firm in Washington and one-time press aide to Dwight D. Eisenhower. Mullen, for a time, had also been head of the Marshall Plan's information service and knew something of my accomplishments in ECA.

The CIA placement officer had told me that the Mullen firm had "cooperated" with CIA in the past. This cooperation was identified as the firm's having established and managed a Free Cuba Committee for CIA. So I inferred that my CIA background would not prove a handicap to employment with Mullen as it had with several multinational firms.

During a second meeting Mullen told me that he was getting on in years, the company was comfortably established and he was casting about for younger successors to take over the management and direction of the firm. One of Mullen's accounts was the General Foods Corporation, whose Washington representative, Douglas Caddy, worked out of the Mullen offices. According to Mullen, with Caddy, myself and an as-yet-unselected individual, Mullen would be able to retire, leaving the business in the hands of this successor triumvirate.

I retired on May 1, 1970, and began working for Mullen on the HEW account, publicizing the plight of handicapped children who needed but were not getting "special education." I was soon made aware that there were other links between the Mullen firm and the Central Intelligence Agency: The accountant was a CIA retiree, as was his eventual replacement. Moreover, a Mullen office in Europe was staffed, run and paid for by CIA. The autumn passed without Mullen's taking discernible steps toward turning the firm's management over to a younger group of successors. Douglas Caddy resigned from General Foods and left the Mullen & Company office in favor of practicing law. Presently Mullen announced that he was selling the firm to Robert Bennett, son of the Republican Senator from Utah. This switch was as unexpected as it was unwelcome. I confronted Mullen with his breach of faith, and from that time on our relations were cool.

Bennett left the Department of Transportation's Office of Congressional Liaison and joined the firm, bringing with him an account with the Hughes Tool Company. In due course Bennett offered me a minority participation in the firm, but on attorney's advice I declined to invest in an undertaking over whose activities and profit sharing I would have no control. Instead, I remained a salaried employee with the nominal title of vice president.

One evening Mullen, Bennett and I dined with a young man named Spencer Oliver, son of a lobbyist occasionally employed by our firm. A Democrat, Oliver had been engaged for some time in an international student exchange which I suspected to be financed by CIA; too, Oliver mentioned several active CIA officers whom I knew. When Mullen and Bennett asked me what I thought of Oliver as a possible partner, I was less than enthusiastic, pointing out that the firm had a solid Republican image which could only be diluted by the addition of Spencer Oliver.

Early in the new year I lunched with Chuck Colson and expressed my dissatisfaction over the turn of events in my public relations firm. Colson told me that he knew Bob Bennett and expressed optimism that we would be able to work constructively together. However, Colson suggested that I consult with the Chicago backers of an organization located in Washington whose evident purpose was to counter partisan media coverage of events in Vietnam.

I met the executive director of the organization, then a few days later met with the backers at Colson's office in the White House. Additional funding was being sought, they told me, and were much interested in employing me to direct the organization. For my part I was less than totally enthusiastic, for I recognized the hazards attendant on leaving Mullen & Company for an organization whose fortunes depended upon the conduct of the Vietnam War.

Like every other resident of the Washington area, I was highly conscious of antiwar demonstrations and demonstrators as they periodically were inflicted upon the capital. During the May, 1971, Moratorium I narrowly escaped injury when demonstrators who had vowed to isolate Washington and particularly the Pentagon rolled a telephone pole down an embankment on Canal Road, narrowly missing my car. As I drove toward my office by a route made indirect by street clashes, tear gas and tire slashings, I was reminded of the postwar religious and political frenzy that gripped India and the senseless and violent internecine slaughter. There was, of course, Washington police intervention and mass arrests, but it was apparent to me that the youth of the nation was taking out on the Nixon Administration its displeasure and disillusionment over what was, in fact, a Kennedy war. Across the nation there were endless student demonstrations, and my own university was not immune. In fact, the Ivy League seemed to glory in emulating student protests elsewhere in the country. But if there were shrill and unpleasant happenings at Brown—such as the 1969 senior class turning its back on Dr. Henry Kissinger when he was awarded an honorary degree—there was alumnus Chuck Colson in the White House and his assistant, an even more recent graduate, Henry Cashen.

Occasional lunches at the White House mess with Colson were almost inspirational experiences for me; I was impressed by Colson's suite of offices in the Old Executive Office Building, the deference shown him by other White House officials and his own staff and the efficiency of his two secretaries, Joan Hall and Holly Holm.

In mid-April, in connection with my work on the HEW account, I attended a convention of special-education teachers and administrators in Miami Beach, Florida. Dorothy accompanied me, and we stayed at the Singapore Hotel on the oceanfront. At Dorothy's suggestion I attempted to get in touch with Bernie Barker by telephone, but there was no answer. Later in the day I took a taxi to the Barker address given by the telephone book listing and left a signed note pinned to the door: "If you are the Bernie Barker who worked for me in 1960-61, call me at the Singapore." That evening Bernie called and we made plans to attend a rally in Little Havana marking the tenth anniversary of the Bay of Pigs and honoring the dead and living of the brigade. I tried also to reach Manuel Artime, but he was out of town on business. So on April 17 the Barkers and the Hunts attended the ceremony—a moving one for all of us —heard Senator Lawton Chiles address the Cuban-American crowd, after which Barker and I greeted old friends among the veterans. Barker referred to me as "Eduardo," my operational alias during the Cuban operation ten years before, and I found that Eduardo was well and favorably remembered in Miami. I was glad to be among the men who had survived the invasion debacle and to whom I felt my country still owed an enormous debt.

By now I knew that Barker was active in Miami real estate and he introduced me to two of his associates, Rolando Martinez and Felipe De Diego.

That night a number of us dined together at a restaurant specializing in stone crabs and discussed at length the past, our present and what the future might hold. Of particular interest to my Miami friends were my views on the possibility of overthrowing Castro or, conversely, recognition of Castro by the United States. I told them that, realistically, I was afraid the concessions made by JFK to Khrushchev, including a no-invasion pledge, would always be invoked to tie the hands of American Presidents who might be interested in or willing to support another anti-Castro effort. However, I said, it was unthinkable that Richard Nixon, who as Vice President had been so strong a backer of our Cuban project, would entertain thoughts of Castro recognition.

Later Barker drove me to Artime's house, where for some hours we met with the former brigade leader—now married and with a substantial family—to discuss the ground we had covered at the restaurant and the possibilities of engaging together in business ventures that might be mutually profitable.

Artime was now an importer of beef from Nicaragua and engaged in other enterprises that required his frequent presence in Managua. Barker had other friends who were connected with the Dominican airlines, with Haiti and Venezuela, and felt that something of mutual interest could well evolve.

Artime was anxious to visit our new home again, it having been several years since he had visited us. So Dorothy and I left Miami with the warm glow of having seen old friends and renewed ties that had too long been allowed to slacken.

On June 13 the New York *Times* began publishing the Pentagon Papers, a leak of classified information which astonished and revolted me. On the twenty-eighth Dr. Daniel Ellsberg was indicted on two counts, theft of government property and unauthorized possession of documents related to the national defense.

Then on July 1, 1971, I received a telephone call from Charles Colson at the White House, a call which was to alter my life and perhaps the future of my country.

13 WHITE HOUSE CONSULTANT; THE "PLUMBERS" FORM

IT is a truism that great events, in retrospect, are often found to have trivial beginnings. Watergate was no exception.

I was unprepared for Colson's call and for the intensive grilling concerning my views of Ellsberg and the publication of the Pentagon Papers. For example, Colson said, "As a good observer of the political scene, what do you think of the Ellsberg prosecution?"

In reply I said, "I think they are prosecuting him for the wrong thing, possession. Isn't there some aspect of the law that focuses on the theft aspect rather than just mere possession?"

Colson said, "I don't know. It may be that there can be stiffer charges as the investigation develops . . . do you think this guy is a lone wolf?"

"Yes, I do, with the exception of the Eastern Establishment which certainly aided and abetted him. I think the whole thing was all mapped out well in advance. Don't you? It seems to me indispensable that he be prosecuted. I think that the temper of the country is certainly such that it is required. I think there is a great deal of dismay and concern among, let's say, the Silent Majority that is our principal constituency, that this hasn't been done."

"Let me ask you this, Howard. Do you think with the right resources employed that this could be turned into a major public case against Ellsberg and co-conspirators?"

"Yes, I do, but you've established a qualification here that I don't know whether it can be met."

"What's that?"

"Well, with the proper resources."

"Well, I think the resources are there."

"I would say so, absolutely."

"Then your answer would be we should go down the line to nail the guy cold?"

"Go down the line to nail the guy cold, yes. And as you know, many people, far many more than myself, have referred to the Otepka* case, you know, by way of invidious comparison. Otepka gave a few documents to a legally constituted Senatorial committee and he's been hounded ever since. And as Jack Kilpatrick said a few nights ago in his column, it depends on whose ox is being gored."

Presently Colson said, "The case now can be made on grounds where I don't see that we could lose . . . this case won't be tried in court, it will be tried in the newspapers. So it's going to take some resourceful engineering. . . ."

I said, "I want to see the guy hung if it can be done to the advantage of the Administration."

"I think there are ways to do it and I don't think this guy is operating alone."

"Well, of course he isn't operating alone. He's got a congeries of people who are supporting him, aiding and abetting him."

"But I'm not so sure it doesn't go deeper than that," Colson mused. "I'm thinking of the enemy."

Colson was referring to the Soviet Union.

I said, "Of course *they* stand to profit the most, no question about it. You've got codes and policy making apparatus stripped bare for public examination, all that sort of thing. Supposing we could get a look at these documents from inside the Kremlin or Peking? Helms could be retired forthwith and you'd cut down 90% of our expenditures over across the river [at CIA headquarters]. If you've got that kind of thing you don't need much more."

Now Colson injected a new idea: "What do you think of the idea of declassifying a lot of these old documents now?"

"I think it's a fine idea. I'm all in favor of it and I would particularly

*A former State Department security officer.

like to see the Bay of Pigs stuff declassified including the alleged agreements that Castro made with JFK."*

On Monday, July 6, Colson called me again and asked me to come to the White House. He had been thinking over our conversation, he told me, and the need for someone with my background on the White House staff. The administrative aspect had been explored, and if I served the White House as a consultant, I could continue to draw my CIA annuity.

"I've got a full-time job," I reminded Colson, "but if you can work it out with Bob Bennett, I'll be glad to help."

"Sure," Colson said, "and the first thing I want you to do, Howard, is to become, let's say, the resident expert on the origins of the Vietnam War. The last administration cleaned out everything, and no one around here seems to know exactly how we got into the damn thing. You and I know it was a Kennedy war, but people, particularly the press, have a closed mind on the subject."

Colson went on to tell me that the White House press office had voluminous clippings of the texts of Pentagon Papers and recommended that I immerse myself in them as soon as possible.

So we agreed in principle, and when I returned to my office, Bob Bennett told me that he had agreed to Colson's request for my part-time services.**

Bennett then told me that a former employee of his named Clifton De Motte was anxious to get back into Washington politics and was volunteering information on the Kennedy clan, particularly the Chappaquiddick tragedy. Bennett suggested I mention this potential source to Colson, which I did the following day.

On July 7 Colson took me to John Ehrlichman's office in the White House proper and introduced me to Ehrlichman for what was to be our one and only meeting. Colson prefaced his remarks by saying I was the Howard Hunt he had been talking about, and Ehrlichman's nod signified that he had indeed heard of me before. Colson said I was going to work on the Pentagon Papers project and Ehrlichman

---

*Colson recorded this conversation and sent the transcript to Bob Haldeman, the President's chief of staff, on the following day. Colson's covering memo said, "I think it would be worth your time to meet him [Hunt]. Needless to say I did not even approach what we had been talking about but merely sounded out his ideas."

**The $100-a-day consultation fee was less than I was earning with Mullen & Company.

asked me if I were still with CIA. I told him I had retired a year before and had been working in private industry ever since. Ehrlichman stood up, shook my hand and thanked me for coming by.

When we returned to Colson's office, Chuck said that I had just undergone the formality of being interviewed and okayed by Ehrlichman, and with that out of the way my hiring papers could be processed.

I spent a short time filling out forms, was fingerprinted and photographed by the Secret Service and issued a temporary White House pass. Space was made for me in a small office on the third floor of the Old Executive Office Building, and a typewriter and a safe were moved in. The combination was set by Secret Service technicians and the combination furnished to me and Colson's secretary, Joan Hall. That afternoon I told Colson about Clifton De Motte, and Colson was immediately interested.

"Does Bennett think he's got inside information?"

"Bob says De Motte worked for the Kennedy entourage back in 1960 and knows the whole gang. Bob thinks he's worth checking out."

"Could *you* do it?"

"I could do it, but—" I shrugged. "If I interview him, there would have to be a rationale for the interview. Who would I be, for instance?"

"Not a White House staffer," Colson interjected.

I shook my head.

Colson said, "You must have done these things before in CIA, Howard."

"I have, but when you're uncertain of a man—as we are of De Motte—you take precautions. In some cases that means disguise and certainly false documentation."

Colson leaned back in his chair. "You've got friends over at CIA. Couldn't they get what you need?"

"They could," I said, "but they wouldn't. It would be too risky for them."

"What would it take to get the things you need?"

"It's been my CIA experience that a call from the White House always produced whatever the White House wanted."

"All right. I'll see what I can do and get back to you."

As special counsel to the President, Colson had an attractively decorated suite of offices adjoining the Presidential "hideaway" in the Executive Office Building.

Because of the proximity of the two offices, Manolo Sanchez, the President's valet, often wandered into Colson's reception room to chat with the secretaries. One morning I was waiting to see Colson when in bounded King Timahoe, the Presidential Irish setter, followed by Sanchez. The dog approached me, sniffed and began lifting his leg on mine. I roared a warning and shoved the dog away before he could stain my trousers. This incident caused great hilarity among the viewers, but left me feeling surly.

Colson's phones were constantly ringing, appointments made and canceled, and invariably there were callers waiting in the outer office to see Colson. One had a sense that Colson was a dynamo around which spun large and powerful wheels. This sense of dynamism which pervaded Colson's office reflected the kinetic energy of the man himself. Everything about Colson moved at superspeed, not a moment to be lost. To and from the men's room he carried papers to read. Tall and articulate, Colson had a ready sense of humor, but did not suffer fools gladly. He made decisions quickly and was totally dedicated to President Nixon. He expected—in fact, assumed—that everyone associated with him would be equally dedicated to the President.

The longer I worked for him, the more I admired him, though I realized that among his White House associates he was probably more feared and envied than liked.

In a day or so Colson asked if I knew Lieutenant Colonel Lucien Conein. I said I had known Conein in OSS and later in CIA.

Colson said, "I thought you probably would," and asked if I could arrange to interview Conein concerning the events leading up to the death of Vietnamese Premier Diem.

"How soon?"

"Right away."

An American citizen of French-American parentage, Conein had served in the French Foreign Legion until the fall of France, then transferred to the American Army. Bilingual in French and English, Conein was quickly transferred to OSS and parachuted into France, where he worked with Maquis groups. Lou and I trained together on Catalina Island and I had seen him again in Kunming just before

Howard Hunt at two years of age.

Already a clandestine communicator at eleven years of age, "Whispers Too Much," underlined for emphasis, Hunt's sixth-grade report card, but straight "A's" in reading.

Hunt, H.

METHOD OF GRADING:
A—Superior Work.
B.—Work Above Average.
C.—Average Work.
D.—Work Below Average.
F.—Failure.

6 B II   7 B II

Attendance Deportment Studies	FIRST TERM					SECOND TERM					Yr's Av'ge
	October	November	December	January	Term Exam.	Term Aver.	February	March	April	May	Term Exam.	Term Aver.	
Days Present	18	19	12½	15								
Days Absent	0	2½	7½	5								
Days not En'd	2											
Times Tardy	0	1	0	1								
Deportment	C	A	C	F	D							
Reading	A	A	A		A							
Language	A	B		A	76	B						
Spelling	B	B	A	A	96	B						
Arithmetic	D	D	F	C	61	D						
Health Ed.	B	B	A	B	85	B						
Hist. & Cit's'p	B	C	C	B	89	B						
Geography	C	C	C	B	79	C						
Writing	C	D	C	C	78	C						
Music	C	B	B	C		C						
Drawing						C						
Manual Arts												
Ind. Arts	B	C	B	C		C						
Normal Wt.												
Weight												

Promoted to 7 B II
Jan. 31, 1930.

In an average group of 100 about 7 will rank "Superior...
In an average group of 100 about 24 will rank "Above Average...
In an average group of 100 about 38 will rank "Average."
In an average group of 100 about 24 will rank "Below Average."
In an average group of 100 about 7 will rank "Failure."

ATTITUTE TOWARD SCHOOL WORK	Oct.	Nov.	Dec.	Jan.	Feb.	Mar.	April	May	June
Indolent									
Wastes Time		X		X					
Work is Carelessly Done									
Copies: Gets too Much Help									
Gives Up Too Easily									
Shows Improvement									
Very Commendable									
RECITATIONS									
Comes Poorly Prepared									
Appears Not to Try									
Seldom Does Well									
Inattentive	X	X		X					
Promotion in Danger									
Capable of Doing Much Bet'r									
Work Shows a Falling Off									
Work of Grade Too Difficult									
Showing Improvement									
Very Satisfactory									
CONDUCT									
Restless: Inattentive									
Inclined to Mischief									
Rude: Discourteous at Times									
Annoys Others				X					
Whispers Too Much	X	X		X					
Shows Improvement									
Very Good									

The author at twelve, sitting between his father and mother while observing the old Buffalo Bisons work out in Ft. Lauderdale.

The horn player (third from left) is Howard Hunt while a student at Brown University.

Ensign Howard Hunt, USNR, fire-control officer on convoy duty in the North Atlantic aboard the destroyer DD422, USS *Mayo*.

Howard Hunt (second from right) at Henderson Field, Guadalcanal, with George Gay (on his right), the sole survivor of the famed Torpedo Squadron 8, the heroic squadron of the Battle of Midway.

Sydney, Australia, 1943, where the author was on Rest and Recuperation on leave as a war correspondent for *Life* in the South Pacific. ↓

War correspondent Hunt on Guadalcanal in 1943, in the picture used by Random House to publicize his novel *Limit of Darkness*, his second book.

Howard Hunt, helmetless, in the center with fellow candidates for the Army Air Force, Miami, 1944.

Howard Hunt shown typing up a story for *Cosmopolitan*, "Others Are Waiting," while a second lieutenant, an instructor in intelligence for the Army Air Force.

The beautiful Soviet agent Marusha Chernikov, with whom OSS operative Hunt had a brief affair, photographed here at the American Club, Shanghai, September, 1945.

The author with children released from Chapei POW Camp, Shanghai, 1945.

Howard Hunt with statues used for target practice at Apple Mission, Hsian, North China.

The author watching coolies fix a flat tire, Kunming, China, spring, 1945.

Sniping near the Yellow River, summer, 1945.

Howard Hunt (center) at a New Year's Eve party in Zurs, Austria, 1948.

On the beach near Hollywood during a stretch of movie scriptwriting in 1947.

Howard Hunt (left), with a friend, while on a Guggenheim writing fellowship at Acapulco, 1946.

The author (left) with a hunting friend from the FBI, after a day's shooting in Mexico, 1952.

Howard Hunt shown directing a documentary film in Vienna during his tour of duty under Averell Harriman, 1948.

CIA agent Hunt (left) skiing in Austria, 1949.

Our CIA man in Montevideo, 1959, shaking hands with the visiting President Eisenhower.

Always a jazz lover, with bandleader Woody Herman (left) in Uruguay.

Dorothy and Howard Hunt in Montevideo, 1959,
where he was CIA chief of station.

JOHN MITCHELL

I accept Gordon Liddy's characterization of the "AG" as a man accustomed to having his orders obeyed without question. As it turned out, Mitchell would have served everyone better, including himself, had he spent less time in splenetic denials of Watergate involvement and more in assuming responsibilities that devolved on him following the Watergate arrests. Mitchell's subsequent courses of action revealed insensitivity to the plight of men jailed for an action he instigated in his capacity as Attorney General.

Did the President know of Mitchell's Gemstone plan?

Given the intimacy between Mitchell and the President, Mitchell's Cabinet post and Mitchell's chairmanship of the Committee to Re-elect the President, it is difficult to believe that Mitchell would have allocated half a million dollars to intelligence collection and convention protection without the knowledge and implicit consent of his former law partner.

According to Liddy, it was Mitchell, the "Big Man," who insisted on a second Watergate entry despite all logical arguments to the contrary. If Liddy's assertion is true, then John Mitchell, more than any other member of the Watergate hierarchy, must assume responsibility for the debacle that ensued.

CHARLES COLSON

Chuck had far more basic courage than Dean, but not enough to assume responsibilities and obligations dropped by others. Colson was a brilliant idea man, committed to Nixon personally and to his administration. From associates and underlings Colson demanded the utmost in dedication and performance, yet he proved unwilling or incapable of reciprocating in equal measure. His self-protectiveness in recording our phone conversations, passing my letters to others and writing *ex post facto* memoranda to "paper" his files turned out to be of no help to him. In the end he pleaded guilty to a lesser charge and he, too, was sentenced to jail.

G. GORDON LIDDY

A keen combative mind, gifted raconteur and good companion, Gordon was an unquestioning believer in the prerogatives of high authority. Impatient with bureaucrats, ambitious and burdened with a sense of mission.

I never found Gordon to be the "kook" of media invention. If anything, he was and is a nineteenth-century man incapable of adapting to the liberalism and permissiveness of the late twentieth century and satisfied with his commitments to the verities of an earlier age. A religious man, Gordon suffers his personal Calvary without complaint and without hope.

JAMES MCCORD

His bombshell letter to Judge Sirica successfully polished the judicial apple and prevented his serving time beyond the five days following his arrest in DNC headquarters. Self-centered, devious and sanctimonious, McCord put his own welfare above that of his companions—and of the nation itself. His double-dealing behind the back of his original attorney was a discreditable extension of his letter-writing to CIA, and his acceptance of a cost-free Democratic lawyer filled out the picture of a weakling determined to save himself at all costs. During his televised testimony I kept wondering why, since McCord had so sensational a story to tell, he took the trouble to embroider it. McCord's recent book, however, demonstrates his inability to distinguish between fact and fiction.

JOHN DEAN

He moved through the corridors of the White House as sleekly as Iago. I mistook his taciturnity for wisdom and guts, but Dean was too young for his job—far too young. Deficient in perspective, unfamiliar with clandestine tradition, he scampered like Chicken Little to the President crying, "Blackmail."

In a post where loyalty to the President was presumptive, John Dean thought only of getting out from under a burden he was incompetent to handle. Thereafter his every action was aimed at justifying and saving himself—despite the cost to others. Even so, Dean was sent to prison, where, one hopes, he will at least gain maturity from the same suffering he caused so many others.

EGIL "BUD" KROGH, JR.

The original Mr. Straight Arrow. Calm, competent and overtaxed with duties, he was swept along in the White House current of reaction to Ellsberg's publication of the Pentagon Papers. Manfully he attempted to assume full responsibility for the Fielding entry, pleaded guilty and went to prison determined to purge himself of sin.

"A country that frees Ellsberg and puts me on trial instead can't be all bad," Krogh is alleged to have said.

Bud, you're far too charitable.

RICHARD M. NIXON

I read the White House transcripts with a sense of disillusionment, betrayal and sorrow. Nixon, the man I had believed in for so many years, turned out to be indecisive, petty and obsessed with self-preservation. Although he assumed "full responsibility" for the Fielding entry, he shouldered none of the blame and watched loyal subordinates enter prison without, as far as can be determined, emotion beyond an inner relief that "there but for the grace of God go I."

Should the former President serve a prison sentence?

My personal feeling is that he should not. Nor do I want others yet unsentenced to serve time. Far more than enough lives have been destroyed over Watergate, and there remains a national future to construct. This cannot be done as long as Nixon and his confidants remain in jail, and prison for others will not restore to me the lost years of my life.

he parachuted into Indochina. After the war Conein accepted a Regular Army commission and was either in or on the periphery of intelligence work for the rest of his Army career.

After the French capitulation in Vietnam, Conein had been taken by General Edward Lansdale to North Vietnam in order to establish a series of stay-behind nets and lay sabotage plans. Lansdale then became a brilliant but erratic CIA station chief in Saigon, and though Lansdale left CIA, Conein stayed on and spent many years in Vietnam, becoming a leading American authority on all things Vietnamese.

I telephoned Conein at his McLean, Virginia, home, told him I had recently joined the White House staff and asked if he would be willing to talk to me about some matters of mutual interest. He expressed willingness to see me and complained that his contract with CIA was about to be terminated. He was retired from the Army and added that he had suffered financial reverses in Vietnam; perhaps I could help him have his CIA contract renewed? I told him we would discuss all these matters and reported to Colson that Conein was on his way.

Colson decided to tape-record our conversation, but there were no facilities either in Colson's office or in mine. John Ehrlichman's office was empty, however, and Colson arranged to have the premises bugged.

When Conein arrived at the White House east entrance, he was passed quickly in and met by me not far from Ehrlichman's office. I took Lou on a brief tour of the East Wing, with which I had become familiar only an hour or so before. We entered Ehrlichman's office and sat down, and presently Joan Hall brought in a tray of scotch, ice, soda and glasses. She withdrew and closed the door, and Conein and I began to talk. Obviously impressed by our surroundings, Conein examined Ehrlichman's desk and appropriated a scratch pad with Ehrlichman's name printed on it. Then he returned to the sofa and I questioned him extensively about his knowledge of the circumstances surrounding the death of Premier Diem and his brother-in-law. I made no attempt to take notes, for the conversation was being recorded. Inevitably we began to discuss Daniel Ellsberg, whom Conein had met when Ellsberg was there as a senior representative of the Pentagon.

Conein mentioned that Ellsberg had once gotten into a fight with a bar owner named Nicolai over a woman of Nicolai's coveted by Ellsberg. We discussed Nicolai's background and narcotics traffic in Saigon, and as we drank scotch, the room temperature seemed to rise and our conversation became more disjointed and garbled.

It was nearly dark when I helped Conein out of the White House and returned to Colson's office much in need of black coffee and rest.

On the following day when I went into Colson's outer office, Joan Hall told me that most of the conversation had not been recorded: The Secret Service had not had time to install a remote microphone and instead had merely concealed a tape recorder in a cushion of the sofa. Compressed by the weight of Conein and myself on the sofa, the tape recorder functioned intermittently, and the portions that would have been of greatest interest to Colson had been lost. Could I reconstruct them?

I tried, but memory failed. Colson suggested I telephone Conein, introduce Colson as "Fred Charles," a member of the White House security staff, and lead Conein into the areas we had covered the previous afternoon and evening. There was a recording device on his telephone, Colson told me, and everything said on the phone would be preserved.

Telephoning Conein, I explained that details of our discussion were lost in an alcoholic fog and asked if he would mind covering significant areas for my friend "Fred Charles." Conein agreed, and with "Fred Charles" interjecting questions from time to time, we managed to reconstruct our conversation of the previous day.

As I was leaving Colson's office, Joan Hall cautioned me never to reveal the use to which John Ehrlichman's private office had been put; Ehrlichman would be furious, she told me, and the Secret Service was uneasy over having entered Ehrlichman's office and abashed at the failure of their tape recorder. I told her that while I was perfectly willing to keep the secret, Conein might not feel himself under similar obligation. One could only hope that he would either forget where he had been or else—as a CIA professional of long experience—hold that it was no one's business but his own.

When Colson indicated that he would want me to interview others from time to time, I asked that he arrange to have my office miked so that I could record conversations and avoid the awkwardness of taking notes. Soon microphones were placed behind the front panel of my desk and minute holes drilled to enable sound vibrations to enter. These microphones led to a Sony recorder in the lower right-hand drawer of my desk, and a switch was installed under the surface of the desk itself so I could activate the tape recorder unobtrusively.

I first used this device when, at Colson's request, I interviewed Major General (ret.) Edward G. Lansdale concerning many of the same things Conein had previously discussed with me.

A few days after the Conein interview I walked into Colson's outer office and saw a shirt-sleeved young man talking with Joan Hall. He was wearing glasses and carrying a sheaf of papers in his hand, and before I sat down, Mrs. Hall introduced me to John W. Dean III, counsel to the President. Dean acknowledged the introduction in an offhand way and strolled in to see Colson. I checked the correspondence folder Mrs. Hall kept on her desk for me, emptied it of memoranda from Colson and carried them to my third-floor office, where I resumed my daily work.

On Saturday, July 10, I was in my office when Joan Hall called to ask that I attend an emergency meeting to be chaired by Ehrlichman's assistant, Egil "Bud" Krogh. The meeting was held in the Roosevelt, or sub-Cabinet, room, and in it were assembled senior representatives from the departments of State and Defense, the FBI and the Secret Service. Although Krogh was young, I was immediately impressed by the skill and decisiveness with which he handled this assembly of older and, for the most part, career government officials. The instant problem was the publication in the New York *Times* of the substance of documents revealing the U.S. negotiating position in the SALT talks. A brief general discussion narrowed the suspect leaker to either State or Defense, a Defense consultant coming under heaviest initial suspicion for having had previous contact with the *Times* reporter.

Remarking that because it seemed unlikely that either suspect would return to his office over the weekend, I suggested that State and Defense security officers open the suspects' safes and inventory their contents. This idea was accepted, and orders were issued. Krogh pointed out that general suspicion was insufficient, and he wanted the identity of the culprit. I suggested the FBI polygraph the suspects, but when the FBI representative seemed disinclined to honor my suggestion, and State said they had no such facilities, I suggested that CIA polygraph teams be called upon to administer the lie-detector tests.

The meeting lasted an hour or so, and the measures taken proved effective: As it turned out, *both* suspects had leaked information to the reporter, but no particular sanctions were ever invoked against them.

Early the following week Joan Hall told me that arrangements had been made for me to see General Robert Cushman, deputy director of CIA. I was to call his assistant, Carl Wagner, for an appointment.

I had known Wagner from my Far East tour when he was a junior officer in Seoul, and I had had dealings with Bob Cushman, first in OPC, then when I joined the Cuba project and Cushman was the Vice President's military aide. Through Wagner I was granted an appointment with General Cushman on July 22.

In the meantime I was discovering that simply reading through the published Pentagon Papers and the press commentaries was getting me no closer to the secret background of the Vietnam War. I had made notes and footnotes and on one occasion asked Colson whether it might be possible to gain access to the pertinent files of the National Security Council. These I felt would have been maintained separately from President Johnson's personal White House files, and as a continuing organization, the likelihood was that the NSC, perhaps more than any other governmental unit, would maintain file continuity.

Colson indicated that he might put the question to Henry Kissinger, but if he did, Colson never mentioned it to me.

The media, always friendly to the antiwar cause, were lionizing Ellsberg and turning him into a larger-than-life figure. Within the space of a few weeks he had become a figure of heroic proportions, David with the pebble of Truth in his sling.

In and around Colson's offices the question was often asked: Why did Ellsberg do it? What was his motivation? Was he madman, martyr, the tool of a foreign power or—that most unlikely of possibilities—an idealist and an altruist?

These were vexing questions. My White House colleagues felt that Ellsberg's challenge could not go unanswered lest others in the government, out of sympathy with the Vietnam War, be encouraged to outdo Ellsberg's deed. The Department of Justice had drawn up indictments and was preparing to prosecute Drs. Ellsberg and Russo. Still, I recalled Colson's admonition: "Ellsberg could be turned into a martyr of the New Left—he probably will be anyway," and I had the visceral feeling that Chuck was right.

From Lucien Conein we had learned little more than that Ellsberg—like many Americans—had known some unsavory people in Saigon. Ed Lansdale's recollections of Ellsberg were even less illuminating, and there seemed no easy answer to the troublesome questions concerning Ellsberg's motivation.

To me, as to others in the White House, Ellsberg's deed seemed the culmination of the lawless mass actions that had taken place across the country during the previous several years: chaos on street and campus, urban bombings and burnings, massive marches and nonnegotiable demands. Finally, the unprecedented spectacle of the nation's capital battling fanatical invaders for its very life.

As we perceived them, these episodes derived from a civil conflict between the legitimately elected government and hostile elements which not only denied the legitimacy of that elected government but arrogated legitimacy only unto themselves.

This hostile, unassimilated minority formed, in effect, a countergovernment with strong ties to the counterculture, both of which were using every means at their disposal—legal or illegal—to frustrate the majority will.

In the case of Daniel Ellsberg, the countergovernment asserted its right to declassify and publish top-secret government documents—and was being applauded by all the pundits of the Left. Meanwhile, from within the legitimate government the countergovernment was sending forth a constant stream of leaks and disclosures to friends and allies in the press. Moreover, the countergovernment disposed of its own journalists, media, clergy, scientists and lawyers, all immediately available to support and urge its claims.

If Daniel Ellsberg viewed the legitimate government of the United States as "criminal," then we perceived him as treasonist and alien. We were deeply concerned by extremist elements: the yippies, hippies and zippies; the mob, the SDS and the movement—all groupings of the counterculture directed by the countergovernment, whose purpose seemed clearly aimed at the destruction of our traditional institutions they could not hope to eliminate through elective process.

These, then, were what Frank Wisner used to refer to as the "atmospherics" of the situation that challenged the White House as it surveyed the country in that summer of 1971.

I recall asking Colson for a classified document and being told by him that I should see Gordon Liddy in Room 16, where sensitive documents were being assembled. So I walked down to Room 16 of the Executive Office Building and introduced myself to Gordon Liddy.

Liddy was a taut, wisecracking extrovert, an alumnus of the FBI and recently a special assistant to the Secretary of the Treasury. In our early discussions I learned that he had been a prosecutor in Duchess County, south of my former Albany home, was married and had several children. He had run unsuccessfully for Congress and had been given a job with the Nixon Administration in payment of that political debt.

Liddy and I liked each other at once. To me he seemed decisive and action-oriented, impatient with paperwork and the lucubrations of bureaucracy. He introduced me to David Young, his immediate supervisor, whom I found to be an agreeable young man, blond and balding, with a passion for tennis. Young had attended Cornell and Oxford and was a recent transfer from Kissinger's staff.

While at Treasury Liddy had helped set up Operation Intercept, which substantially reduced the importation of Mexican marijuana. He was keenly interested in the narcotics problem and was frequently consulted by Walter Minnick, another occupant of Room 16. Bud Krogh, I learned, directed the unit (later called the "Plumbers" by the press), but on that occasion I did not grasp the unit's basic function.

The secretary, Kathleen Chenow, had transferred to the White House from the Hill, where she had worked in the office of a New England Senator. Like myself, all seemed to work long hours uncomplainingly and were always among the last to leave the White House at night.

As I turned increasingly to Room 16 for reference to sensitive documents, I became aware that Liddy and the others were receiving periodic reports from the FBI on Daniel Ellsberg and his associates. One of the offices where Krogh occasionally worked had been converted into a sort of situation room. Pinned to the wall was a makeshift PERT chart indicating the status of projects and individual assignments. Documents originating in Room 16 were stamped with the sensitivity indicator ODESSA to differentiate them from other routine classified documents circulating within the White House.

A skillful raconteur, Liddy provided frequent comic relief for us that was much in contrast to the grim miens encountered elsewhere in the White House. Instead of using the pat John Doe to refer to an unknown person, Liddy energized the identification with "Tondelayo Schwarzkopf." A flying enthusiast, Liddy had photographs of himself taken in the classic barnstormer poses of an earlier time. We began lunching together in the White House cafeteria and occasionally had an afterwork drink at one of my downtown clubs.

On July 22 I was driven in a White House limousine to the Central Intelligence Agency and escorted to the private elevator used only by the director and his deputy. On the seventh floor I was shown into General Cushman's office and shook hands with him and Carl Wagner, his administrative aide.

I asked Cushman if we might not speak privately, and Wagner departed to leave us alone.*

General Cushman, I noted, seemed rather portly. I thanked him for having Wagner withdraw and said, "I've been charged with quite a highly sensitive mission by the White House to visit and elicit information from an individual whose ideology we aren't sure of. And for that purpose they asked me to come over here and see if you could get me two things: flash alias documentation which wouldn't have to be backstopped and some degree of physical disguise—for a one-time op, in and out."

Cushman said, "I don't see why we can't."

I told him I wanted the matter as closely held as possible and suggested that I meet someone in a safehouse.

"Tomorrow afternoon would probably be the earliest it could be accomplished," I said, "so if someone could do it by tomorrow afternoon, it would be great."

---

*More than a year later I was to learn that General Cushman had recorded the entirety of our conversation.

We turned to the problems of gaining weight in sedentary occupations and Cushman said, "The only way I can lose weight is to be miserable, relatively miserable."

I told him I had the same problem and remarked that since retirement, the thing I missed most about CIA was the gymnasium facility. Cushman said, "Well, I don't use it. I ordinarily trot or jog for thirty minutes in the morning at home. If I wait until afternoon I'm too tired. I'm just getting to that old-age point where, when I get home in the afternoon, I may work in the workshop or do a little bit of work in the yard but I don't feel like running."

Then Cushman said, "I can get in touch with you at the White House, can't I—to give you what address to go to and so forth?"

"Right. So we can lay it on. Do you think tomorrow afternoon is ample time?"

"I'll give it a try, yes. I haven't talked to anybody yet. I suppose they can do it. I haven't been in this business before—haven't had to."

"Well, Ehrlichman said that you were the—"

"Yes, he called me. I mean I haven't been in the cover business so I don't know if they operate real fast, but I suppose they do."

"Well, I know they can. It's just a question of getting some physical disguise."

"What do you need? That will be the first thing they'll ask."

"Well, I'll need—let's see, what have I got here?" I examined the contents of my billfold. "I'll probably need just a driver's license and some pocket litter."

"Driver's license?"

"Driver's license in any state at all," I told him.

"Pocket litter?"

"Yes, that's what they call it."

"You don't care in what name?"

I told him I wanted the first name to be Edward. "Because I'm being introduced to this gentleman by just one name. He was told early this morning that somebody by the name of Edward would be getting in touch with him."

"And any state for the driver's license?"

"Yes, any state. It doesn't make any difference. I'm just going to check into a hotel and I'll use this alias documentation for that."

Cushman asked me to repeat my telephone number and I suggested that he call Colson's office, since my office was unattended. I told him Joan Hall answered Colson's phone and said he could give her the time and the address of my meeting in the safehouse. As I rose, Cushman said, "If you see John Ehrlichman, say hello for me."

"I will indeed."

"He's an old friend of mine from previous days. . . . How's that Domestic Council working out? You don't hear about it much in this business."

I told Cushman it was working out pretty well and remarked that the Pentagon Papers affair had electrified the White House.

Cushman said, "Well, John—I think John is in charge of the security overhaul, isn't he?"

"That's right."

Cushman said, "Well, let me get to work on this. I'll get the word back to you."

I told him that the less my name came up, the better, knowing the CIA penchant for intramural gossip.

On that note we parted, and I returned to the White House and telephoned Clifton De Motte. We set up a meeting date for some days later in a motel at the Providence airport. It was near the GSA installation where he worked and I did not want to be bothered renting a car and driving to Providence to meet him at, say, the Providence Biltmore Hotel. Besides, I had asked Cushman for only the most superficial of documentation, and I had no plans to use it with sharp-eyed car-rental agents.

Next morning I received a telephone call from Carl Wagner telling me to go that afternoon to a safehouse on upper Wisconsin Avenue near the National Cathedral. A man from CIA's Technical Services Division would be waiting for me, and his operational alias was "Steve." He would know me as "Edward."

At the safehouse Steve outfitted me with thick, nonrefractive glasses and a brown wig, which he showed me how to don and adjust. He was experimenting, he told me, with a voice-altering device, which he hoped I would be willing to use and report upon. Accordingly, he made a dental cast of my mouth and palate and with dental equipment in the safehouse fashioned a replica of my upper palate. Fitted into my mouth, the device—a false palate—interfered with normal tongue placement and produced a lisping effect.

Steve had brought with him a number of documents made out in the name of Edward J. Warren, and I signed them in his presence, as well as a receipt for everything supplied me. I asked also for some calling cards imprinted with my alias and with the notional New York City address that appeared on related documentation. Steve said he would deliver them at a later time.

So I flew to the Providence airport and checked into a motel room, where Clifton De Motte joined me at the appointed time. At first he seemed cautious and edgy, and I purposely kept the light low in the room to avoid his taking particular note of my physical disguise. We sat on opposite sides of a table, on which I had placed a small home tape recorder and its microphone. I asked if he objected to our conversation being recorded and he said that he did not. De Motte inquired about Bob Bennett and told me that he hoped to become active in the coming Presidential campaign—this time on the Republican side—for he was sick of his GSA job at Davisville, Rhode Island.

Preliminaries over, De Motte told me that in the summer of 1960 he had been employed as "public relations man" by a Cape Cod inn which lodged such Kennedy staff luminaries as Pierre Salinger. As De Motte explained it, his duties included keeping the Kennedy guests happy, and as the summer went on, De Motte became increasingly involved with members of the Kennedy staff. He told me several stories about Pierre Salinger and others that dealt with the general reputation of the Kennedy family on Cape Cod, including their notorious delays in paying local bills. None of this was particularly interesting to me, and I asked him if he had, as a native of the region, any particular information on the tragedy at Chappaquiddick. De Motte floundered with this one, then indicated that he would be willing to make inquiries, knowing as he did a number of local figures on Chappaquiddick Island. We had dinner together in my room and De Motte continued to talk about events which, however piquant, had occurred a decade earlier and had no current utility.

At the conclusion of our discussion I gave De Motte money for future expenses and suggested that after he had explored the Chappaquiddick situation he telephone Bob Bennett, who would convey the message to me.

I stayed overnight at the motel and in the morning flew back to Washington, where I prepared a memorandum to Colson covering my discussions with De Motte, using the taped record to assist my recollections. Colson thought I had done the right thing in pursuing the Chappaquiddick aspect of the investigation and asked me to keep him posted on future developments.

I now began to find myself spending increasing time with the Room 16 group, which, I learned, had an in-house title: the Special Investigations Unit. There I became aware of considerable dissatisfaction with assistance rendered the White House by the FBI and the Department of Defense. Liddy was in contact with both, particularly General Counsel J. Fred Buzhardt of the Department of Defense, and as a matter of daily routine I began reading the reports submitted to the White House by the Department of Defense and the FBI on the Ellsberg-Pentagon Papers investigation.

An example of FBI lassitude—and inexactitude—in its coverage of Daniel Ellsberg arrived at Room 16 in the form of a report from a highly rated Bureau informant stating that Ellsberg and his wife, Patricia, took part in orgies at the Sand Stone Club in Los Angeles. A telephone check by Liddy and myself failed to locate the Sand Stone Club, so the Bureau was asked for more details: location, membership, etc. No response from the FBI was ever forthcoming. However, in late 1972 a magazine article described Sandstone as a reputable and legitimate institution for the group treatment of sexual dysfunction—hardly the orgy club reported by the FBI.

Liddy and Young, both lawyers, believed the indictments against Ellsberg sloppily drawn, and Liddy made this known to Robert Mardian at the Department of Justice. According to Liddy, J. Edgar Hoover referred contemptuously to Mardian as "that Lebanese Jew." In fact, Mardian was of Armenian descent and a Christian. Mardian was also assistant attorney general in charge of the Internal Security Division of the Department of Justice under Attorney General John Mitchell.

As Daniel Ellsberg became increasingly the object of media admiration, he acquired a useful image as an apostle of truth, a courageous loner against the hated and war-prolonging Nixon Administration. With Ellsberg's new status as a public figure, curiosity spread within the White House concerning the motives for his thefts and revelations. From FBI reports we learned that Ellsberg and his first wife had experimented with hallucinogenic drugs, that he had numerous mistresses and that his sex life between marriages could easily be described as bizarre. Furthermore, he had been amorously involved with two foreign women: one Indonesian, one Swedish. On a holiday from Vietnam Ellsberg had visited the latter woman in Sweden before returning to the United States.

Through my Agency years in European counterintelligence I was familiar with the ease with which Soviet agents could enter Sweden via Finland and thence to Western Europe. Too, it had been reported to us that copies of Ellsberg's Pentagon Papers had been delivered either to a Soviet agent or to a Soviet Embassy before their publication by the New York *Times* and other newspapers.

And there was an FBI report so couched as to suggest it was based upon a telephone intercept: Ellsberg was reported to have called his Beverly Hills psychiatrist, Dr. Lewis Fielding, and told Dr. Fielding of his immense relief that the task was now completed.

Taken together, all these circumstances, far from throwing more light on Ellsberg's motives, suggested a variety of conclusions that could be drawn. His intimate involvement with foreign women while he himself held high-level security clearances and the alleged prior delivery of copies of his stolen documents into Soviet hands suggested the possibility that Ellsberg was a Soviet agent. Moreover, Ellsberg had attended Cambridge University in England, historically a fertile hunting ground for Soviet recruiters. The call he made to psychiatrist Fielding, however, focused our interest, and we discussed it at some length, concluding that although Ellsberg had not been a patient of Dr. Fielding's for a number of months, it was likely that Dr. Fielding's patient files might well provide answers to our more pressing questions.

We were also concerned that, once embarked upon an unpopular prosecution, the government might be faced with an insanity plea. If Ellsberg's psychiatric file were to provide a basis for such a plea, then the White House recommendation to the Department of Justice would be that the charges be dropped, at least against Dr. Ellsberg.

I suggested to Krogh and Young that we request CIA to provide a psychiatric profile of Dr. Ellsberg. In the past, I told them, CIA performed this service routinely on foreigners of interest to the United States government. Although these profiles were, of necessity, indirect and at least once removed from the subject, they had proved useful guides in the work of both the Department of State and the Central Intelligence Agency. I cited a lengthy psychological profile performed by the Agency on Fidel Castro, a study which had proved a valuable source of information for propaganda themes and other clandestine activities against the Cuban dictator.

I made a preliminary call to Dr. Barney Malloy and invited him to Room 16 in the White House for a conference with me and some of my associates. After checking with his superiors, Malloy complied.

We explained the Ellsberg problem to the Agency psychiatrist. Before he left, we provided Dr. Malloy with much of the classified information that had been collected on Daniel Ellsberg and asked that he provide us with an "indirect personality assessment" as soon as possible. But when it was delivered, we found it superficial and perhaps prepared by a partisan of Ellsberg's. So we asked that a second study be prepared and gave Malloy additional documents, plus a chronology of the most significant events in Ellsberg's life.

Disheartened by CIA response to our request, Liddy and I began discussing alternate means of resolving the Ellsberg enigma: It was obvious to both of us that securing Dr. Ellsberg's psychiatric files could be of paramount assistance in making a binding determination concerning the feasibility of Ellsberg's prosecution.

In the meantime, I had kept Colson informed of our findings with regard to Ellsberg and the disappointing results of the CIA psychiatric study. Colson then asked me to prepare a memorandum giving my thoughts on steps that might be taken to neutralize Daniel Ellsberg, and I provided such a memorandum, one line of which suggested acquisition of psychiatric material on Ellsberg from Dr. Fielding's files. If the files could be obtained, their information would be used for two purposes: to determine the prosecutability of Daniel Ellsberg and to damage Ellsberg's heroic image.

The more Liddy and I discussed both the problem of, and the opportunity presented by, Dr. Fielding's file, the more apparent it became that the file should be photographed by surreptitious means.

We made such a proposal to Bud Krogh and David Young and told them that as an initial step, it would be necessary for us to make a feasibility study of Dr. Fielding's office and office building.

Neither Young nor Krogh had any experience in entry operations, so I went into the matter fairly thoroughly with them, describing techniques and practices with which I was familiar and which could be employed if an entry were authorized. However, I told them, the feasibility study was essential, for without that we were simply discussing the proposal in theory without practical knowledge on which to base a decision.

At Krogh's request we drew up a budget for the feasibility study, which amounted to little more than the cost of plane tickets and hotel rooms in Los Angeles. The request was promptly approved and Bud Krogh authorized us to take the initial steps.

During our initial discussions of a surreptitious-entry operation I had told Liddy of the physical disguise and alias documentation provided me by CIA. Liddy now asked that I have CIA issue him similar materials. I did so by calling "Steve" at CIA and arranging to have him meet Liddy and myself at the Wisconsin Avenue safehouse.

Liddy decided on the alias of "George F. Leonard," was given a black wig, alias documentation, pocket litter and a heel-lift device that Steve wanted him to field-test. The device was supposed to make the wearer limp, as, in fact, it did. It was a rather unsophisticated item, however—a pebble would have done as well—for the heel lift simply pained the wearer so much that he favored the foot and automatically limped.*

On August 25 Gordon Liddy and I picked up our airline tickets to Los Angeles. Under our aliases we checked into the Beverly-Hilton Hotel, which we had determined by prior map reference was only a few blocks from the office of Dr. Fielding. This was the first of many trips that Liddy and I were to make together, and after we had walked to and around Dr. Fielding's office building and back to our hotel, I was surprised to see Gordon do a hundred or so push-ups before we retired. Liddy was a physical-fitness enthusiast who watched his diet carefully and drank only moderately.

Early in the morning I phoned Tony Jackson and asked him to breakfast with us en route his office. Thus Jackson and Liddy met for the first time, though I introduced Liddy to him as George Leonard, a White House associate of mine. Jackson did not inquire the reason for our presence in Los Angeles but I gave him the impression that we were there on a narcotics mission, and Liddy supported this

---

*During our Beverly Hills survey Liddy became so incensed over the pain-inducing device that he threw it away, but often resurrected its memory with pointed jibes at CIA.

misdirection by speaking knowledgeably of Operation Intercept.

My purpose in having Jackson meet me was to discuss with him the possibilities of West Coast financing for the Latin American business opportunities that Barker, Artime and I had discussed the previous spring and that were still very much in my mind.

After Jackson departed, Liddy and I donned our physical disguise and I shouldered my personal 35mm camera. We photographed the target office building from 360°, the access and escape routes, and the exterior windows to Dr. Fielding's office, which overlooked a driveway and a parking lot. To blunt curiosity among passersby, I posed Liddy in front of the office building, so that it would appear that I were photographing him rather than the background building. Next we rented a car and scouted Dr. Fielding's residence, which we also photographed from three sides.

I said to Liddy, "We've got Fielding's name and address. Couldn't we get his automobile license number from the local FBI office?"

"Sure we could, but they'd start asking questions. I know these guys, and the first thing they'd do would be to telex J. Edgar for permission. No, let's see if we can't dig it out ourselves."

Back we went to Fielding's office building, and there in the parking lot, in the slot assigned by name to Dr. Fielding, was a Volvo. We photographed it and returned to our hotel room, where we wrote down all the information we had acquired. All that remained was to survey the scene at night under simulated operating conditions.

For inside photography Steve had provided Liddy with a small camera concealed in a tobacco pouch. According to the headquarters technician, the camera was loaded with film so sensitive that it would photograph objects in a fairly dark room. As Liddy fumbled with the camera's concealed shutter mechanism, he grumbled, "First your guys give me this heel lift that's crippled me for life and now a camera I can't even see."

Due to jet lag, we were tired and turned in to sleep until after dark. We dined late in our room and set out on foot for the target building. Again I photographed the exterior of the building and noted which windows were lighted.

Above Dr. Fielding's office there appeared to be an apartment; its lights were on and the rooms were occupied. The main entrance to the building was closed by large glass doors, giving us a view from the street of the entire first-floor corridor. At the far end was a charwoman. I put away my camera in an attaché case and Liddy got out his tobacco-pouch camera and a corncob pipe. The front door was open, so we entered the corridor and took the stairs toward Dr. Fielding's office on the second floor. As we neared the office, the charwoman stepped out of a nearby door and (because she appeared to be Mexican-American) I said to her in Spanish, "Señora, we are doctors and friends of Dr. Fielding. With your permission, we would like to go into his office for a moment and leave for him something he has been expecting."

She looked at us suspiciously. I said, "Please, we promise not to take anything."

"Very well, *caballeros*," she said with a shrug, produced a pass-key, opened the door and turned on the reception-room light. While Liddy entered, tobacco-pouch camera in hand, I conversed in Spanish with the cleaning woman until Liddy's continuing absence disturbed her and she said to me, "What's he doing in there?"

"Writing a message to the doctor," I told her, and just as she began to enter the office in search of Liddy, my companion walked briskly toward me and said in English, "Well, I left it. I hope he understands."

I tipped the cleaning woman, thanked her for her courtesy, and as we left the building, Liddy aimed his tobacco pouch to take several more photographs of the building's interior.

I said, "Did you have time to get any shots?"

"A few, but Jesus, I kept thinking she was going to charge in on me!"

We left the building and returned to the hotel garage for our rented car. Over the next three hours we checked the building's immediate area at fifteen-minute intervals, noting the cleaning woman's directional progress from office to office and her final departure at midnight. After she left, we tried the front door and found, to our surprise, that it was open. So was the back door. We drove into the adjacent parking lot and stayed there, lights out, checking for police cruisers, but none appeared.

From where we sat we could just make out a portion of the Beverly-Hilton Hotel and decided that if the entry operation were authorized, we would book rooms in that visible part of the hotel to give us line-of-sight communication with the target building.

I called Steve at his home and asked him to meet me at Dulles Airport in the morning, telling him I would have some exposed film that I wanted developed. On our way to the Los Angeles airport to catch the Red-Eye Special, Liddy said, "While you were doing some of that outside photography, I went off in that little park and stretched out on a bench for some sun. First thing I knew I was being cruised by a seven-foot Navajo faggot and I almost had to fight him to get rid of him. Christ, what a town!"

The TSD technician, as bidden, met us in the morning at Dulles, and I asked for blowups to be ready for me during the course of the day. Liddy and I went to our respective homes, slept a few hours and regrouped at the White House, where we began preparing a step-by-step operational plan for the proposed entry.

In midafternoon a White House limousine took me to a safehouse not far from the present location of the Watergate Special Prosecutor's office, where Steve delivered to me the developed photographs. I returned to the White House and incorporated the prints into the operational plan, using transparent overlays with easy-to-understand colored symbols. Before our feasibility study was forwarded, I reported to Mullen & Company and spent the rest of the day at my normal work.

On the following day Liddy informed me that we could plan on the entry, but with one reservation: Neither he nor I was to be permitted anywhere near the target premises. Previously, I had not considered it necessary to involve anyone other than Liddy and myself. Now I would have to turn to others for help.

From Room 16 I telephoned Bernie Barker and asked him if he could put together a three-man entry team, telling him only that the target was a traitor to the United States. Barker responded affirmatively, and I asked him to provide me the names of his assistants as soon as possible so they could be checked out in Washington. When Barker phoned back, he gave me the names of Rolando Martinez and Felipe De Diego. I passed the names of all three men to David Young and told him that in view of Krogh's injunction, these three Cuban-Americans would be making the entry rather than Liddy and myself.

"It would be a hell of a lot easier if Liddy and I could do the job," I told him.

"Do you think they can do it?"

"If everything goes according to plan," I told him, "but they've never worked together before."

Liddy and I had suggested Labor Day weekend as the optimum time for the entry. It was unlikely that the professional building would be occupied over the long weekend; most of the physicians would probably be elsewhere vacationing. Additionally, cleaning services would probably be performed on Friday night, the second of September, and surely no later than the following day. Thus we would have Saturday, Sunday and Monday nights to perform the entry.

I instructed Barker to fly to Los Angeles from Miami and check into the Beverly-Hilton with his men under assumed names. Then Liddy and I made plans to fly to Los Angeles via Chicago, where we would stop off and acquire camera equipment and walkie-talkies. The purchases were to be made in Chicago rather than Washington or Los Angeles to avoid the possibility of their being traced back to Liddy and myself in the event the entry team was apprehended.

Our suitcases packed and ready, Liddy and I waited in Room 16 for Bud Krogh to provide operational funds. Time passed and we became increasingly nervous, fearing we would miss our flight. But at the last minute Krogh appeared, handed Liddy an envelope and said, "Here it is. Now for God's sake, don't get caught."

Liddy said, "We won't."

Krogh shook his head. "I'm going to give you my home phone number," he told Liddy. "As soon as the operation's over —whatever happens—call and let me know. I'll be waiting." He wrote down a number and handed it to Liddy, who tucked it in his pocket.

"I'll call from a pay station," Liddy told him. "I'll be George —honest George Leonard." He smiled. "What'll I call you?"

Krogh grimaced. "Just call me Wally," he told Liddy.

"Wally?"

"Yeah—Wally Fear."

Amused by Krogh's honest revelation of his nervousness, we hurried out of the White House and caught a cab to the airport.

So, on September 1, Liddy and I flew to Chicago, overnighted and made our purchases the following day, leaving in the afternoon for Los Angeles. Barker, Martinez and De Diego were already at the hotel, and after dark I conducted them to the target area in order to familiarize them with its approach and escape routes as they would look during the actual operation. On the following day further items were purchased at widely separated stores: work uniforms for the three men, a large suitcase, entry tools, a length of stout nylon rope and black muslin to cover the windows. The nylon rope was to be the emergency means of exit from Dr. Fielding's office.

I had acquired airfreight manifests at the airport and rubber stamps and RUSH labels at a nearby stationer's. These I placed on the suitcase to give the appearance of an airfreight delivery to Dr. Fielding. The photographic equipment, black muslin and nylon cord went inside the suitcase, the scheme being to persuade the cleaning woman to permit the "delivery men" to leave it inside Dr. Fielding's office. This pretext entry had two purposes: to deposit the heavy equipment in the target office so the entry team would not be burdened with it when they returned later that night to the building; and the "delivery men," on leaving the target office, would punch the inside doorknob lever, leaving the lock disengaged.

We adjusted and ran tests on the four walkie-talkies, finding, to our consternation, that the frequency was also utilized by radio cabs in the Los Angeles area. Still, we felt our signals would be strong enough for the short distances involved and developed an easily memorized plain-language code for use during the operation.

On the night of the third we took up our assigned positions, Barker and De Diego wearing the physical disguises that had been issued to Liddy and myself. From a pay phone I called Dr. Fielding's office but the ringing went unanswered. I then telephoned his apartment, and when a male voice answered, I hung up. Dr. Fielding was home.

I drove one of the rented cars to the vicinity of Dr. Fielding's apartment building, while Liddy, in another car, surveyed the target area, then stationed himself in the empty parking lot, from where he could observe any passing police cars and alert the entry team.

As I drove past Fielding's apartment house, I saw his Volvo in the drive. I parked two blocks away, leaving the walkie-talkie in it, and strolled past the apartment house again. The Volvo was still there and there were lights in Dr. Fielding's apartment windows. All was as it should be, and I wondered how matters were progressing in the target area.

For the next hour or so I alternately walked and drove past Fielding's apartment. Finally I saw that his apartment lights were extinguished. The chance of his entering his office for the rest of the night were next to zero.

While I watched Dr. Fielding's apartment, my thoughts turned to other entry operations I had been involved in over the years for the government and regretted that this time I was posted so far from the scene of action. I wondered if the team had encountered any difficulties and whether they were actually in the target office photographing Ellsberg's file. I felt a temptation to raise Liddy on the walkie-talkie and ask him for a progress report, but that would have violated our rule of radio silence except for an emergency situation.

I returned to my car, sat there for a few minutes and started the engine. I drove slowly past the apartment house and braked to stare at the driveway.

It was empty; Dr. Fielding's car was gone.

I glanced up, and the apartment was still dark. Did Fielding know his office had been entered? Had a concealed alarm been tripped and warned him? Were the police there even now? Were my friends under arrest?

I drove around the block, stopped the car and extended the W/T antenna out of the window.

"George," I called. "George, this is Edward. Report. Repeat: George, this is Edward. Report."

From "George Leonard" nothing.

I transmitted again, repeated the call, then once more. Now there was nothing I could do but drive to the office building and warn the team away—if a warning was not already too late.

I sped east through the night, past the Los Angeles Country Club and along Wilshire, heading toward the heart of Beverly Hills. As I neared the office building, I slowed, transmitted again and again, but there was still no answer from Liddy. Now I telescoped the antenna and laid the W/T under the car seat. If stopped by police for any reason, I did not want the walkie-talkie to raise questions.

I turned the car down the street and crawled past the office building. No police cars. I turned into the alley and glanced up. The windows of Dr. Fielding's office were dark. To the right, fifty yards away, sat Liddy's darkened car. I could barely make out the figure of a man in the driver's seat. Was he asleep? I drove to the far end of the alley, locked the car and jogged back to Liddy. He had seen me approach and sat up, alert. As I got into the car, he said, "What's happened?"

"I put Fielding to bed, but"—I glanced at my watch—"fifteen minutes ago his car disappeared."

"*What?*"

I nodded. "Where are the boys?"

"Hell, they're inside."

"I thought they'd be out by now."

"Well, the goddamn cleaning woman closed up early tonight. The boys had barely dropped off the suitcase inside the office and she took off. Naturally, she locked both doors, so the boys had to break into a ground-floor window so they could get upstairs. That's what took so long."

"Any word from them?"

"No."

I shook my head. "I shouldn't have lost Fielding. The car was there; fifteen minutes later it was gone. Where the hell would he go this time of night? If he was a general practitioner, he might be off seeing a patient, but not a shrink. After six o'clock shrinks don't budge. Believe me, I know."

Liddy picked up his walkie-talkie. "George to Leader," he called: "George to Leader. Come in. Come in."

No answer. Liddy looked at me. "What the hell's going on?"

"We'd better get them out of there," I told him.

Liddy looked at the walkie-talkie in his hand and laughed bitterly. "I know how to do it too—heave one of these mothers through their window. That'll bring 'em!" He shook his head in disgust. "This goddamn Mickey Mouse gear!" he said explosively. "If we ever do another op like this we're going to go first cabin, believe me." Again he gazed at the walkie-talkie. "For two box tops you get one of these and an Orphan Annie ring." He pushed the antenna into the body of the W/T. "Let's go get them."

We got out of the car and were walking toward the alley when we saw movement against the dark side of the building. An exchange of whispered hails assured us that the three men were out of the building. To Liddy, I said, "Okay, back to the plan. I'll head for the hotel room, and we'll all meet there."

"I hope to hell your buddies didn't leave anything up there."

"We'll find out soon enough."

I was the first one back to the hotel room, then Liddy came in a few minutes later. By then I was cooling a bottle of champagne and getting glasses ready for the five of us. Liddy pulled off his coat and flung it on the bed. With a grin he said, "I bet Krogh's pissing his pants. Wally Fear, for God's sake!"

The three men from Miami came in together. They were sweaty and disheveled, and one of them had cut himself on broken window glass. We gave each other *abrazos*, then Barker said, "Eduardo, there was nothing there."

I stared at him. "*Nothing?*"

He shook his head. "We went through every goddamn file in that office, Eduardo, and there was nothing there. Nothing with the name Ellsberg on it." From his pocket he pulled the scrap of paper on which Liddy had printed the name Ellsberg and given it to Barker only minutes before the entry began. "If this was the name, I tell you there was no file there with that name on it."

Liddy and I exchanged glances. "You're absolutely *sure?*" Liddy asked.

Barker nodded, as did Martinez and De Diego. They had pulled off their wigs and were mopping their faces with towels. Liddy swore.

"I'm sorry, George," Barker said, "but that's how it was." From his pocket he produced some Polaroid photographs and gave them to us. "Like you told us to, we photographed the files before and after, and there's what it looked like."

I saw a file cabinet whose drawers had been pried open. The files inside were out of focus, so it was impossible to read the headings.

"Well," I said, "I guess it's time for champagne."

The team agreed. I popped the cork and filled our glasses.

Clearly unhappy, Liddy said, "Well, this isn't the kind of victory celebration I figured we'd have, but at least nothing went wrong."

"Except that we had to break into the building," Martinez said and drank thirstily.

De Diego mopped his face again and gave a Latin shrug of resignation.

Barker said, "I found a lot of files—looked like old income-tax returns, and I even went through them, but there was nothing about

Ellsberg." He chuckled. "I got the idea maybe the doctor wasn't reporting all his income."

"Macho," Martinez said, "don't be an idiot. If it was his income-tax returns, then he reported his income." His eyes rolled heaven-ward.

I said, "Where's the suitcase and the rest of the gear?"

"In the trunk of the car," Barker told me.

"I'll take the car key," I told him. "George and I will clear out the trunk in the morning and turn the cars back in. The three of you take the next plane out of here for Miami. Go to your rooms, pack and get out. I'm still worried about what happened to Fielding's car, where the doctor went. For all we know, we were trailed here, so let's get moving."

"Macho, make your plane reservations from a pay phone," Liddy called, and when the three men had left the room, Liddy said, "I'd better call Wally now."

I looked at my watch. "It's about six o'clock in Washington," I remarked. "Time to end his suspense."

As Liddy started to leave, I said, "There're no flights out of here for Washington until around noon, and I don't think we ought to wait that long. While you're down there, get us a couple of seats on the next flight for the East Coast."

Liddy nodded. "Right on," he said and gave me the clenched-fist salute. The door closed behind him.

Wearily I began to pack my bag. We had gone to a lot of effort and taken a number of risks—for nothing. All we had established was that Ellsberg's file was not in Fielding's office. Where was it, then? What did psychiatrists do with inactive files, the files of former patients? Or had Fielding—who had twice refused to discuss Ellsberg with the FBI—been alerted by the Bureau visitations and sequestered his former patient's file in a safer place? Perhaps a safe in his apartment? These thoughts coursed through my mind as I finished packing my bag and got into bed. It might be worth an entry operation in the good doctor's apartment, I reflected, but for that we would need a further authorization. In Washington all we would be able to report was failure—and the possibility that Ellsberg's file was in the Fielding apartment.

Liddy came in, locked the door, sat on the bed and pulled off his shoes. "Wally was so relieved he almost cried. He's so happy we weren't caught he doesn't really care that we didn't find anything." He looked at his watch. "Well, we can get a few hours' sleep. The next plane east goes to New York. We could take the shuttle down from there."

"Better leave a call with the operator," I suggested. "We've got to get the equipment out of the cars before we turn them back in."

Liddy grunted. "What a hell of a way to spend a Labor Day weekend. If I hadn't been out here, I could have been up in Poughkeepsie with my family."

After Liddy left a wake-up call with the operator, we turned out the lights. I said, "Do you think there *is* an Ellsberg psychiatric file?"

"There *had* to be one. Unless Fielding destroyed it, he's got to have it at his apartment. I'll suggest the entry to Bud." He chuckled. "Krogh'll go bananas."

Our flight reached Kennedy International Airport after dark that same night, and rather than take a late shuttle down to Washington, we decided to get some much-needed sleep in a hotel. At the Pierre we registered under our true names and showed our White House passes; this entitled us to a discount on our rooms.

In the morning we had breakfast in our room, walked from Fifth over to Park Avenue and around the block, crossed over to the Plaza fountain, then back up to the Pierre, where we paid our bill and checked out. By midday we were back in Washington. It was Sunday, September 5, and the next day was a national holiday. Liddy thought he might put in a few hours at the office, but I was less certain, for the day marked the end of the summer swimming season at my country club, and my children would want to be taken there for a final swim. In fact, I thought, I could use a little sun myself; it seemed as though I had been seeing nothing but moonlight for weeks. I was pale and tired from the nervous drain of the entry operation. No, I was not going to my White House office on Labor Day. The following day would be soon enough.

On Tuesday morning, September 7, I drove from my home to the Executive Office Building and carried in the operational suitcase filled with heavy photographic and entry equipment. I took it to my third-floor office, opened the special lock on the door and took the suitcase inside. I put it in the corner beside my two-drawer combination safe and was about to open the safe drawer to put in the Polaroid photographs Barker had taken inside Dr. Fielding's office when I had another idea.

I left my office and went down to the main floor, entered Colson's reception room and sat down. Because I had been out of touch with him for several days, I thought I owed him something by way of explanation. When Colson strolled in, he said, "How's the boy?" and kept walking toward his office door. I stood up, got the Polaroid photographs from my pocket and said, "Chuck, I'd like to show you these. They concern what I was doing over the weekend."

Without pausing in his stride, Colson said, "I don't want to hear anything about it," and went into his office, closing the door behind him. For a moment I stood there, surprised at the rebuff, then shrugged and pocketed the photographs again. I should have realized, I told myself, that the principle of compartmentation was observed as fully at the White House as it was at CIA.

Over the next few days Liddy and I prepared a brief proposal to Krogh for an entry attempt at Dr. Fielding's apartment. This proposal, presumably, was reviewed by John Ehrlichman. When I heard nothing further about it, I asked Liddy if he expected the proposal to be approved.

He shook his head. "It's on the back burner," he told me. "Way, *way* back."

So ended our efforts to obtain information from a file which might no longer have been in existence at the time we searched for it. And although we scanned Los Angeles newspapers for several days after that Labor Day weekend, we found no mention of the Beverly Hills break-in.

The operation itself was to remain secret until revealed by John W. Dean in April, 1973. By then Liddy, myself, Barker and Martinez were in the District of Columbia jail, serving time for our parts in two entry operations that were to follow and which were to become known around the world as Watergate.

In a display of majestic irony the charges against Dr. Ellsberg *et al.* were dismissed in 1973 when it became known that the office of his psychiatrist had been entered by our White House team. Nevertheless, dismissal of charges against Ellsberg neither eradicates nor vindicates his thefts and illegal revelations. And it should be borne in mind that while Ellsberg acted unilaterally in publishing our country's secrets, the team that sought his personal secrets was authorized to do so by high and competent government officials, including the President's chief domestic-affairs adviser, reacting to the largest raid on national security in our country's history.

Ellsberg is free. The entry team was tried and convicted along with John Ehrlichman.

14 GENESIS OF GEMSTONE

IN the aftermath of the unproductive Beverly Hills entry operation, Liddy and I discussed the need for more solid alias documentation than we had been furnished by the Central Intelligence Agency. I asked "Steve" to see what he could do about getting valid credit cards issued to us under the names of Edward Warren and George Leonard, also a New York telephone number which, when called, would ring in Langley, and either "Leonard" or myself would be notified of the incoming call. These were standard CIA operational amenities, and I perceived no difficulty in their being provided.

At the same time it was apparent that the Room 16 stenographer, Kathy Chenow, was heavily overburdened with work from five men, and I suggested to David Young that I attempt to get the loan of a CIA secretary who was familiar with the preparation, handling and safeguarding of highly classified documents—as Miss Chenow was not. I repeated the request to General Cushman's assistant, Carl Wagner, but in a few days Bud Krogh told me that the Agency was unwilling to extend us the requested courtesies.

Krogh added, "I think there must be some people over there that don't like you, Howard."

"No doubt about it," I told him. "You don't spend twenty-one years in a place without acquiring nonadmirers."

CIA had, however, furnished me with a Uher tape recorder, which had inputs for two microphones and could be used by two

177

participants in a give-and-take interview, for I had been thinking I might have to reinterview Clifton De Motte.

But De Motte telephoned me at Mullen & Company and once at my home concerning rumors on Chappaquiddick. De Motte's information was highly speculative but Colson indicated that it formed part of a larger, though subterranean, pattern: unrevealed circumstances of Miss Kopechne's death, the cover-up and whitewash, etc. Colson hoped De Motte would be able to provide further hard information, but I was not optimistic about the man's abilities, and my contacts with De Motte gradually tapered off.

I also reported to Colson that my researches into the origins of the Vietnam War had reached an impasse: Studying only the Pentagon Papers as supplied by Daniel Ellsberg, I was limiting myself unnecessarily, I thought. What I proposed was a search of the chronological cable files at the Department of State to not only authenticate the cables that Ellsberg had revealed, but to search for other cables, perhaps even more critical and revealing than those which Ellsberg published.

Colson approved the procedure, and in late September David Young sent a memorandum to Mr. Macomber at the Department of State asking that I be given full access to the department's chronological cable files, particularly for the period of the Vietnam War. Permission was quickly granted, and I began a long and thorough examination of State's cable holdings from 1954 through the Diem assassination in 1964.

The cable files turned out to be miniaturized photocopies of the cables themselves, and I selected several hundred for duplication by the departmental archivist. My file survey revealed two points of interest: Many cables were stamped to indicate that they had previously been copied by the John F. Kennedy Memorial Library; the other, and perhaps related, point was that the closer one approached the assassination period in 1963, the more frequently were cables missing from chronological sequence. After a week or so of this intensive work I reported my findings to Colson, who said, "The full story isn't there, then?"

"No, but anyone who read the cables as I have could never doubt the complicity of the Kennedy Administration in the death of the Vietnamese Premier."

"How many cables did you say were missing?"

"It's hard to say, but certainly no less than twenty. Perhaps forty or fifty."

Colson whistled. "Aren't there one or two cables that would pretty definitely establish that the Kennedy gang was responsible for Diem's assassination?"

"No. You'd have to take a sequence of three or four cables, be aware of their context and speculate on what was contained in the cables missing from the sequence."

Colson pursed his lips. "*You* know and *I* know that the New Frontier was responsible for those murders."

I nodded.

"Got any ideas?"

"Sure," I said. "I could fabricate a couple of cables that could be substituted for two of the missing ones. I'm familiar enough with the writing style of the principals in Washington and Saigon that I could produce credible fabrications. That's the easy part. The tough part is to produce replicas that would withstand a technical scrutiny."

"What do you mean?"

"Well, for example, the cables that originated at State or here at the White House have distinctive typefaces. Those same typewriters should be located for use in making the fabricated cables. Any typewriters other than the originals could only approximate the typefaces and would be easily detectable with a magnifying glass, if not the naked eye. As I said, I can create credible texts; but to go beyond that, I'd need technical help. The Secret Service ought to be able to help me."

Colson shook his head. "Uh-uh. Too sensitive, Howard."

"Then whatever I can produce can be used only for our personal edification," I told him. "I'll do as well as I can, but remember that what I turn out won't be able to withstand any sort of technical examination."

"Well, they may not have to." He smiled. "Let me see those two cables you were showing me."

I handed him the two most damaging authentic cables I had been able to locate in State's files. Quickly, Colson reread them, handed them back and said, "See if you can't improve on them."

With a nod I left his office and returned to mine.

Presently author Clifford Irving announced himself as the official biographer of Howard Hughes. McGraw-Hill bought his manuscript and *Life* magazine the first serial rights. At Robert R. Mullen & Company we became active in publicizing the Hughes position that the claimed biography was false, and in this connection I was visited by Bill Lambert, a Pulitzer Prize-winning investigative reporter for *Life* magazine. As a former *Life* correspondent, I.was in an excellent position to argue the matter with Lambert on professional terms. He, however, was convinced of the manuscript's authenticity, and we spent long hours together in my office arguing the pros and cons. During these meetings I learned that Lambert had had previous contact with Chuck Colson, and I told Lambert that I was now working for Colson as a part-time consultant. Finally, Lambert left on a trip South, where he was to check out the numerous locations where Irving alleged he had met and interviewed Howard Hughes, and by the time he returned, the Irving hoax had been pretty much exposed.

By now I had produced texts of two cables that I thought might answer Colson's purposes: One was an apparent query from the Saigon embassy concerning White House policy in the event that Diem and his brother-in-law should request asylum from the American Embassy. The second was a negative response, couched in State's typically Aesopian language. After Colson approved the texts, I began working with typewriters then available in the Executive Office Building and produced, with the aid of a Xerox machine, two cables which might be visually convincing to the reader, though not—as I had warned Colson—invulnerable to technical examination.

Colson suggested that I show Bill Lambert my entire collection of authentic State Department cables, with particular emphasis on the two fabricated cables I had produced. He would notify Lambert that I had something of interest to show him, but, though Lambert was to be permitted to read and copy the texts of the fabricated cables in my office, he was not to be permitted to take them from the office for photocopying, as he might be expected to request.

Lambert was elated with the cable texts, seeing in them a news scoop of national proportions. As anticipated, he wanted to borrow the cables long enough to photograph, but I explained this was expressly forbidden by Colson. For some reason Lambert never asked me the direct question: "Are these two cables authentic?"

Had he done so, I would have found some way to pass off the question rather than lie to him, for by now I had begun to feel compunctions over my fabrications. Loyal as I was to Colson, I was unwilling to deceive a journalist of Bill Lambert's professional integrity and make him innocent party to a deception of international proportions.

Not long afterward Lambert telephoned me to say that his office was greatly interested in the cable story but wanted copies for examination prior to running them on the cover of a forthcoming issue of *Life*. I repeated the reservation established by Colson, and Lambert remarked that he was going to try to put pressure on Colson through John Mitchell, whom he knew well. The Attorney General, he felt, would be able to shake the cables loose despite Colson's "reluctance" to permit their reproduction.

I reported Lambert's plan to Colson, but never learned whether Lambert ever presented his case to the Attorney General. Abandonment of the plan was a source of relief to me, and I hoped it would not be revived.

The several hundred authentic State Department cables remained in my locked two-drawer safe in my White House office, and the fabricated cables, in their various phases from text draft to completion, were placed in manila files captioned "Fab. I" and "Fab. II." These files, among others, were to be extracted from my safe by John Dean and eventually destroyed by the acting director of the Federal Bureau of Investigation, L. Patrick Gray.

Some weeks later Colson summoned me to his office and told me that one of the major networks was doing a special TV documentary on the Vietnam War. Many former New Frontiersmen had been interviewed for the network's cameras, as well as Major General Lansdale and Colonel Lucien Conein.

He had heard, Colson told me, that Conein's portion of the documentary was flabby, in that Conein failed to lay responsibility for the assassinations squarely at the Kennedy Administration's doorstep. It was urgently necessary, he told me, that I contact Conein, show him the fabricated and the authentic State Department cables and persuade him to have the network refilm his interview.

From Colson's office I telephoned Conein, who was at first mystified, then agreed to come to my White House office. After that Colson sent me to see John Scali,* who was at that time White House resident adviser on radio and TV communications. When I told Scali that Conein had additional information which he was willing to impart to the network, Scali phoned the network and, as the camera team was still in Washington, arranged a refilming of the Conein interview.

When Conein came to my office, I showed him the significant cables. He read and accepted them as genuine, remarking, "Funny, the things you don't know about when you're working in the field." I agreed that people at the cutting edge were often the last to know and Conein said he would be glad to set the record straight. He told me that he was now working on contract for Walter Minnick in the drug field and felt that this interesting and productive job had probably flowed from his contact with me last summer. With that Conein went off to the Hay-Adams Hotel, where the camera crew was waiting for him.

When I viewed the network documentary a few weeks later, Conein's remarks, revised in good faith, were well received by the White House.

During my months of association with Colson I had come to realize that he was the administration's point of contact with special-interest groups, so I was not surprised to see Frank Fitzsimmons, successor to James Hoffa as chief of the Teamsters Union, waiting occasionally in Colson's reception room. On one occasion Colson introduced us, and not long afterward Colson remarked to me that Fitzsimmons, through a union contact in Nevada, had learned that a pair of Las Vegas show girls were able to provide information damaging to Senator Ted Kennedy, and Colson was hopeful that this information would be more useful than Clifton De Motte's. From time to time thereafter I would remind Colson of Fitzsimmons' alleged information, and Colson would jot down a reminder, but if the union chief ever provided Kennedy information to Colson, Chuck did not pass it along to me.

Colson occasionally asked me for information on Cuban-American political leaders in the Miami area. In the past some of them had been associated with the Nixon election effort, and others were

*Now United States Ambassador to the United Nations.

volunteering their services for the 1972 campaign. Through Barker and his friends I was able to provide Colson with most of the information he needed.

Then Colson showed me a series of articles appearing in the Long Island paper *Newsday* which were unfavorable to the President's friend Bebe Rebozo. The source of the derogatory information on Rebozo's financial dealings in Miami and on Key Biscayne was, according to Colson, a banker named Hoke T. Maroon. Through my Miami contacts Colson wanted a report on Maroon with emphasis on any derogatory material that could be developed. As in the past, I assigned the task to Barker, who, after a week's investigation, was able to report nothing unfavorable on Mr. Maroon. On the contrary, Barker found Maroon a man held in high esteem, particularly by the South Florida banking community, and he was believed to be a man of unimpeachable integrity. Rebozo, on the other hand, Barker continued, was not well thought of by the Cuban-exile community, which tolerated him only because of his close friendship with the President.

This report was, of course, not what the White House had been seeking, and as far as I know the episode was forgotten.

About this time CBS-TV commentator Daniel Schorr became aware that an FBI investigation was being conducted into his life and background. When the investigation surfaced, Schorr demanded an explanation and was told that he was being considered for a White House job.

This explanation was laughable on the face of it, for Schorr was manifestly hostile to the administration and, as was later demonstrated, figured on the White House "Enemies List." From what I was able to glean inside the Executive Office Building, the administration had heard a rumor that Mrs. Schorr had at some time in the past been associated with organizations which, if not Communist, were of the Marxist Left. It was this "vulnerability" which the FBI investigation was supposed to authenticate, presumably for later use against Dan Schorr. Public exposure of the investigation quite naturally ended it, although in media circles there was understandable resentment over it. And the administration's explanation that Schorr was being considered for a White House job continued to be viewed with extreme skepticism.

On one occasion Colson discussed with me the fact that Daniel

Ellsberg's chief counsel was Leonard Boudin. Boudin was a well-known advocate for persons accused of Communist and Leftist activities, and his daughter, Kathy, a Weatherman, was on the FBI's most-wanted list. From FBI reports I pieced together a summary of Boudin's long involvement with the American Communist party and the fact that Boudin represented not only Castro Cuba, but the Marxist government of Chile as well.

From this FBI information I put together a story which Colson eventually passed to a Detroit newspaper correspondent named Jerry Ter Horst.* Ter Horst was later to publish an article concerning the defense team of Daniel Ellsberg, but how much of my findings he included is a matter of controversy.

As the autumn progressed, I saw less of Colson than before. And what work I did at the White House focused increasingly on Room 16, where Liddy and David Young were finding it increasingly difficult to accommodate to each other. Young I regarded as principally a paper pusher, whereas Liddy was demonstrably a man of action, and so my sympathies tended to lie with him. Upstairs Colson's staff was increasing, and from the talents of the new arrivals it was apparent they were to play a part in the 1972 electoral campaign. Coincidentally there were departures from other quarters of the White House to the Committee to Re-elect the President (CREP), whose new offices had been established within sight of the White House and directly across the street from the office building in which Mullen & Company was located.

My next-door EOB neighbor, Katharine Balsdon, asked me if she could store several cartons of books in my office. I agreed, and in a few days workmen delivered approximately seven heavy cartons to my office and stacked them in an out-of-the-way corner. The top carton was open and I saw that it contained copies of Edith Efron's book *The News Twisters*. The other cartons, unopened, were marked with the name of the publisher, and I assumed that they were packed with Ms. Efron's books.

I had forgotten this incident until, a few days before President Ford's scheduled nomination of a Vice President, both Jack Anderson's column and a number of news services reported allega-

*Later press secretary to President Ford.

tions made by a Philadelphian named Hamilton Long that the seven cartons stored in my office contained 7,000 documents of material allegedly derogatory of Nelson Rockefeller, a presumptive candidate for the Vice Presidential nomination. The name of Sam Sheppard was given in the news accounts, a man described as a former CREP official who, acting on instructions of my wife, just after the Watergate entry, spirited away the seven cartons in question. These palpably false stories infuriated me, and I saw in them a squalid means of disqualifying Rockefeller by invoking my already notorious name. Accordingly I gave an immediate interview to the New York *Times* setting forth the truth of the matter and pointing out that Sheppard could not have received any "instructions" from my wife, for she was then in Europe on the date alleged. Although my interview denying the Long/Sheppard allegations appeared on page 16 of the August 18, 1974, issue of the New York *Times*, it may have persuaded President Ford that the allegations were false and reassured him that Howard Hunt, at least, knew of no reason why Nelson Rockefeller should not be nominated to become Vice President, as in fact occurred the following day.

Toward the end of November I was working in Room 16 on a narcotics-intelligence proposal when, late in the day, Liddy entered the office, closed my door and sat down. Obviously buoyant, he said, "If you mention to anyone what I'm going to tell you, I'll be finished, so for God's sake keep it to yourself."

I looked up from my work and nodded.

"It's the damnedest thing," Liddy said. "I've just come from John Dean's office, and you'll never guess what the Attorney General wants me to do."

"Replace J. Edgar?"

"No—but it's not a bad idea." He grimaced. "Dean told me the AG wants me to become general counsel for the Committee to Re-elect the President!"

"That's great. Congratulations."

Liddy sat down on the corner of my desk, and his voice lowered. "But here's the most important thing—get this: The AG wants me to set up an intelligence organization for the campaign. It'll be big, Howard, and important. They don't want a repetition of the last campaign; this time they want to know everything that's going on. Everything."

I sat back and looked up at him, feeling a proposition was unfolding. "Care to tell me about it?"

"That's the bones of it, and Dean tells me there's plenty of money available—half a million for openers, and there's more where that came from. A lot more." He gazed at me. "What I want to know is, can I count on you? Will you help me?"

"From what you've told me so far, I can't think of any reason not to."

"That's great," he said enthusiastically. "I'll need you and Macho and all the rest of the guys if we're going to make this work. The AG doesn't want any trouble—like Chicago—at the San Diego convention, and he wouldn't mind causing the Democrats a little trouble in Miami. That's where you and the Cubans come in. We ought to be able to have informants in every hotel along Miami Beach."

"So what's the drill?" I asked.

"Well, I've got to run this past Krogh. Bud's my boss and he's got a big future with this administration. Dean understands I can't make a move unless Krogh approves."

"Bud shouldn't object."

"No, but I want to do this by the numbers. I've asked for an appointment with Krogh and maybe I'll get to see him tomorrow. Meanwhile, I wanted to make sure I could count on you, Howard."

"Sounds good," I told him, and looked down at my nearly finished work. "Let's go out and have a drink on it."

Within the next few days Liddy told me that Krogh approved his transfer and that he, Liddy, was now working out details with Jeb Stuart Magruder, the young acting chairman of the Committee to Re-elect the President. Already they had clashed, Liddy told me, on such basic matters as salary, office space and secretarial assistance. "If he gives me any more trouble," Liddy said jokingly, "I'll tell him I'm going to kill him."

Apparently the AG intervened and resolved the problems to Liddy's satisfaction, for before the Christmas holiday my friend was cleaning out his Room 16 desk and gave me the telephone number at his new office across the street from mine.

Even though no longer on the White House payroll, Liddy continued to carry a White House pass, and so we were able to lunch together at the White House cafeteria or the dining room maintained for middle-level members of the White House staff.

Late in the year Dorothy and I were invited to "An Evening at the White House." The entertainer was opera star Beverly Sills, whose husband, Peter Greenough, and I had been Air Force friends at Orlando during World War II. When Dorothy and I passed through the receiving line, a Presidential aide presented us to Mr. Nixon. I said, "I'm working with Chuck Colson now, Mr. President."

"Oh, yes," the President replied with a ready smile, "I know about that," and passed us along to Pat. I was, of course, pleased and encouraged by this knowledge of Presidential awareness of my work for Charles Colson. But it was not for many months and following the development of the Watergate investigation that the full significance of the President's words struck home.

Gordon and Frances Liddy spent New Year's Eve at my home, and while our wives talked, Gordon and I withdrew to discuss some details of the requirements being laid on him by Jeb Magruder and John Dean. By now Liddy was adopting the clandestine principal of seldom if ever referring to true names. Unless he was reviling Jeb Magruder, Liddy used the phrase "my principals." This was sufficient for me, for Liddy had already identified his principals as the Attorney General, John Mitchell; the counsel to the President, John Dean; and Jeb Magruder, who had, like Liddy, also been a White House aide.

Moreover, when we began to make our initial outlines of the intelligence organization, our discussions were held in Room 16 of the Executive Office Building, where we sketched charts and drew up a paper organization calculated to be responsive to his "principals' " requirements. I kept copies of these drafts and notes in my third-floor office safe, not only to isolate them from the David Young operation but to have ready access to the notes for weekend and afterhours work, as was my habit.

My task was to create projects to protect the Republican Convention at San Diego, establish an intelligence-collection network directed against the Democratic National Convention in Miami, organize groups able to counterdemonstrate at the Democratic Convention and to maintain in standby status the entry team that had searched Dr. Fielding's office. There was, Liddy told me, an additional requirement: for electronic surveillance.* He assumed it would be placed into effect against whomever the Democrats nominated, but that nomination was still half a year away. In the meantime, he suggested I locate one or more CIA retirees who were skilled in electronics and/or physical entries—particularly a lock-and-key man.

I remembered the CIA security officer from the Guatemalan project, and a Christmas card told me that Jack Bauman was now retired because of a heart condition and living in Winter Park, Florida. I wrote him for nominees and at the same time telephoned the CIA placement service, asking for résumés of CIA retirees whose work experience qualified them for the contemplated job. Bauman had no independent suggestions, but at my request interviewed a candidate whose résumé had been given me by CIA. The retiree was not interested.

I named the overall project Gemstone, and the projects it comprehended were given as cryptonyms the names of precious or semiprecious stones: Ruby, Diamond, Sapphire, Opal, Crystal and so forth. On a matching chart cryptonyms were not used, but the projects themselves were briefly described, together with their dollar figure costs.

This was in keeping with clandestine practice, and Liddy was charmed with the technique.

We referred to my portion of the operation and its budget as the human-resources section; the rest of it comprehended the electronic-surveillance capability and included hire of a "chase plane" which would be capable of intercepting air-to-ground communications between the Democratic candidate and whoever was in touch with him by radiotelephone. Taken together, the entire budget ran close to a million dollars, and as Liddy pointed out, there was plenty of fat to cut in case Attorney General Mitchell was unwilling to go that high.

Early in the new year I asked for an appointment with Colson,

---

*Until June 19, 1972, the Attorney General was empowered to authorize electronic surveillance in both criminal and national-security cases. On that date a Supreme Court ruling required future domestic criminal electronic surveillance to be accompanied by a court order but did not limit the Attorney General's power to authorize electronic surveillance in cases involving national security.

during which I told him that I assumed he knew I was collaborating with Gordon Liddy on the massive intelligence-collection and political-action program engendered by the Attorney General.

Colson nodded. "In fact, I supplied your bona fides to the AG."

"Well," I said, "as a result, I expect to be spending so much time with Liddy that I'll have little, if any, time left to work for you. Besides, there hasn't been a great deal for me to do here the past few weeks."

Colson nodded. "You can be of more help over there," he told me. "The only thing is, I wish you were heading it up—not Liddy."

"I'm satisfied with the arrangement," I told him. "Liddy and I get along well together, and we'll work well together. Unlike David Young, we're both action-minded and see things the same way. Besides, I wouldn't have enough time to be in charge of the GA's operation. My work at Mullen is a full-time job, I've usually got a book in progress, and what I'm doing for Liddy takes up the rest of my time. I assume I can keep my office upstairs and the safe."

"Sure—no problem, Howard."

So I continued to make use of my office in the EOB, even though I performed only occasional chores for Colson.

Soon Liddy told me he had been given a show-and-tell appointment with the Attorney General in the latter's office at the Department of Justice. Magruder and John Dean were to be present, and Liddy was preparing charts from which to brief them.

On the afternoon of his initial presentation I waited in Room 16 to learn the outcome, but when Liddy returned, he was dejected. He had briefed both Magruder and Dean before going over to the Department of Justice with them, and the AG's two subordinates had seemed enthusiastic over the Gemstone proposal. But, said Liddy, during the presentation the Attorney General was horrified by the cost of the operation and told Liddy to cut it at least in half. "And there they sat," Liddy said disgustedly, "Dean and Magruder, like two bumps on a log. All they are, for Christ's sake, is yes-men." He shrugged. "So it's back to the drawing boards."

"Electronic surveillance is the biggest cost factor," I remarked. "Maybe that's the place to start cutting."

"Yeah, but the AG still wants it. The trouble is, I haven't been able to set down any realistic figures, but I know a guy who used to work for your old outfit who can give me a hand. He's a pro—actually in the electronics business—and he'll be able to give me the figures I need. Why don't you take a crack at cutting down the San Diego costs? Hell, I've got a better idea, why don't we go out there and take a look around? If we're supposed to supply covert protection for it, then we ought to know what the place looks like. Right?"

"Right."

Over the next weekend we flew to Los Angeles and checked into the Beverly-Wilshire Hotel, planning to leave by plane for San Diego in the morning. But when Liddy phoned his office, he learned that a Washington delegation was en route to inspect the convention sight, including Secret Service men, John Dean and several others.

"So I guess I'd better go down alone, because if you show up with me, all kinds of questions will be asked. Think you can find something to do?"

"In Los Angeles on a Saturday night?" I nodded. "I'll take Tony and Nancy Jackson to dinner."

When Liddy returned from San Diego, he told me that the convention site was indefensible. "There's nothing around it but railroad tracks on one side, and if two hundred thousand demonstrators all charge it at the same time, it'll take the entire California National Guard to stop them. Besides, that isn't the kind of image we want the country to get—particularly when everyone's still uptight over Kent State. If you want to take a look for yourself, be my guest."

I shook my head. "You're the voice of experience," I said. "I'll take your word for it, Gordon."

Back in Washington I helped prepare Liddy's negative recommendations and suggested incorporating one of the many counterculture leaflets that called on America's disenchanted to converge on the San Diego site and make a shambles of it, as had been done at the Chicago Democratic Convention in 1968. A further factor militating against the San Diego site was the fact that the hotel which was to house the President and his party that summer had not yet been built. This vexed the Secret Service, and their concerns, together with Liddy's negative report, were probably responsible for the eventual rejection of San Diego in favor of Miami.

Soon Liddy was given a second opportunity to present the scaled-down Gemstone proposal to the Attorney General. As before, Liddy prepared charts and budget figures, but now the electronic-surveillance portion was substantially reduced, Liddy having obtained the cooperation of his as-yet-unnamed electronics adviser. I had been able to eliminate protective costs for the San Diego site from the budget, anticipating that the Republican Convention would be held in Miami and so benefit from whatever protective arrangements the city of Miami Beach made for the Democrats.

Even so, Liddy reported back to me that the Attorney General had found the nearly half-million-dollar figure too high and ordered further cuts. "Magruder and Dean tell me everything's fine, then I trot in there, go through my soft-shoe dance and get cut off at the knees by the AG. All Dean and Magruder do is nod their heads sagely. To hell with them!"

Privately, I had decided that Gemstone was never going to get off the ground. During twenty-one years in CIA I had often witnessed the sudden enthusiasm of senior officials for projects dwindle away with the passage of time, the influence of new factors or an unexpected turn of events. This I was sure had happened to Gemstone, so although I helped Liddy prepare a third version of the program—this one scaled down to bare, bare bones—I was convinced it would never be approved.

Without telling Liddy, I telephoned Bernie Barker and instructed him to suspend the developmental work he was doing: contacting veterans of the Cuban invasion brigade and locating friends and potential informants in the complex of hotels along Miami Beach. Disheartened, Barker asked me if I thought the undertaking was off. I told him I thought that if it ever took place, it would not be on anything like the scale we had originally envisioned. I discouraged him from spending more time on the activity and suggested he devote himself for the foreseeable future to his real estate interests and to the Central America business projects we had discussed with Artime and others.

My employer, Bob Bennett, asked if I thought his nephew, Robert Fletcher, might be able to find summer-vacation employment at CREP headquarters through the influence of Gordon Liddy. I told Bennett that Liddy and I planned to place agents in the offices of leading prospective Democratic nominees, principally Senator Muskie, whose star was then in the ascendant. Bob Fletcher was not interested in this kind of work, but he recommended a young Mormon from the University of Utah, Thomas Gregory, whom, in due course, I interviewed in Washington and hired. Gregory, a slack-mouthed, disheveled youth, fitted easily among the scores of Muskie volunteer campaign workers, and from him I began receiving regular reports on Muskie contributors and finances and the Muskie position on subjects of national importance.

Presently Liddy informed me that his associates had planted an agent at Muskie headquarters who was able to photograph mail and other documents at Muskie headquarters. Liddy asked me to meet the agent's handler on a weekly basis and receive from him the agent's photographic take. Liddy described the handler's physical appearance to me—portly, gray-haired and tall—and so the handler—whom Liddy referred to as "Fat Jack"—and I began periodic meetings in downtown Washington.

At intervals Fat Jack* would tender me a bill for the cost of photographic development, and at the next meeting I would give him an envelope containing cash provided by Liddy. These contacts ended when Senator Muskie abandoned his quest for the Democratic Presidential nomination and our attention turned to Senator McGovern, then the front-runner.

Tom Gregory was able to switch from Muskie to McGovern headquarters but Fat Jack's agent was not. Thus Gregory became the Republicans' sole window on McGovern finance and policy.

Earlier Liddy told me that he had been charged with investigating a curious set of circumstances: A young, plump and bespectacled man appeared at several state Republican headquarters, indicated that he came from "high levels" in Washington and volunteered to assist state chairmen in sewing doubt and confusion in Democratic ranks. "Donald Simmons," as the man identified himself, was believed to be the instrument of a Democratic scheme to infiltrate Republican campaign machinery, and Liddy said it had been requested that Simmons be located and neutralized. In the meantime, a warning was circulated to all state Republican chairmen, and Liddy and I waited for word of another Simmons contact.

Several days passed, then Liddy announced he had been told to drop the Simmons investigation. Simmons, Liddy had been

*Later identified as John Buckley, an OEO official.

warned, indeed worked for a "high level" in Washington, but now the bluntness of Simmons' approaches had brought his usefulness into question. For that reason Liddy and I were asked to meet Simmons in Miami and evaluate him in terms of future campaign usefulness. Accordingly, Liddy and I interviewed Simmons in his room at the Frolics Motel in Miami using our aliases of Warren and Leonard. We had decided in advance that we would use the good-cop-bad-cop routine with Simmons and I was to be the heavy. We listened to Simmons' description of pranks already carried out and future pranks planned and were as unimpressed by them as we were by Simmons himself. While I absented myself to use a pay phone outside the motel, Liddy said to Simmons, "There's one thing about Warren you ought to know. We have trouble with him."

"Trouble? What kind of trouble?" Simmons asked.

"Well," Liddy told him, lowering his voice, "Warren tends to kill without orders."

According to Liddy, Simmons paled at this unwelcome information, and when I rejoined them, I noticed Simmons was reduced to monosyllabic responses.

When we returned to Washington, Liddy and I agreed that Simmons and his unbounded enthusiasm could become a campaign liability, and Liddy said that he would recommend Simmons being dropped by his "sponsor," later identified as Dwight Chapin.

About this time Bob Bennett returned from a business trip to Los Angeles and Las Vegas for his Hughes Tool Company account. Bennett told me that he had heard a rumor in Las Vegas that Las Vegas publisher Hank Greenspun had been heard to say that if Ed Muskie received the Democratic nomination, he, Greenspun, had enough information on Muskie to "blow him out of the water." I assumed Bennett wanted me to relay this information to Gordon Liddy, which I did in a brief memorandum.

Liddy responded promptly, saying that independent information from Las Vegas tended to verify Bennett's report and that Liddy's "principals" would be grateful for further specific information on the kind of derogatory information Greenspun allegedly possessed. I passed Liddy's comments to Bob Bennett, and in a day or so Bennett invited me into his office, where he introduced me to a man named Ralph Winte, whom Bennett identified as a former FBI agent now in charge of security for the Hughes interests.

The Hughes Tool Company was engaged in extensive litigation with former Hughes executive Robert Maheu, and I was given to understand that Maheu and Greenspun were political allies in Nevada. I was told further that Greenspun was believed to have documentary information concerning corruption among high Nevada officials and that the acquisition of this information would benefit the Hughes organization in their litigation with Maheu. Thus, Bennett suggested, there was a commonality of interests between CREP and the Hughes Tool Company.

Winte and I retired to my adjacent office, where Winte told me that his firm was disposed to cooperate with me. I confessed that I had never been in Las Vegas, although I understood it to be well covered by the federal government—FBI and IRS agents, in particular—and that it was foolhardy to telephone from even a pay telephone. I knew Winte employed the private investigation and security firm of Intertel and assumed that through its resources—in addition to the leverage represented by Hughes ownership of casinos in Las Vegas—we would be able to acquire further hard intelligence on Hank Greenspun's rumored claim.

In general terms Winte and I discussed an entry operation should further information indicate that the Muskie information was, like the supposed corruption lists, kept in Greenspun's safe. From his years with the FBI, Winte was familiar with "bag jobs," and we agreed it was essential to determine whether there was, in fact, a safe in Greenspun's newspaper offices. Winte said he would attempt to produce a floor diagram of Greenspun's offices, and in response to a question from me, he said that in the event we decided on an entry operation he would be able to provide hotel rooms and transportation facilities for an entry team.

This concluded our initial conversation, after which Winte gave me his business card and private telephone number, and I told him that when I was on the West Coast in the fairly near future, I would contact him in Los Angeles for further discussion.

These developments gratified Liddy and in mid-February we flew to Los Angeles and met with Winte at our hotel room, using Liddy's operational alias of George Leonard. Winte produced a floor diagram of the Las Vegas *Sun* offices, but said he had been unable to determine whether there was a safe on the premises. Winte reaffirmed his ability to provide lookouts, safehouses and ground transportation, and Liddy, always the aviation enthusiast, asked if Hughes Aircraft might not be able to provide a "getaway" plane.

Presuming a successful entry operation, Liddy thought that the entry team, with the fruits of the operation, could board the waiting aircraft and fly perhaps to Baja California, where division of the spoils could be made according to our separate interests.

Winte replied that he himself could not authorize a plane but would have to obtain such authorization from his superiors and would let us know.

Subsequently Liddy and I learned that the Hughes Company declined to provide the requested aircraft, and a short time later it became apparent that Senator Muskie would not be the Democratic Presidential candidate. For that reason nothing further was discussed in connection with publisher Greenspun.

Despite our negative recommendations concerning Donald Simmons, Liddy informed me that Simmons' sponsor wanted his work to continue and I was asked to monitor his activities and keep him out of trouble. I met once more with Simmons in a Miami motel, at which time he showed me samples of posters and leaflets he had used for primary-campaign disruptions elsewhere in Florida. He also provided me with a West Coast answering service through which he could always be reached, and a mailing address as well. In turn, he requested the name of a "reliable" printer in the Miami area, and through Bernie Barker I provided him the name of a Cuban exile who had been active in printing clandestine leaflets for both the anti-Batista and anti-Castro undergrounds.

15 DITA BEARD, THE "GOLDEN GREEK" AND J. EDGAR HOOVER

TIME had passed since Gordon Liddy's second submission of the Gemstone budget to the Attorney General, Jeb Magruder and Presidential counsel Dean—so much time that I had put Gemstone in the back of my mind and moved on to other things.

Late one afternoon I was working in Room 16 when Gordon Liddy came in. He sat down, and after some opening remarks in which he criticized Jeb Magruder's youth, inexperience and obstructionism, he said, "You know, I'm hoping for a pretty decent post in the next administration, but Magruder's at the committee, Mitchell has already said he won't be in the next Cabinet, and as for John Dean, who knows whether he'll be around? The point is," Liddy went on, "I'm known as a Mitchell man, and the strong man in the White House—the one who's likely to stay on with Nixon—is Chuck Colson. If Colson would endorse me for a job in, say, the Department of Justice, it would carry a lot of weight, but my problem is I don't know Colson. You do." He paused. "If you'd be willing to set it up, I'd like to touch base with Chuck, let him know I'm around and alive, then let him form any judgments on me based on my performance with the committee. Would you do that?"

"Why not?" I said and called Joan Hall, Chuck Colson's secretary. "Joan," I said, "I don't know what Chuck's appointment book looks like, but I'd like to bring around Gordon Liddy to introduce him. It shouldn't take long, and the sooner, the better."

"I'll check," Joan told me, and in a moment, "if you wouldn't mind coming after office hours, he might be able to see you for a minute or two."

I repeated her suggestion to Liddy, who nodded, and then I said, "About what time?"

"Oh, five thirty, a quarter to six?"

"We'll be there," I told her and hung up.

Liddy said, "That's great. I'll meet you here."

After a short wait in Colson's reception room Joan Hall told us to go in, and when Colson rose, I said, "Chuck, I'd like you to meet Gordon Liddy. As you know, he's working across the street now."

Colson acknowledged the introduction and made some perfunctory remarks before reseating himself. Liddy sat in front of Colson's desk facing him, and I, mission accomplished, withdrew to the far side of the room, where I sat down, filled and lighted my pipe and began looking through magazines. Colson's telephone rang from time to time, and he was either placing or receiving phone calls. Finally I noticed Liddy rise, as did Colson, and the two men shook hands. I joined them at the door and Colson said, "Good to see you, Howard. I hope you're keeping busy."

I said, "Plenty busy," and left his office.

Liddy and I passed through Colson's reception room and went out into the marble-floored corridor. "Well," Liddy said with satisfaction, "I think I may have done us some good." He glanced at his wristwatch. "I've got to hurry along to beat the traffic rush. See you tomorrow."

As he walked away, I realized for the first time that Liddy must have been discussing Gemstone with Colson, and I felt a sense of irritation for having been maneuvered into a somewhat false position. Still, I thought, Colson was a big boy, perfectly capable of making his own decisions concerning any urgings Liddy might have made. Besides, from my previous talk with Colson in January, I knew Colson was generally familiar with the Attorney General's proposed intelligence-collection and political-action program. In any case, the incident passed unremarked by me until, somewhat to my surprise, Liddy informed me in buoyant tones that Gemstone had finally been approved—though for an initial sum of only $250,000. Still, Liddy remarked, there was more where that came from, and additional subprojects could be approved on an individual basis. The important thing was: The word was Go.

I notified Bernie Barker that he was to resume contacting potential informants and told him that "George" and I would be down to see him in the near future.

Columnist Jack Anderson now published what purported to be a memorandum from ITT lobbyist Dita Beard to one of her company's superiors in which she mentioned a supposed agreement with Attorney General Mitchell concerning financial considerations to be provided by ITT in return for use of Sheraton Hotel facilities during the Republican Convention in San Diego, the Sheraton chain being an ITT subsidiary. The media immediately picked up this "revelation" and for a time there was little else in the newspapers. John Mitchell denied he had ever held such a conversation with Mrs. Beard, and ITT executives denied that any such "deal" with the Attorney General had ever been made. Presently Mrs. Beard herself disappeared from her usual haunts, and there was considerable speculation over her absence from Washington until from Denver, Colorado, came an announcement that Mrs. Beard was a heart patient at the Rocky Mountain Osteopathic Hospital.

Some days later I received a call from Colson, who asked me to come to his office as soon as I could. When I was admitted, I noticed half a dozen men, whom I took to be White House aides, grouped and deep in conversation, some in shirt sleeves. The atmosphere was of anxiety and urgency. Some of the faces were familiar; most were not. Standing apart from the group with me, Colson said, "Would you be able to fly to Denver and interview Dita Beard?"

"I guess so. How soon?"

"As soon as we can set it up." Colson beckoned to a younger man who had been watching us intently. When he came over, Colson said, "Howard, this is Wally Johnson.* Wally, Howard Hunt." Then to Johnson he said, "I want you to know this about Howard: He's one of a very few people in the world I would trust with my life."

Johnson said, "Chuck, did you fill him in?" and Colson replied, "No, I'm leaving that to you."

I followed Johnson down through the lower levels of the White House into the office suite of Clark MacGregor, the White House chief of Congressional relations. When we were in Johnson's office, he closed the door and began a series of telephone calls, occasionally asking questions of me, and when he had finished, he turned to me.

---

*Wallace Johnson was later an assistant attorney general.

"Here are the arrangements," he told me. "Dita Beard's daughter, Lane, works on the Hill. She will be telephoning her mother to tell Dita that "Edward Hamilton" will be coming from Washington to talk to her. Before you leave, however, Glee, a friend of Lane's—the woman I've been talking to—will drive her to meet you. I guess Lane wants to make sure you're okay, though Glee should be able to convince her. In any case, after you've talked to Lane, head for the next flight to Denver. Chuck said you've got some physical disguise, so wear it, because we don't want you traced back to the White House."

"I understand."

He described the car and said it would meet me across from the Washington Monument at four o'clock, giving me time to drive home, pack an overnight bag—including my physical disguise—and get back to downtown Washington.

"That's fine," I told him, "but what am I supposed to talk about with Dita Beard?"

"Two main things," Johnson told me. "First, is that memorandum authentic, or is it a forgery? Second, why the hell did she leave town and hide out in Denver? Meanwhile I'll prepare some notes, a sort of aide-mémoire for you to study on the flight out."

"When do you want the answers?"

"As soon as you can get them." He considered for a moment. "Call Chuck Colson at home, but use a pay station."

"Okay."

"What about money?"

"I don't have a lot on me—" I began, but Johnson said, "Never mind, we'll get some cash for you. You get on back with Chuck and work out the details, and I'll get these notes up to you."

When I returned to Colson's office, the meeting seemed to be breaking up. His attractive secretary, Holly Holm, consulted the airlines and booked a flight for me from Dulles Airport to Denver.

Colson said to me, "I don't know if you should tell Dita or not, but the FBI has checked over the memorandum, and they say it's a fabrication. You'll have to play that one by ear—anyway, you and I will be in contact through the night. Right?"

"Right."

In a little while Gordon Liddy appeared and handed an envelope to Colson. He thanked Liddy and, when Gordon was gone, handed the envelope to me. "This will take care of your plane fares and hotels," he told me. "The important thing is to get going. Now, after you've talked with Lane—and assuming everything goes okay with her—drive out to Dulles and phone Wally Johnson before you board the plane. That's a couple of hours from now, and he may have additional matters for you to take up with Dita. Or by then we may want to call off the whole thing." He shook my hand. "I'm damn glad you were available for this, Howard. It's one hell of an important thing."

"Glad to be of service," I told him and we shook hands.

Returning to my Mullen office, I told Bennett I was leaving at once and would be out of town a day or so on business for Chuck Colson. "Denver?" Bennett asked and I nodded.

At home I packed, donned my brown wig and put in my pocket the special billfold in which I kept nothing but alias documentation issued me by the Central Intelligence Agency. At the appointed time and place I met Lane Beard and her driver, Glee, who, I inferred, worked for the Senate Republican Caucus.

Dita Beard's daughter was deeply troubled and obviously was having second thoughts over whether she should have encouraged her mother to see me.

"Who, exactly, do you represent?" she asked.

"High Washington levels who are interested in your mother's welfare," I told her.

"Could you be more specific?"

I shrugged. "Your friend's already told you I come well recommended."

Glee nodded. "That's right, Lane," she told the girl. "Besides, your mother needs help."

Lane gave me the name of her mother's physician and said he would be expecting a call from me when I reached the Denver airport. As an afterthought, she asked to see some form of identification, and I displayed the New York driving license made out in the name of Edward J. Hamilton, a business card and some pocket litter. She seemed satisfied, so I thanked her and got out of the car, in which the entire conversation had been held. From there I drove directly to Dulles Airport, bought my ticket and telephoned Wally Johnson at the White House.

"There's something else you should know, Howard," he told me. "If Dita denies knowing Jack Anderson's secretary, tell her we have a photograph showing the two of them together at a party in the Carlton Hotel."

"Anything else?"

"That's it. The word is Go."

It was after dark when I arrived in Denver. I telephoned the hospital and was connected with Dr. David Garland, Mrs. Beard's physician. He had been expecting my call, he told me, and suggested I come at once to the hospital. His patient had been upset by the prospect of our interview, and he was anxious that it take place as soon as possible.

I checked in at a Ramada Inn near the airport, left my bags in the room and took a taxi to the hospital. Dr. Garland met me in a reception room and asked for proof of my identity. I showed him the documents I had exhibited to Lane Beard, after which he told me he hoped I would avoid questions that could cause his patient to suffer stress. I said I hoped so too, but as he knew, a great deal was at stake, including Senate confirmation of Attorney General-designate Richard Kleindienst. The physician told me that he had resisted a Senate committee invitation to have Dita testify in Washington. Instead, a subcommittee of Senators would visit at her hospital bedside within the next few days.

As we walked toward the hospital room, I reflected how little I really knew about Dita Beard. Brief and possibly inaccurate press accounts identified her as a onetime Washington debutante who had married, borne several children and been abandoned by her husband. She had managed to turn her social contacts into professional ones and had been employed by ITT as a Washington lobbyist for many years. Beyond that, I knew nothing.

The physician entered her room first and after a few moments beckoned me in.

"Dita," he said, "this is Mr. Hamilton."

Lidded eyes examined me, peering through the semidarkness of the room. She was lying on one side, facing me, her hair disheveled, her face bloated, and it occurred to me that she might be an alcoholic. Her appearance brought back memories of Marie Dressler as Tugboat Annie.

"Who're you?" she grunted.

"Your daughter's already told you about me, Mrs. Beard."

"Lane?"

I nodded. "Lane. We were together only a few hours ago."

She plucked at her nightgown. "What did you come here for?"

I turned to the physician. "Doctor, could we possibly speak alone?"

He nodded. "Would you mind if I sat over in the corner? I'll be out of earshot there, but I'll still be able to watch my patient."

"Fine," I said and drew up a chair beside Dita's bed.

"I didn't get my Christmas bonus," she complained. "I was counting on it to pay the taxes and mortgage on my house. I've done that every year. Now the bonus hasn't come through. What about that?"

"Doubtless a misunderstanding," I ad-libbed and noted her complaint on a pad of paper. "The principal questions," I told her, "are whether the famous memorandum is authentic and why you left Washington."

She laughed bitterly, then coughed. The physician half rose, reseated himself. "I don't remember writing the memo, and I came out here to get away from the press." She stared at me almost pleadingly. "I don't know what to do; everyone in the office stayed away from me. I heard they were going to fire me, and I couldn't talk to Hal. You know Hal Geneen?"

I shook my head.

"I'm sick," she went on, "just ask the doctor. I've got a heart condition. That's why I'm here."

"There's a pretty strong rumor around Washington that you gave the memorandum to Jack Anderson's secretary, Opal Ginn."

"Eh? I don't know her," she said petulantly.

I leaned forward. "Mrs. Beard, there's a photograph showing you and Jack's secretary together at a party for the Carlton's headwaiter. Do you remember that?"

One hand waved vaguely. The doctor rose. "Mr. Hamilton, Mrs. Beard is getting tired, and I'll have to ask you to leave. Perhaps after I've checked her over, you can come back later."

Standing, I looked down at Mrs. Beard. She seemed huddled protectively, indrawn. What a lousy job this was, I thought, and went out into the corridor.

When the doctor joined me, I said, "I'd like to get to a pay phone, but not one in the hospital. Do you know where the nearest one is?"

"I'll take you there," he volunteered. "Wait downstairs for a while, and I'll be with you."

When we drove away from the hospital, he said, "I've had to

administer oxygen. She's really very tired, and I hope you won't be hard on her."

"I'm trying not to be," I told him, "but I don't think she's being fully candid."

"She's pretty sedated, so that may account for her inability to respond to your questions."

"I hope that's all it is."

Near a darkened drugstore the doctor stopped the car and I got out. From the outside pay phone booth I dialed Colson's private home number and heard him answer. I summarized the conversation as far as it had gone and told him I was not sure the physician would permit me to continue questioning her.

"Is she really sick?"

"As far as I can tell—but of course I never saw her before tonight. Maybe she always looks like that."

"Any trouble with the doctor?"

"No. He's being helpful, but he's got an obligation to his patient."

"Think you can ask her more questions?"

"I'll try."

"Well, get back to me as soon as you can."

I returned to the car and we drove back to the hospital. An oxygen tube was taped into Mrs. Beard's nostrils and as we began to talk, she seemed neither more nor less alert than before. Dr. Garland cautioned me that she was getting progressively weaker and urged me to end the interview as soon as I could.

Referring to the aide-mémoire, I resumed the interrogation, jotting down Mrs. Beard's replies. She was concerned about her salary, she told me, and wanted assurances it would be paid.

"Who've you been talking to," she asked suspiciously. "Hal?"

"A friend of his," I reassured her.

"What about the Christmas bonus?"

"I'll have word on that before I leave Denver."

Colson had told me that he would confirm this before my second call to him.

I led her through a jumble of dates and a sequence of events involving ITT internecine rivalries, her high-level Washington contacts and again the question of the memorandum. Her recollection seemed to have improved, for she now told me she could *not* have typed the memorandum, for she was unable to use an electric typewriter, though on one occasion she had permitted a Naval officer friend to use it one night in her office. Back to the pay phone again and another call to Colson.

"Tell her not to worry about the Christmas bonus, Howard. There was some sort of administrative hang-up," Colson told me. "That's solid."

I paraphrased the information she had supplied me, hardly understanding its significance myself and feeling more of a conduit than an active participant in this clandestine White House operation.

Again the hospital bed, more questions and a hodgepodge of answers that I hoped would fit the jigsaw puzzle being assembled in Washington by my superiors.

Finally the doctor told me he could authorize no further disruption of Mrs. Beard's routine and ushered me from her room. In the morning, he suggested, I should phone him to determine whether she could again be seen.

The hospital desk called me a taxi and I returned to my motel, placing a final call to Colson from the pay phone in the lobby. Then I went to my room and, dead tired, fell asleep.

In the morning I telephoned the hospital and spoke with Mrs. Beard's physician, who agreed to allow a final brief interview.

When I entered her room, her son was just leaving. I had brought flowers with me, and Mrs. Beard brightened when she saw them, although she asked Dr. Garland to have them checked for electronic "bugs."

She was in better condition than the previous night, and her attitude was less suspicious and hostile than before. I had no new questions to ask her but, at her urging, reaffirmed that her Christmas bonus would be paid, as would her past salary and hospitalization expenses. I added that her friends were anxious that she get well and repeated that her job at ITT was waiting for her as soon as she could return.

With that I left, went to the airport and called Colson for a final report. He seemed satisfied with the information I elicited and told me to return to Washington.

During the flight I was able to doze on the plane, but even so, when I reached Washington, I felt too tired to go to the White House and instead went home to sleep.

That evening Colson telephoned me to say he wanted a complete report of my interview, typed and in his hands by nine thirty the next morning. He suggested that I go to the office early, use the Dictaphone in my office and as the Dictabelts were completed, pass them to his secretaries, who would be waiting for them in his office before he arrived.

The next morning I reached the White House about six thirty and began dictating. Colson's secretaries produced an eight-page single-spaced memorandum, and when the Mullen & Company offices opened at nine thirty, I was there and ready to work, for a change, on the HEW account.

The Mullen & Company office had become the locus of a triangular operation devoted to preparing a statement for issuance by Dita Beard to the press. Bob Bennett was in touch with the office of Senator Hugh Scott and with Dita Beard's attorneys, one of whom I believed to be at her hospital bedside, the other in Washington and in touch with ITT. During the course of the day a press statement agreeable to all parties was developed, drafts were transmitted between Washington and Denver by facsimile copiers and the statement was released.

Colson complimented me on my work and remarked that John Ehrlichman had been well pleased with my eight-page memorandum.

For weeks I had been preparing a public-service television commercial which we hoped Julie Nixon Eisenhower would make to aid America's handicapped children; negotiations with her secretary and with a local television studio consumed a good deal of my working time. Finally the White House approved my script, and Mrs. Eisenhower set a date for the shooting, which, when it took place, I supervised and directed.

I was still meeting Tom Gregory and Fat Jack. Too, I was receiving sporadic reports from Clifton De Motte concerning his findings on the Chappaquiddick case. Among others, De Motte had interviewed the district attorney who had "prosecuted" Senator Kennedy following the tragic death of the Senator's midnight passenger. Through these interviews, a new theory of the incident evolved: Unknown to the others in the cottage party, Mary Jo Kopechne had gotten into the Senator's car and fallen asleep in the backseat. Later Kennedy emerged with another woman and the two of them drove toward the beach for a supposedly romantic interlude. Through mischance the Senator's car had gone over the bridge at Chappaquiddick, but both Kennedy and his companion escaped. When they returned to the cottage, someone asked if they had seen Mary Jo, after which a frantic search for the missing girl began. The lips of everyone involved had long been sealed, but if the Senator had not known of the sleeping girl in his car, revelation of that fact would have been far less damaging to him politically than the less creditable circumstances the world had come to believe.

I reported these findings to Colson, who put them in a locked drawer behind his desk, first showing me photographs of Senator Kennedy and an attractive Frenchwoman taken when they were leaving a Paris nightclub when the Senator was in France for the burial of former French President de Gaulle. There were other similar photographs, Colson implied, and if Kennedy were to become the Democratic nominee, they would be used against him. However, Colson went on, it now seemed clear that Senator McGovern would be the Democratic nominee.

On the twenty-ninth of the month I submitted to Joan Hall what was to be my final time voucher for services rendered to the White House, even though I continued to work there a few hours each week on narcotics matters, Room 16 affairs and what seemed to be the endless search for the origins of the Vietnam War. I did not really need the money, and I felt that it would be petty to request a fee for my sporadic work. I still considered myself a White House consultant, however, and maintained my office and its safe as before.

Some days after I left Denver a group of Senators visited Mrs. Beard at her bedside and asked her a number of the questions that I had propounded during our nocturnal meeting. Her answers must have satisfied the Senators, for within a short space of time Richard Kleindienst was confirmed by the Senate as successor to John Mitchell as Attorney General of the United States.

Of Dita Beard I was to hear no more until long after the Watergate arrests that summer.

A secretary in the firm whose offices adjoined my Mullen & Company office was raped in the rest room on our floor, and a similar assault was perpetrated at the USIA offices down the street. Our secretaries were becoming apprehensive and reluctant to work after normal office hours. Then in the New Executive Office Building across the street a government official was murdered in a washroom. Because I worked late, not only at the White House but also at

Mullen & Company, I brought my wife's .25 caliber Browning pistol to my Mullen & Company office and kept it there, letting the secretaries know of its presence. After the rapist was apprehended, I took the pistol to my White House office and kept it in the safe, where it was discovered by those who drilled open and ransacked my safe.

Liddy abruptly came to me with a strange request: He asked me to fly to Chicago, taking an envelope filled with cash. I was to go to a certain office, announce myself as Edward Warren and hand the envelope to an unidentified young man who would respond and claim it. What was odd about the transaction was the name of the office: a foundation named after millionaire philanthropist W. Clement Stone.* Stone, as the entire world knows, was a multimillion-dollar contributor to Richard Nixon's Presidential campaigns. So it seemed unusual to me that in place of money traveling from Chicago to Washington, this time it was I who was taking money from Washington to the offices of W. Clement Stone.

In the privacy of the recipient's office I handed him the envelope Liddy had given me. He asked if I wanted a receipt and I told him none was required. He suggested that he count the money in front of me but I said the formality would be meaningless, for I had no idea how much money the envelope contained. With that I departed and caught the next plane back to Washington.

I was not to think of the episode again until I read that Mr. Stone was one of a number of well-to-do Republicans who were raising defense funds for then Vice President Spiro Agnew.

Before final Gemstone approval, and at a time when Liddy was providing funds for our developmental activity, I asked him where the money was coming from.

Liddy said, "They found some money left over from the '68 campaign. It was in a safe-deposit box, and that's the dough we're using."

"If they've got the money, then what's Mitchell's problem with the Gemstone price tag?"

"Can't figure it. He braces me with 'half a million dollars for openers,' and since then it's been a fight for every nickel. Magruder's the only logical answer. Jeb's giving me a really hard

*The W. Clement and Jessie V. Stone Foundation.

time and I've decided to get out from under him. Maurice Stans is coming aboard and I'm going to transfer to his office as general counsel for the Finance Committee to Re-elect the President. Stans is a hell of a guy, self-made, and a man who has no problems making decisions."

Liddy used some rough language about Jeb Magruder and said, "There seems to be some kind of weird parallel operation going on up in New York. Caulfield—that gumshoe of Mitchell's—seems to be in charge, and they've told me to go up and take a look at it."

"What's involved?"

"Something about one of the broads who was at the Chappaquiddick party—you know, one of the survivors. I gather they've set up some sort of fabulous pad and it's run by another ex-New York cop. The idea seems to be to have the broad fall in love with the ex-cop, and while they're in bed together, automatic cameras are supposed to whir and buzz like *From Russia with Love*." Liddy shrugged. "Anyway, I've got committee business in New York, so the trip won't be a total waste."

"Maybe the guy will turn out to be Don Simmons in disguise."

Liddy laughed. "Christ, anything could happen. These cops of Mitchell's are murder. Anyway, I'll tell you about it when I get back."

When Liddy returned from his New York inspection, he telephoned me at once and we met. Shaking his head and laughing, he said, "The setup's unbelievable. This middle-aged guy who's in charge of the 'operation' has an accent I can't place. And the pad! It's got to be a cop's idea of an East Side bordello in the 1880's—secondhand furniture, red plush sofas—and the Golden Greek's trying to build a fake wall—a partition—so he can get cameras behind it." Liddy laughed uproariously. "I can just see him making out up there. The gal'll take one look at the pad and shriek for help. That's how subtle it is. And the dough they're spending on it. . . ." He shook his head. "It's about as sophisticated as a Mack Sennett comedy."

"And you told it like it is?"

"Yeah. I don't know who the hell's idea it was, but here's the Golden Greek pounding up this great partition all day long and dating the broad at night. My guess is that the broad'll be finished with the Golden Greek before he's finished with the wall."

"Anything salvageable?"

"Well, we could have a garage sale or a street sale and try to get rid of the crummy furniture, but otherwise nothing. For months down here they've been thinking the Golden Greek had a great seduction setup in New York and once the broad was compromised, she'd tell the true story about what happened that night at Chappaquiddick." Liddy chuckled. "The Greek hasn't been getting very far with her, so now he figures she must be a dyke."

"Anything's possible."

"I suppose so, but I don't think there were any dykes in that boiler-room gang of Kennedy's."

Later I heard that the seduction suite had been dismantled and the Greek* directed to other pursuits.

From Liddy I learned that he had passed a large sum of money to his as-yet-unidentified electronics expert, and essential items were being acquired or on order. "I'll tell you this about him," Liddy said. "He was not only with your old company, but with mine as well, so he ought to know what he's doing. In addition, he's been working as a bodyguard for Mitchell."

"Martha?" I asked.

"No, the AG—hell, maybe Martha as well."

One evening Liddy came to my Mullen & Company office and showed me a series of checks for large amounts of money. He asked me if I thought that Barker would be able to negotiate them through his business in Miami and return the cash. I telephoned Barker and found that Bernie foresaw no difficulties in meeting the request. So on our next trip to Miami Liddy turned over the checks to Barker, and in due course the cash was forthcoming.

I had noticed that some of the checks were drawn on a Mexico City bank, but made no comment, for I knew that Liddy was the committee's foremost expert on the new election law with its complicated restrictions on campaign contributions. These checks, it was later to develop, derived from Gulf Resources and Chemical Corporation of Houston, from Kenneth Dahlberg and from Dwayne Andreas, and were to become the focus of a fruitless and controversial FBI investigation that led into Mexico.

*Not until the Ervin televised hearings was I able to identify ex-New York policeman Anthony Ulasewicz as Liddy's "Golden Greek." In a subsequent incarnation he became "Mr. Rivers."

Next Liddy informed me that his "principals" desired that a "bug" be placed in the campaign headquarters of Senator George McGovern, near Capitol Hill. We cased the headquarters externally, and from Tom Gregory I began receiving reports which included a floor diagram of the office and the office habits of Gary Hart and Frank Mankiewicz.

About this time Liddy brought to my Mullen & Company office his so-far-unidentified electronics expert and introduced him to me as James McCord. McCord and I chatted about CIA employees whom we might mutually know, but because McCord's Agency career had been almost entirely in Washington, our sole common contact was Director of Security Howard Osborn. McCord brought me up-to-date on the current state of electronics art and indicated that he was commercially purchasing several items that had been developed for CIA. Liddy remarked that McCord was also procuring some small but highly effective walkie-talkies. "Not like those Mickey Mouse monsters we used in L.A." And McCord smiled confirmation. These new walkie-talkies were expensive, McCord said, but fitted easily into a coat pocket.

I learned also that McCord, on Liddy's instructions, had previously rented an office adjacent to Senator Muskie's headquarters, but the office had been vacant ever since CREP decided that McGovern rather than Muskie would be the Democratic Presidential candidate.

During that same meeting there was a brief discussion of Democratic National Committee headquarters at the Watergate office building, and I inferred that DNC headquarters might be an eventual electronic target.

Then, on May 2, J. Edgar Hoover died, and preparations were made for a lying-in-state under the Capitol Rotunda.

As early as the previous autumn, the Special Investigations Unit had been discussing possible replacements for J. Edgar Hoover, whose nonresponsiveness to the administration had become an extremely sore point in the White House.

Among us we had drawn up a list of possible successors for Presidential consideration. Because Hoover was long past retirement age, his retention in office had to be approved each January by the President, and there was considerable White House reluctance to reappoint J. Edgar Hoover as director of the FBI. I remember contributing three names and Liddy several more. Supreme Court Justice Byron "Whizzer" White, however, was the man deemed most likely to succeed—if, in fact, the jurist would accept the post. Although a Kennedy appointee, Justice White was not known as an active antagonist of the Nixon Administration, and we felt that as director of the FBI, White would not only administer the Bureau effectively, but restore the bureau's long-sagging morale, which had been further lowered by internecine struggles among Hoover's closest aides and advisers.

On the other hand, there was vocal fear that replacement of Hoover might alienate large numbers of voters who had come, over the years, to regard Hoover as a superman. In any event, through lethargy, inaction or internal White House decisions, the proposal to replace Hoover was not acted upon and President Nixon once more extended Hoover's tenure.

Late that evening Liddy came to me and said that a high-level requirement had been laid on him. "There's going to be a peacenik rally on the Capitol steps featuring Jane Fonda, Kunstler, Donald Sutherland and, grab this, Daniel Ellsberg. They're all going to be there while Hoover's lying in state in the Rotunda. According to our information, there are going to be a lot of inflammatory speeches, and as you know, the antiwar Left has always regarded Hoover as one of its chief villains. There's concern that the peacenik crowd will surge around into the Rotunda and maybe turn over Hoover's catafalque. Do you suppose Bernie could get some fellows together to come up and try to prevent it?"

"All I can do is ask him."

I telephoned Barker, explained the situation and asked if he could come to Washington the following day with perhaps as many as a dozen well-motivated friends.

When Barker arrived next day, he telephoned me first from the airport, then from his hotel, and I asked him to come to my Mullen & Company office. Gordon Liddy joined us—still using his George Leonard alias—and showed Barker photographs of Ellsberg, Kunstler and some of the other countergovernment luminaries. Barker told us that actor Donald Sutherland had flown up on the same plane with him, so the men from Miami were already able to identify Sutherland, at least.

Liddy and I briefed Barker: He and his men were to circulate among the crowd listening to the antiwar activists. Then, lest the bystanders assume that the audience was entirely in favor of the speakers' propositions, the Miami men were to shout "traitor" from time to time, and if altercations ensued, they were to defend themselves.

"But most important," Liddy said, "is to take away any Vietcong flag they might unfurl."

"Is that part of their plan?" I asked.

"That's what I've been told," Liddy said.

We explained further to Barker that if the inflamed audience should make a surge toward the Rotunda, where J. Edgar Hoover's body was lying in state, he and his men were to attempt to group themselves around the casket to protect it from desecration by the antiwar crowd until police arrived.

"The crazies have always considered Hoover their number one enemy," I said to Barker, who nodded agreement, then, "Bernie, after it's all over, phone me here at this number, where George and I will be waiting for your report. Understood?"

"I've got it all." He left us to return to the hotel where he and his men were registered. Liddy and I discussed Gemstone matters for a while, then went out for dinner, returning to my office in the early evening.

We listened to the radio, drank coffee and waited for the telephone to ring. Liddy said, "I hope they get that flag. Colson really wants it."

"*Colson?*"

"Yeah. Chuck really wants it."

This was the first time Liddy had alluded to a specific White House individual's interest in this operation. I felt it odd that Colson had not communicated with me, but then realized it would have been inappropriate had he done so, since Liddy was known by Colson to be the man at CREP who got things done.

Time passed.

Finally the telephone and Barker's breathy voice. "I'm calling from a pay phone, Eduardo, and outside of some shoving and pushing, not much happened. Frank traded punches with somebody and a cop grabbed him and led him away from the scene."

"Anyone arrested?"

"No, but the crowd didn't like to hear Ellsberg called a traitor."

Oh, yes. The cop who collared Frank Sturgis said he was glad to see that there were some Americans willing to take issue with what the speakers had been saying, and then some radio reporter had an interview with Frank."

Liddy got on the phone to question Barker more closely. Then we arranged to pick up Barker in front of his hotel within half an hour so he could give us a fuller report.

There had been, said Barker, no Vietcong flag.

For half an hour we drove around in my car, Liddy, Barker and myself, Martínez and Felipe De Diego, all of whose stories matched.

It was now dark, and I drove past McGovern headquarters on Capitol Hill, parking a couple of blocks away. We walked back and through the side alley, taking note of the building's rear entrance door. The area was illuminated by a high-powered streetlight, which Liddy remarked would have to be extinguished a day or so before we attempted the pretext entry. Inside McGovern headquarters lights were burning, and it was obvious that the workers were active well after normal office hours.

From there we drove down Virginia Avenue past the Watergate complex, and Liddy, pointing at the Watergate office building, said, "That's our next job, Macho."

"What is it?" Martínez asked.

"Democratic National headquarters," Liddy told him, "and after McGovern's nominated, it'll be his headquarters, too."

"There's a report," I told Barker, "that Castro's been getting money to the Democrats. He's Hanoi's favorite, too, and if McGovern's elected, he'll simply pull out our troops and the hell with everything else."

"Hell, that rumor's all over Miami," Barker grunted. "You don't have to tell me any more about it."

"The idea," I told him, "is to photograph the list of contributors the Democrats are required to keep. Once we have those lists, we can have them checked to determine whether the contributors are bona fide or merely fronts for Castro or Hanoi money."

"Just like the Fielding operation," Martínez remarked, and I said, "Yes, but this time I hope we can find what we're looking for."

In the morning the Miami men departed, leaving Liddy disappointed over the lack of media interest in the vocal protests that had been shouted during the discourses of Ellsberg, Kunstler, *et al.* If the radio correspondent's interview with Frank Sturgis was ever aired, neither of us ever heard it, and the incidental episode was to pass for the most part unnoticed until it was disclosed a year or so later during investigations by the Ervin committee and the Office of the Special Prosecutor.

From time to time Liddy expressed enthusiasm over the progress made by James McCord in obtaining the needed electronic equipment. Occasionally I met with McCord to continue our casing of the Watergate office building and, at McCord's request, introduced him to Thomas Gregory.

At my suggestion, Gregory had developed the habit of working late at McGovern headquarters. This gave him an opportunity to check the day's final tally of contributions received through the mail and to acquire exemplars of press and scheduling material before their release the following day.

I had also asked Gregory to locate a place within the offices where he could conceal himself after the last employee had left McGovern headquarters for the night. McCord's request to him was somewhat more complicated, but it was accomplished by having McCord go to McGovern headquarters late one evening and ask at the door for Gregory. Passing himself off as Gregory's out-of-town uncle, McCord made a reconnaissance of McGovern headquarters, with attention to the offices of campaign managers Frank Mankiewicz and Gary Hart. McCord's additional information, added to the rough floor diagram already provided by Gregory, gave McCord all he felt he needed to implant an electronic device in the offices of either Mankiewicz or Hart. The key was Thomas Gregory.

Gregory's function, very simply, was to remain inside the offices and, when the building was empty, admit McCord through either the front or back door. McCord had said he needed no more than five minutes to install his bug, and so a date and time were set for the operation.

On that night, however, Gregory was detected in the building by a fellow employee and had to leave, telephone McCord and abort the operation for that night. Talking to Gregory later, I was not encouraged by the young man's apprehensions. McCord's avuncular attitude was able to calm Gregory somewhat, but the youth was becoming a bundle of nerves, and so I began to devise an alternate solution to the problem.

Our pretext entry into Dr. Fielding's office had worked so well in Los Angeles, I remembered, that a similar operation with modifications might be effective at McGovern headquarters on Capitol Hill. Gregory had reported that deliveries were constantly being made to McGovern headquarters—office machines, stationery, furniture and the like—and when I had worked out the details, I presented them to Liddy.

"The problem with Gregory," I said, "is that he spooks when he has to stay alone in that little furnace room. Things that go bump in the night bother him, and so we'll plan around him."

"How?" Liddy asked.

"Most of the volunteers leave around six o'clock; a few stay on until nine or after, including Gregory. Let's say sometime after nine a delivery is made to the front door of McGovern headquarters. Gregory is in the area and indicates he's heard something about a delivery, so the men come in: Barker and Martínez carrying a couple of heavy boxes, with McCord as their supervisor, all three of them in work uniforms. While Barker and Rolando unpack whatever is being delivered, McCord will get his five minutes—if not more—to splice in his bug. Delivery made, the three men leave, and if anything should go wrong then or later, Gregory would run little risk of being implicated."

"Sounds good to me," Liddy said. "I'm for anything that doesn't involve that gutless wonder of yours."

A day or so later, however, the Gutless Wonder reported that there had been an attempted burglary at McGovern headquarters; as a result, the premises were guarded by a Burns Agency guard around the clock.

Liddy was dejected over the news, but I persuaded him that a professional guard might be more easy to con than one of McGovern's volunteer zealots.

"All we do," I said, "is show the delivery manifest to the guard."

"What if he signs for the delivery but won't let the men take the boxes in?"

"The boxes will be so damn heavy the guard won't be able to move them by himself. Second, Rolando's a pretty good shouter, and he can work himself up into a rage over the guard's lack of cooperation. If the guard insists on watching the two men open the boxes and unpack them, great. That will give McCord time to disappear and do what he has to do. So I think we've still got a good chance of pulling off the operation."

"That means we'll have to put it off until we get the guys from Miami up here again."

I nodded. "We're only waiting for McCord to assemble his gear."

"He swears he'll have the stuff in a week or so, but I don't know—he's been wrong before," Liddy remarked.

"All I want is plenty of walkie-talkies," I told him. "No more of those Dick Tracy marvels we used in Beverly Hills."

"You'll have them."

On May 15 Governor George Wallace of Alabama was shot by a would-be assassin at a Maryland shopping center. Later I watched television coverage of the incident, saw a guard wrestle the gunman to the ground, then hurry him away in a police car. Throughout the evening I listened to news bulletins issued from the hospital, and though I was no admirer of Governor Wallace, I felt that this country's recent political history had been far too often marred by violence. On the following day I received a telephone call from Charles Colson.

"Howard, do you know anyone in Milwaukee?"

I thought for a moment. "Some fellows from college, but I haven't seen them since 1940."

"Know the city? Ever been there?"

"No. Why?"

"This fellow who shot Wallace—Bremer. He lives in Milwaukee, got an apartment there." There was a long pause. "Could you go out there, take a look at the apartment and let me know what you find?"

"Chuck," I said, "according to the press, the FBI's got the place sealed—after reporters had been tramping through it for a couple of hours."

"I know, god damn it! That's the trouble. Every time there's an assassination in this country the press blames the political Right. Weeks later the truth seeps out—like Oswald and Sirhan Sirhan, who were Lefties. Just once I'd like the truth to come out—if Bremer's a Marxist himself."

"Jesus, Chuck, how in the hell am I going to get in a sealed apartment that's being watched by the FBI?"

"Maybe you could bribe the janitor, get another key—something like that. You know—like your CIA experiences."

"Even if I got in—which I seriously doubt I could do—what would be left? By now the newshawks have picked the place clean. And what the FBI may have taken out. . . ." I left the thought unfinished.

"Well—give it some thought, will you? And check on flights to Milwaukee, Howard. This is a goddamn serious thing, and we'd like to know what in hell's lying around Bremer's apartment."

"You could always ask the Bureau."

"Very funny," Colson said. "Just get on standby, will you?"

Reluctantly I began to pack a bag, adding to it the shaving kit that held my CIA-issue physical disguise and documents.

Dorothy noticed my desultory packing and said, "What does Chuck want now?"

I told Dorothy, who shook her head disgustedly. "He's got to be insane. Call him up and tell him you can't do it."

"Can't or won't?"

"I don't care. This is one mission he can find somebody else to do." She turned and left the bedroom.

I called several airlines and found that the only available flight would put me in Milwaukee about eleven o'clock that night. Would Colson provide Bremer's address, or would I have to find it in the telephone directory? Or, if Bremer were a drifter, as news reports indicated, would he even have a phone?

I knew I would be going in cold, colder than I had ever undertaken a mission before. Colder by far than my trip to Dita Beard's bedside. I liked none of it; still, Colson had turned to me, and Colson was close to the President. If Colson was assigned to inventory Bremer's apartment, it had to be on orders from the Oval Office. How could I refuse? Against that was Dorothy's opposition, and Dorothy's intuition had seldom failed.

Even supposing I could locate the apartment janitor and bribe him for a key, wouldn't the Bureau have men inside the apartment? How could I credibly explain my presence? Once in the Bureau's hands, I could quickly be identified and traced back to the White House, and that was something Colson wanted to avoid.

For the next hour or so I watched television and listened to radio reports of Governor Wallace's condition; there was added information about Arthur Bremer, but nothing concerning his political orientation. If I were going to catch the flight to Milwaukee, I would have to leave the house soon.

Again Dorothy attempted to dissuade me, but I told her I felt an obligation to Colson and would do whatever he desired. Then the telephone rang and I heard Joan Hall's voice.

"You don't have to travel, Howard," she told me. "Chuck says thanks, anyway."

"I'm just as glad," I told her and hung up.

Dorothy was immensely relieved, and I was glad to be off the hook. Moreover, I had responded affirmatively to another of Colson's requests, and I felt that I was continuing to justify the faith and confidence he had placed in me when almost a year ago he had brought me into the White House.

16 WATERGATE I

THROUGH our casings of the Watergate office building, McCord and I found three ways to reach Democratic National headquarters on the sixth floor: by elevator, which meant passing in front of a guard desk; by the stairwell, whose door was near the guard desk, and through an entrance two levels down which gave out into the office garage; lastly, a subterranean corridor connecting the office building's stairwell and elevator with a banquet room in the Watergate Hotel—the Continental Room.

I elected the corridor route for several reasons: First, the corridor floor was carpeted and footsteps were not likely to be heard. Second, from the corridor one could enter the stairwell at that level without being observed—presuming the stairwell door could be opened; third, an elevator could be summoned to the corridor level, then ridden to the sixth floor—the only risk being the off chance that the guard might happen to glance at the nearby locator panel and see marker lights ascending.

But to gain the subterranean corridor meant initial access to the Continental Room, which I had once been in as a business-luncheon guest.

It occurred to me that by hiring the Continental Room for a banquet, I could provide legitimate access to the building for the entry team, and as business banquets tend to go on until late hours of the night, the presence of a group of men in the Continental Room would not be likely to arouse undue suspicion. I discussed the

concept with McCord, who agreed, and one afternoon we entered
the Continental Room, which was vacant, and noted that the door
between the Continental Room and the corridor was equipped with
a magnetic alarm system. McCord said he was familiar with the
system and would be able to defeat it when the time came. Meanwhile, he told me, he would set about familiarizing himself with
guard schedules in the office building, as well as the times when the
alarm system was on and off.

I flew to Miami and was introduced by Barker to Virgilio González, a Cuban exile who had been for many years a Presidential
bodyguard and was now a successful locksmith in the Miami area. At
lunch Barker explained the mission we had in mind and told González that I was "Eduardo" of Bay of Pigs fame, and González agreed
to take part in our mission. Later I told Barker I had selected the
Watergate Hotel's Continental Room as a staging area for our entry
and had decided to hold a banquet there to provide the pretext for
our presence. All that was lacking was the name of some sponsoring
organization under whose auspices the banquet could be held.

Barker responded promptly. Sometime before, he told me, he
had formed a small and now inactive corporation called Ameritas.
He still had letterhead paper, and the return address of the corporation was valid, actually that of his attorney, Miguel Suárez.

I told Barker that in addition to his three-man entry team, I
wanted three guards or lookouts. He suggested Felipe De Diego,
who had worked with us in Beverly Hills, and Frank Sturgis, who
was known, during CIA days, as Frank Fiorini. I had not previously
met Sturgis, nor had I met Barker's other guard candidate, Rolando
Pico, one of the men brought by Barker to prevent desecration of J.
Edgar Hoover's catafalque.

I mentioned that another man would be accompanying them, a
former Agency employee, who would be there on electronics business of his own. He would be, I told Barker, a sort of electronics
hitchhiker, and the team's prime function, as he knew, was photography. What "Jim" did was no business of theirs. I told Barker it
was my responsibility to get Jim safely in and out of the target area
but stressed that the photography mission was paramount.

I returned to Washington and asked my wife to telephone the
Watergate Hotel saying she represented the Ameritas Corporation

and wanted to book a banquet into the hotel's Continental Room for the night of May 26. There would be between ten and a dozen guests, she was to tell the management, then select a menu sufficiently impressive to lend authenticity to the affair.

Meanwhile, from Miami, Barker had his secretary telephone the Watergate Hotel and book several rooms to house his contingent. When these arrangements were completed, I gave Liddy a status report and learned that the walkie-talkies had not yet reached McCord's hands.

Within a day or so McCord and I met with Thomas Gregory in the lobby of the Howard Johnson Motel across the street from the Watergate office building. Our meeting had to do with our sidetracked effort to bug McGovern headquarters, and when Gregory departed, McCord told me he had rented a Listening Post upstairs in the same motel. He took me to the room, which was then unoccupied, but showed indications of another inhabitant, whom McCord described as an employee of his who would monitor the electronic transmissions from Democratic National Committee headquarters across the street. So far there was no equipment in the Listening Post, though McCord said he expected to be able to install it in the near future—certainly by the twenty-sixth, which had become our target date for the Watergate entry.

Liddy now began passing me increments of operational funds*: for team travel from Florida, for the operational banquet, for team hotel lodgings, and a sum of $10,000, which he asked me to keep in my White House safe. That $10,000 he described as a contingency fund to be used in case of emergency.

"Like what?" I asked.

"Well—you know, suppose the guys get picked up and jailed. . . . Use the money to hire a lawyer, pay collateral and get them out of town. I'll give Barker an extra few thousand to bribe any guard who might walk in on them. That way we're covered in both directions. Any other problems?"

"I hope McCord gets his equipment on time."

"He swears he'll have it by the time we need it, but I think he's cutting it pretty thin."

---

*Of whose source I was never certain until FBI investigation disclosed that at least a portion came from CREP.

"So do I. We may have to use those Buck Rogers walkie-talkies again."

"I've checked the catalogue: We can do better with Green Stamps."

While renting the Continental Room from the Watergate Hotel, we learned that a large convention would be occupying most of the hotel's other rooms. Transpo '72 would be in town and this was welcome news, for the presence of a large crowd would be helpful in giving anonymity to our group. So, inexorably, the plan went forward under what appeared to be cloudless skies.

On May 22 Barker, Martínez, González, De Diego, Pico and Sturgis arrived from Miami and registered at the Hamilton Hotel pending availability of their rooms at the Watergate. Leaving National Airport, Frank Sturgis encountered columnist Jack Anderson, and they exchanged pleasantries, Anderson and Sturgis having known each other during Sturgis' involvement in anti-Castro activities. This encounter, however, was not mentioned to me and I was not to learn of it for many months.

Over the next few days the Miami men familiarized themselves with the two target areas: McGovern headquarters and the Watergate office building. James McCord and Thomas Gregory were introduced to them, and during a late-night walk-through Liddy shot out the streetlight at the rear of McGovern headquarters with an air pistol.

McCord also took the Miami men to the sixth floor of the Watergate office building, where they briefly viewed the entrance to DNC headquarters. This was done overtly, the men signing the guard's book and riding the elevator to the sixth floor.

On the twenty-fourth I went to the glass entrance doors of DNC headquarters and pressed a lump of plasteline against the door lock. From this I made a plaster cast from which "Villo" Gonzalez was to be able to determine the kind of lock-picking devices he would need for the entry.

On the twenty-sixth the entry group moved into the Watergate Hotel, and late that afternoon McCord brought four new walkie-talkies to my Mullen & Company office. That left us short two W/Ts for the operation and the nickel-cadmium batteries for the four we had required lengthy charging. We began this process in the room

Liddy and I had rented at the Watergate Hotel, and as banquet time approached, McCord announced that he was not going to be present. He had other things to do, he said, by which I understood him to mean installing monitor equipment in the Listening Post at the Howard Johnson Motel across the street.

During the afternoon I had rented a motion-picture projector and a travelogue film from a camera store on L Street. This I now took down to the Continental Room and set up not far from the banquet table, facing a built-in projection screen on the wall. I checked the door leading to the corridor and again noticed the burglar alarm. So far McCord had said nothing about his plans to defeat the system, and I telephoned his Listening Post to ask him what he planned to do.

"They don't arm the system until eleven o'clock at night," he told me. "By then everyone ought to be out of the Continental Room and in the target offices."

"Suppose someone's working there past eleven o'clock?"

"Then we'll abort for the night."

"That wasn't the plan, Jim," I told him irritably. "Now our flexibility's reduced."

"The last few nights there hasn't been anyone in the target office past ten o'clock, so I'm not going to worry about it."

During the banquet we tried to relax and enjoy ourselves, lingering long over dessert and drinks and finally dismissing the waiter with a handsome tip, telling him the board meeting was about to begin. He insisted on clearing off the table, however, leaving us with the small bar and several carafes of coffee.

While the motion-picture travelogue repeated itself endlessly, we discussed the developing situation. Because of the W/T shortage we would have no use for De Diego or Pico, and the four available W/Ts were assigned as follows: one to McCord's Listening Post for use by his monitor, one for McCord himself, one for Sturgis, and the fourth for Liddy and myself in the Command Post room.

At ten o'clock the group dispersed, Villo and myself remaining in the Continental Room, hoping to leave it and proceed through the corridor before the alarm system was armed at eleven. About ten thirty a building guard opened the door and said we would have to leave. We agreed to do so, but when he left, we turned out the lights in the Continental Room and concealed ourselves in a closet. From there we could still communicate by W/T with McCord across the street, who reported that, unfortunately, lights were still burning in the target office. I translated his report for Villo, who shrugged philosophically and settled down for what was now going to be a long wait. Shortly before eleven o'clock we heard a guard lock the door—the one leading from the inner court into the Continental Room—and after half an hour or so Villo and I left our closet and he began working on the lock with his picks and tools. That door, we knew, would not be opened until midmorning, if then, but despite Villo's best efforts, the lock would not yield. By now, we assumed, the rest of the party had turned in for the night under more comfortable circumstances than ours. Every hour or so a flashlight appeared at the glass courtyard door and swept the inside of the Continental Room. I mixed myself a highball and sipped it, reflecting that the entire banquet subterfuge had been wasted, for if McCord had neutralized the corridor alarm system as promised, I felt confident the entry team would even now be in the target area completing its work.

Dawn came, and we stretched our stiff bodies waiting for six o'clock and the shutoff of the alarm system. At six Villo began moving toward the corridor exit, but I said, "Let's give it another fifteen minutes," and so at six fifteen we opened the door and strode briskly down the corridor to the nearest exit.

Villo went to his room and I to mine, where Liddy was blissfully asleep. Rousing him, I said, "Lucky we weren't caught, Gordon. Now we'll have to try the other way."

"Through the garage-level door?"

Pulling off my clothes, I got between the sheets. "Thanks to McCord," I told him. "Tell Jim to plan on a garage-level entry tonight—it's that or nothing. We can't go through that banquet routine again."

In the late afternoon I woke, drove home for a change of clothing and returned to the Watergate Hotel at nightfall. I parked my car in the hotel basement and walked from there to the office-building garage. The doors, which McCord and I had checked out before, were double and wide, suitable for furniture deliveries and removal of large trash containers. Making sure I was unobserved, I pressed the doors' release bar and went inside. Nearby was a freight elevator and beside it the entrance to the stairwell. I turned the knob and opened the door. Now, at least, it was unlocked.

I retraced my steps and went to my room in the hotel. Presently Liddy arrived, and soon McCord joined us. We would tape the spring locks, he said, and so gain access according to our alternate plan.

After McCord left, I had Barker and Martínez join us with the camera equipment. While I watched, they simulated setting up the lights and camera and photographing documents. The exercise over, I repeated to Barker my earlier instructions: "According to our information, there're a lot of file cabinets in the offices. Obviously you won't be able to photograph every document, so it's your job to go through the files until you find something with numbers on it—account books, contributor lists, that sort of thing. If you have any questions, call me here, and I'll make the decision."

Barker nodded. "What about Jim? How long will he take?"

"I don't know, but if he's finished before you are, let him leave. You're not responsible for his work and he's not responsible for yours."

After the guard change at eight o'clock and the guard's inspection of the office building, McCord taped the garage-level door permitting entry to the stairwell. He then crossed the street to the Listening Post and by walkie-talkie reported his accomplishment. In our Command Post the air was tense with expectation. A suitcase containing the photographic equipment was opened and reinspected, as was a small hatbox containing the Polaroid camera and film supply.

A little after ten o'clock McCord reported that the last light had been extinguished on the sixth floor of the target building. With that the team made ready to go.

At the garage-level entrance McCord met González, Barker, Martínez and Sturgis. Together they climbed the stairway to the sixth floor, where González began working on the door lock.

All this was reported tersely to Liddy and myself in the Command Post, and we waited for word that the lock had been defeated.

A half hour passed, then an hour. Finally Barker came on the air to report that González was unable to pick the lock. "He says he doesn't have the right tools," Barker told us disgustedly. "What do we do now?"

"Leave the building and report back here," Liddy told him and sat back shaking his head. "I don't understand it," he said. "Villo even had your cast of the lock. Why the hell couldn't he get in?"

When the team returned, I excoriated Barker and Villo for nonperformance and told Barker I wanted Villo to return to Miami in the morning, pick up whatever tools he might need and return by nightfall.

Villo shrugged resignedly.

Barker said, "I'll have my wife meet him at the airport, drive him to his shop, then back to the airport. That way we won't lose too much time."

"Good idea," Liddy said and stood up to stretch. "It's been a long night, fellows," he said, "better get some rest. We'll all meet back here again tomorrow evening."

McCord nodded.

"At least," I said, "now we know what's needed. What about the door tapes?"

"I removed them," McCord told us and left the room.

To Villo I said, "Are you sure you can't find what you need in Washington?"

He shook his head. "Not here. Everything's down there, Eduardo."

It was now Sunday morning, so I slept for a few hours, then drove to my home to spend the rest of the day with my family. My wife, conditioned by years of exposure to clandestine operations, sensed that things were not going well. However, for a year she had grown accustomed to the unorthodox work I was doing for the White House, and so she asked no questions. Besides, Dorothy was busy with plans to take David and Kevan to Europe for most of the summer.

In the late afternoon Barker telephoned to say that Villo had returned with the needed equipment, so after dining with my family, I drove back to the Watergate Hotel prepared for a final attempt upon the Democratic citadel.

Liddy joined me in the room, then McCord appeared to report that little activity had been observed in Democratic headquarters that day. The blinds had been conveniently raised, permitting observation from the Listening Post, and as matters stood, only one employee was in the sixth-floor offices. "If he follows the pattern of other Sundays," McCord remarked, "he'll leave fairly soon, so we should be able to get started early."

The walkie-talkie batteries had been recharging all day, and McCord now placed them in the walkie-talkies. Taking two of them, he left for the Listening Post to continue observing the sixth-floor target windows.

Soon Liddy and I were joined by Barker, Martínez, Sturgis and González. Villo, despite his day of travel, was in good spirits and confident that with his additional equipment he would be able to defeat the door lock.

From the Listening Post, McCord made radio contact to tell us he had taped the garage-door locks as before, and all that remained prior to entry was the departure of the final DNC employee.

Toward nine thirty the last light on the sixth floor was extinguished and McCord reported that the man had left the office building. Because it was Sunday night, I was certain that there would be no further activity in the target offices, and at eleven o'clock Liddy and I gave the word to go.

McCord and the four Miami men rendezvoused at the garage entrance and proceeded up the staircase to the sixth floor, where Villo set to work on the lock. Within fifteen minutes Barker announced: "We're in."

Liddy and I embraced each other Latin-style and settled down to monitor the progress of the operation.

Outside, Virginia Avenue was quiet. Across the street the Listening Post was dark. The tension made us thirsty, so Liddy and I drank Cokes while we waited for word from the entry team.

I had expected queries from Barker, but none came; evidently, I thought, he was having no difficulty in locating the target files. Then, shortly after midnight, came word from Barker that the team was leaving. Liddy and I exchanged glances and I shrugged. Liddy said, "I thought they'd be in there all night."

"So did I," I agreed, "but maybe they're fast workers."

By one o'clock all five men reappeared in our room and McCord announced that he had concluded his business to his satisfaction.

Collecting the walkie-talkies from Liddy and Barker, he bade us good night and departed.

Barker explained that rather than commence searching the file cabinets as instructed, he had found on Lawrence O'Brien's desk a pile of correspondence. This he and Martínez had photographed while McCord worked elsewhere in the office suite. Martínez opened the Minolta camera, extracted a 35mm cassette from it and handed it to me. From his pocket he took another. "We shot one roll and part of another, Eduardo."

I looked at Barker. "What was the big rush to get out?"

Barker shrugged. "Jim—I guess he didn't want to hang around."

I was disappointed over what I felt to be their premature departure, for photography had been the priority mission, and the team had managed to expose fewer than two cassettes when I had expected upward of a hundred frames.

Barker said, "Anything else?"

Liddy shook his head. "That's it, boys," he said and slapped Barker on the back. "Macho, this has been a good job." Then he shook Villo's hand. "Good man," he said, and Villo smiled.

"Jus' took the right tools, George. Me, that's all I need."

Barker returned the contingency money to Liddy, who reimbursed Barker for the cost of the men's plane tickets and Villo's extra flight. Barker estimated their combined hotel bill and fair compensation for time lost by each man from his job. Liddy added that sum to what he had already given Barker and when they were about to leave, Frank Sturgis said, "Without a walkie-talkie I felt real naked out there, George."

Liddy laughed. "At least you didn't need one," he said and showed them to the door.

When we were alone, Liddy said, "I'll have McCord develop these films. He says he's got a man who can do it."

But a week later Liddy came to my Mullen office to tell me that McCord's "man" was out of town and unable to process the two rolls of film. "Think Barker can handle this too?"

"I think so," I said, telephoned Barker in Miami and said I would be coming down on the tenth and would bring some film for development. In the meantime, I asked him to make sure the film could be processed promptly, as I intended to stay in Miami only one day.

I turned to Liddy, who said, "Think your phone's safe?"

"Funny you should ask." I pointed to a fiber ceiling panel above my desk. "I found that on the floor the other morning when I came in, and the building maintenance man had to replace it. Even before that I noted flakes of paint from the ceiling on the carpet."

Liddy tensed. "Maybe I should have McCord sweep the place."

"Might not be a bad idea. But when I asked the maintenance man about the panel, he said there was some rewiring going on because of office refurbishing next door." I gestured toward the far wall. "Anyway, I have this radio here and we ought to turn it on when we talk."

Liddy grimaced. He seemed reluctant to talk. I said, "What's on your mind, Gordon?"

He shook his head. "I hate to say it, but I think McCord screwed up."

"How?"

"I don't know. Put a bug in the wrong place or tapped the wrong line. All I know is, my principals [Mitchell, Dean and Magruder] are going bananas, and I've got to straighten it out with McCord. I'm praying there's something worthwhile on these films. With Magruder on my ass all the time I don't need another flap right now."

"Are you going to Miami with me?"

"No. I've got work up here, but I'll want to know what progress Macho's been making in organizing his informants along the beach hotels. Oh, something else: They want to know if Barker can get a bunch of hippies to carry McGovern signs around the front of the Doral Hotel. The idea is to have them splash around in the pool there—maybe tear off their clothes—anything likely to attract the television cameras and outrage the country. Think he can do that?"

"That's a tough one, Gordon. The hippies, obviously, would be for McGovern. How can we get them to work against their idol?"

"Christ, I don't know." Liddy shook his head. "Sometimes I think these guys figure we can do miracles. But ask Macho, will you? He's always come through before."

"Sure, I'll ask him. Have they made up their minds about the houseboat?"

Liddy shook his head. "Scratch it. They say it's too expensive. Anyway, it's probably too late now to rent it."

On an earlier trip to Miami, Liddy and I, with Barker's help, had located a houseboat in the river in front of the Fontainebleau Hotel. It was to be used by McCord as a Listening Post for bugs he planned to plant in the rooms that would be Democratic National headquarters during the convention. The houseboat rent would be about $1,000 a month, with a minimum rental of three months. After Liddy had reported this to Mitchell, Dean and Magruder and we were again in Miami, Liddy told me that one of his principals —presumably Magruder—had suggested using the houseboat as a place of assignation. "The idea," Liddy explained, "is to line up some cool chicks who'll work for us and spot top-level political aides around the bars, drag them down to the houseboat and, action, camera, you're in living color."

I grunted. "Sounds like the Golden Greek all over again. Somebody's fascinated with the idea of compromise. Why can't we just run a straightforward intelligence operation?"

"Why is it there are so many more horses' asses than there are horses? They lay something like that on me, never stopping to wonder how we could locate the girls, how we could persuade them to work for us, what motivation we could give them, how to identify the target Democrats, and—grab this—how do we all of a sudden install silent cameras and conceal them with some guy to operate the cameras without remodeling the houseboat from deck to ceiling?" He shook his head disgustedly.

"They should have thought of those things months ago," I said. "If we could have gotten Gemstone off the ground around the first of the year instead of in March, we might have a prayer of being able to handle side jobs in addition to the main ones. And whose bright idea was it to bug Convention Hall? Every network plus PBS will be covering everything that takes place in there from morning till night. Nobody needs to bug the place. Anybody who wants to see and hear what's going on can sit in an easy chair and turn on the tube."

"At least I talked them out of that one," Liddy remarked, "and before we'd rented that safehouse near Convention Hall. Saved a few dollars, anyway."

On the morning of June 10 I flew to Miami and was met at the airport by Barker and Martinez. As it was midday, we drove to a restaurant and I ordered lunch, then gave the two rolls of film to

Barker with instructions to have them developed immediately and large prints made of each negative. Cost was no object, I assured him, and Barker said he understood. Before my lunch was finished, Barker returned and said we could expect the developed film by late afternoon. That suited my schedule, for I was returning to Washington on an evening plane.

From the restaurant Barker drove us to his office, where I asked him if there was any possibility he might be able to recruit a group of hippies to cause confusion outside the Doral Hotel.

"I know a realtor in Coconut Grove who rents pads to hippies," Barker told me.

"Coconut Grove?"

"Yes, Eduardo. Since the time when you lived there twelve years ago in our Bay of Pigs safehouse, the place has changed. You wouldn't recognize Coconut Grove now. It's hippie haven. About how many hippies does George want?"

"To make any sort of an impression I think we'll need at least a dozen. Twenty would be better, if you can get them."

Martínez said, "A contact on the Miami police force tells me the police are going to seal off the causeways connecting Miami Beach with the mainland to prevent the kind of trouble that took place in Chicago four years ago."

"That means our hippies would have to be on the beach before the bridges are raised," I remarked, and Barker nodded agreement.

From local newspaper clippings Barker had put together the hotel location of the delegations of the principal Democratic contenders. I scanned it and said, "I think we can forget everyone but McGovern. That means coverage only for the Fontainebleau and the Doral hotels."

"What if my boys pick up information on some of the other candidates?"

"Pass it along to me," I told him. "George may be able to use it."

Martínez drove me to the airport, where I was joined by Barker, who handed me a thick envelope.

"Here they are," he said, beaming. "Just like you wanted."

I opened the envelope, noting that it bore the address of a commercial film developer. This surprised me, but I assumed that the man who did the actual developing was a contact of Barker's and would not talk about the negatives. The blown-up prints showed papers and letters flattened down for photography by hands wearing surgical gloves. This detail would lend a dramatic touch that, as Liddy remarked, seemed to entrance his principals.

I reimbursed Barker for the film processing and flew back to Washington, delivering the package to Liddy the next morning.

On the afternoon of June 14 Liddy called my office and told me he was coming over. When we were alone, my radio playing, Liddy said, "We've got to go into DNC headquarters again, Howard."

"Why, for God's sake? Wasn't the photography sufficient?"

Liddy shook his head. "Oh, they liked the photos, and they want more. But McCord's screwed up somehow. Evidently he bugged the wrong telephone line. He was supposed to tap O'Brien's."

"Isn't it a little late for that now?" I asked. "According to the papers—and from what McCord says—O'Brien's already in Miami. Why tap the man's phone when he's left the office?"

"I don't know," Liddy said resignedly, "but those are my orders. And they want a lot more photographs. Have Macho buy another camera and bring up a lot of film. They want everything in those file cabinets photographed."

"How soon are we supposed to do all this?"

"As soon as possible."

"I'm against it, Gordon," I said. "My men got McCord in and out of the target premises, and if he fouled up his part of the operation, I don't think we should be asked to go in again."

Liddy absorbed what I had been saying. Thoughtfully he said, "Makes sense to me. Besides, Jim tells me the Democrats have even started moving out their files."

"Sure. They'll be sending them down to the Fontainebleau. If Mitchell, Dean and Magruder want another crack at them, the Fontainebleau's the place. Not here." I studied Liddy's face. "Gordon, from the start of this Watergate operation, it's been McCord who's fouled things up. His equipment doesn't arrive when it's promised. My team gets him into the premises and gives him all the time in the world to do whatever he was supposed to do. Even then he seems to somehow have managed to tap the wrong phone."

"It's worse than that," Liddy told me. "He put a bug in an office and it's not transmitting properly. Or if it is, the building's too well shielded and they can't pick it up across the street."

"Meaning McCord has to repeat the work he's already done."

"That's about it." Liddy shook his head again. "I agree with you. We shouldn't be asked for a repeat on this, but I'm under pressure. I'll argue against, but I'm not hopeful."

"Well, do what you can. Be a strong advocate, Gordon. Doing an entry operation in Washington is like working in a fishbowl. I'd be a hell of a lot happier if we could do the repeat—*if* we do a repeat—in Miami Beach. There, at least, we'll have more going for us, and with all the preconvention confusion operating conditions should be a hell of a lot better."

"Okay. I'll get back to you."

Later that day Liddy got back to me. His arguments had been unavailing, he told me, and the order had been confirmed for a second Watergate entry.

I went over the same arguments with Liddy and added some new ones.

"Will McCord have enough walkie-talkies—the minimum six?"

"He says he will."

"These are my men, Gordon, and I'm the one who's responsible for them. I don't have my heart in this operation, and you're putting me in the position of ordering them into something I don't believe in."

"The Big Man [Mitchell] says he wants the operation."

"What about McCord?"

"Jim doesn't like it either. He's mad about having to repeat his work; but damn it, if he'd done his work right the first time, we wouldn't have to do it a second."

I hesitated, weighing whether I should tell Liddy I refused to mount another operation. He sensed my quandary and said, "Look, we're soldiers in this thing, Howard. If I've got a future, it's in government, and when the Big Man tells me to do something, either I do it for him or he gets someone else who can."

"Like who?" I asked sardonically.

"Caulfield, maybe."

"Or the Golden Greek?"

We allowed ourselves some laughter.

"All right," I said finally, "I'll put Bernie and the others on a standby basis, but we're not going to move unless McCord has six walkie-talkies. Understood?"

I left the building with Liddy and entered the Executive Office Building, where I went to Room 16. I dialed Barker's office telephone and asked if he could reassemble the entry team and come to Washington on Friday the sixteenth.

"I can try, Eduardo, but what's up?"

"Apparently Jim's gear isn't working and he's got to redo his work. Besides, they want a lot more photography. Pick up a Minolta that's a duplicate of the one you used and a bagful of film. The idea is to photograph everything in the files."

"*Everything?*"

"Those are the orders."

"According to the Miami papers, O'Brien's moving down here and so's Democratic headquarters. What will be left to work on?"

"I don't know, Bernie, I'm just telling you what George told me. If I don't sound enthusiastic, it's because I'm not. In any case, phone the Watergate Hotel and get a couple of rooms, will you?

"For how many?"

"For the four of you: yourself, Martínez, Villo and Sturgis. We did without the other two guys the last time; we won't need them now. Besides, I'm not sure another two walkie-talkies will be available."

"Okay, Eduardo," Barker said with his customary responsiveness. "I'll get in touch with the boys, get the hotel rooms and call you back. Not much notice, is it?"

"No, but it isn't as if we haven't been there before. Thanks a lot, Bernie. I'll be waiting for your call."

Overnight I again debated with myself the advisability of the second operation. To me it seemed to have no sound basis. O'Brien was in Miami, and for all we knew, the very files we were supposed to photograph were already on their way.

When I saw Liddy that morning, I repeated my opposition to the entry, but Gordon was even more insistent. I gathered that for him the mission was an either/or proposition.

"Gordon," I said, "I could have told you Bernie couldn't round up the team, but that wouldn't be true. The boys will be flying in on Friday the sixteenth. This is one of those things that have to be argued on their merits, not on the basis of passion, enthusiasm or preconceived notions. I can understand your people wanting more photography, more file material—after all, that's what we went in for originally—but to mount another operation just so McCord can replace some electronic bugs doesn't make sense to me. Barker confirms that O'Brien's in Miami. Why in hell should we tap the phone in his Washington office? If O'Brien has already taken up offices in the Fontainebleau, chances are his files are with him. What's the rationale? As a friend, colleague and fellow professional, I'm asking you to go back to Mitchell, Dean and Magruder and reargue the case. If you want to get off the hook, tell them you're having problems with me. I've never dealt with them, so I'm an unknown quantity. You can put it that I'm jumpy or truculent or however you want to describe my resistance."

For a time there was silence between us. Finally Liddy said, "Okay, I'll try again, but I hate to do it. They look to me to get things done, not argue against them. Otherwise I wouldn't have been given this job. Some clown like Caulfield would have it or, God forbid, the Golden Greek. Call it professional pride on my part, but they didn't put me in charge of Gemstone to give them trouble."

"As I told you: As far as they're concerned, let me be the troublemaker. I went into the White House only because Colson asked me to; after the election I certainly don't intend to stay on. Once I get rid of all this, I want to start working on some of these deals Macho and I have had pending for damn near a year. I couldn't care less about working in the White House—or at Mullen, for that matter."

"Your position's different from mine, Howard. In a way you've got it made, but I'm on my way up. Suddenly I'm fighting the guys who can make or break me in the next administration." He shook his head unhappily. "Okay, I'll give it one final try. But—the boys are coming, aren't they?"

"I said I'd have them here and they'll be here. You went back three times before you got Gemstone approved," I reminded him. "If anything, that justifies a third try on this."

But on the fifteenth Liddy told me that his final try had only produced a blast of criticism. "So it's Go," he told me. "And while the boys are here, we might as well have another try at the McGovern offices."

"When?"

"Well, if the boys can get into DNC headquarters tomorrow night, we can do McGovern on Saturday. Or Sunday, for that matter."

"I suppose so," I said wearily. "I'm meeting Gregory tomorrow, so I'll alert him for weekend duty."

Friday, midday, I met Thomas Gregory in the lobby of the Roger Smith Hotel by prearrangement. In the park outside waited James McCord, who was to discuss Gregory's part in the McGovern operation. But as we left the hotel together, Gregory said to me, "You didn't get my note?"

"What note?"

"I gave Bob Bennett a note for you. He was going to give it to you this morning."

We were approaching McCord, who rose from his park bench to meet us. I said, "What was in the note, Tom?"

Gregory licked his lips. "I'm resigning," he told me. "This is getting too deep for me."

"I've sort of sensed it," I told him. "Okay. I don't want any unwilling workers."

McCord put out his hand to Gregory, who shook it perfunctorily.

"Jim," I said, "Tom's copping out," then turned to Gregory. "Did you bother to write up a report of your week's activities?"

With a shrug he produced a folded slip of paper from his shirt pocket and handed it to me.

"I'll pay you for the balance of the month," I told him, "and your fare back to Utah—or wherever you're going to."

At that point I couldn't remember whether Gregory hailed from Michigan, Utah or New Jersey. In one of those places he had a girl with whom he was contemplating matrimony. "I'll give Bennett your money in an envelope. If you have time, send me back a receipt by the same channel."

Gregory nodded. He seemed abashed.

In an attempt to smooth over a deteriorating situation, McCord remarked that he had enjoyed working with Gregory, but was sorry things were not to be carried to their logical conclusion.

Limply, Gregory returned McCord's handshake and shuffled away. As we watched him head toward a bus stop, I said, "I hate to pay the little son of a bitch anything, Jim. But if there's one thing I've learned from years of agent handling, it's 'leave them smiling.' "

"Couldn't agree more," McCord said philosophically, and we sat on the park bench and discussed how we would alter the McGovern entry plan to compensate for Gregory's loss. We agreed, finally, on a pretext delivery as previously decided, with heavy conning of the Burns guard.

"Anyway," I said, "McGovern and his whole staff will be down in Miami within a short time, so I don't think we ought to bust our guts to bug him up here."

McCord nodded. "We might be better off without Gregory," he remarked. "The last time I was in the headquarters with him I noticed he was sweating. I don't think he was cut out to be an agent."

We turned to final plans for the evening entry. The other two walkie-talkies had arrived, McCord told me, and I said I was expecting word of the team's arrival from Miami. "Bernie will call me as soon as he's in the hotel to let me know what rooms they've been assigned."

"Good. I'll be at the L/P. You can call me there and let me know." He grimaced. "I kind of wish we didn't have to do this again."

"I've been arguing against it for days," I told him, "but Liddy's boss is adamant."

"That's the impression I get. See you later tonight." Rising, McCord walked away and I returned to my Mullen & Company office.

In midafternoon Barker telephoned to say the team was lodged in rooms 214 and 314 and was awaiting my further orders. I suggested they try to rest, for I anticipated a long night's work. "Did you get the extra Minolta?" I asked.

"We've got it and a lot of film too," Barker told me. "Anything else, Eduardo?"

"Not for now. See you later."

"Any idea what time?"

"Well, after dinner—say between nine and ten o'clock."

As yet neither Barker nor the other members of his team knew they would be asked to enter McGovern headquarters the following night, and I wanted to delay informing them as long as possible.

I left my Mullen & Company office at the usual time, drove through sluggish traffic to my home in suburban Potomac. By now

Dorothy, Kevan and David had left for Europe, so that night I dined with my other son and daughter, St. John and Lisa.

Although we had no reason to suspect it at the time, it was a last supper for our family. Henceforth, our lives were to be uprooted and torn apart as though by unending hurricanes. And when I kissed my children good night, I told them I would be with Mr. Liddy that evening and would see them on Saturday morning.

17 WATERGATE II *ET SEQUITUR*

IT was well after dark when I drove my Pontiac Firebird to the Watergate Hotel and into the underground garage. I parked, left the car and reconnoitered the underground area, eventually passing the garage-level doors that had admitted the team on the prior entry.

From there I went to Room 214 and found Barker and Martínez had just returned from dinner. After Liddy joined us, Barker summoned González and Sturgis from their room directly above. We checked over the photographic equipment, and Barker and Martínez demonstrated their technique for using two Minolta cameras with maximum efficiency. While one man photographed documents, the other unloaded, then reloaded the spare camera, substituting it when the roll in the first Minolta was exhausted. There were spare bulbs for the high-intensity lights and, of course, the Polaroid camera with its film pack.

After a while McCord arrived with four walkie-talkies, giving one to Barker and the other to Liddy. He had another pair of walkie-talkies, but their batteries were not yet charged; in any case, there were no "guards" to use them.

It was then about ten o'clock and McCord said there were still lights in the target offices, adding that he had just taped open the locks on the garage entrance doors.

Before McCord returned to the Listening Post, I gave him a set of alias documentation papers that once was prepared for me by the

239

Central Intelligence Agency and another set to Barker. Liddy turned his George Leonard papers over to another member of the team. And after McCord left, Liddy gave Barker money to be used as during the prior entry for emergency purposes.*

Now there was nothing to do but wait. Sturgis went out and brought back bottles of Coca-Cola. From the Listening Post McCord reported by radio that there seemed to be only one worker in the target offices.

Liddy and I discussed the defection of Thomas Gregory in deprecatory terms. After a while Liddy and I left the room and crossed the street to the Howard Johnson Motel. From the sidewalk we could look back and up at Democratic National headquarters and saw that a portion was still lighted. We went into the restaurant and had a light snack, after which I drove my car out of the parking garage and positioned it in front of the Watergate Hotel. Returning to the room, I rode the elevator with French film actor Alain Delon, who was, ironically, in Washington for the filming of *Scorpio*, a story involving a fictitious CIA agent.

Finally McCord reported that the last sixth-floor light had gone out, and he would be coming over to join us. The lassitude that had prevailed in our room was shattered. We were tense now, alert and expectant. It was a longer wait for McCord than we had anticipated, and when he came into the room, he said that he had checked the garage entrance doors and found his tapes torn off. He had retaped the locks, and now the team could proceed with the operation.

"Let's junk it," I said, meaning scratch the operation for the night.

"I don't think the building guard took off the tapes," McCord objected. "There was a big stack of mailbags nearby; I think when they were taken out, the mailman took the tapes off the doors."

Liddy looked at me, and I shook my head. "Scratch it," I repeated, but Liddy began talking with McCord. I walked away from them, mentally and physically separating myself from the decision Liddy was in the process of making. I did not hear or even try to listen to the exchanges between Liddy and McCord, but I saw the

*For some reason Barker did not take all the money with him when he led the team into the Democratic National headquarters offices that night. Instead, he left a portion of it in his room. These sequentially numbered one-hundred-dollar bills were traced by the FBI to Barker's bank in Miami and the check from which the bills were the proceeds traced into Mexico and eventually to an illegal political contribution to the Finance Committee to Re-elect the President.

Miami men get up and head for the door. Liddy came over to me and said, "McCord wants to go, Howard. It's his show, so I let him."

"We're doing this because McCord did a lousy job the first time," I reminded Liddy. "It may be 'his show,' but there are four others with him who are my responsibility."

Barker came over and almost wordlessly we shook hands. I watched them file out of the room, and when the last man left, Liddy locked the door.

From McCord's black attaché case he took out a car radio antenna, extended it and jacked it into the walkie-talkie that was our sole means of communicating with the team and with the Listening Post across the street. A long wire led from the walkie-talkie to the antenna, which Liddy set up outside on the balcony to enhance radio reception. Then he turned on the television set and sat down in an easy chair. I drank a glass of Coke and began going through the evening paper. It was now after midnight, and according to McCord's casing information, the office building guard made his rounds at midnight. I hoped the team would be inside the office building before the guard left his post at the main entrance. It never occurred to me or to any other member of the team, for that matter, that the guard would check the garage-level doors through which the team had entered.

Time passed. Together Liddy and I watched an ancient motion picture on the television set. After a while Liddy said, "They ought to be inside by now. Wonder why Macho doesn't contact us."

"He probably figures McCord will let us know when they've made the entry."*

After that conversational sally we resumed watching the movie when, suddenly, breathily through the walkie-talkie came the urgent query: *"Any of your guys wearing hippie clothes?"*

Gordon Liddy sat bolt upright, grabbed the W/T and barked, "One to Three. Repeat."

"Any of your guys wearing hippie clothes?"

I exchanged glances with Liddy. He said, "One to Three, negative. Our guys are in business suits. Why? Over."

"Three here," came the voice of James McCord's monitor from

---

*Months later Martínez told me that just before they entered the target area, he asked McCord if Jim had removed the garage-level tapes, and McCord assured him that he had. That McCord failed to do so was noticed by the building guard, who summoned the police.

the balconied Listening Post in the Howard Johnson Motel across Virginia Avenue. "There's four, maybe five guys running around the sixth floor. Lights are going on. One's wearing a cowboy hat, another a sweat shirt. Oh, oh, they've got guns. Looks like trouble."

"Keep reporting," Liddy told him and stood up. "One to Two," he snapped, calling the entry team in Democratic National Committee headquarters. "Two, come in. There are lights on your floor. Any trouble?"

From the W/T only the low rushing sound of the carrier current. "One to Two," Liddy repeated, voice louder now. "Come in. This is an order. Repeat: *Come in!*"

My throat and mouth were dry, my stomach hard. By now I realized the entry team was in trouble. I looked around our Command Post—Room 214 in the Watergate Hotel—automatically cataloguing what we would have to take with us. The monitor again: "I can see our guys now, hands in the air. Must be cops with them."

Galvanized, Liddy gripped the W/T in one hand. Then a disembodied voice spoke: *"They've got us."* The entry team had responded at last.

Stepping onto the balcony, I looked up at the rear windows of DNC headquarters in the adjacent office building. Lights were on but no one was in sight. The two upper floors were also lighted. I returned to Liddy, who was receiving a moment-by-moment description from the monitor across the street: ". . . filing out with them now, guns drawn. Police wagon pulling up at the entrance below, also some marked police cars. . . ."

"Keep talking," Liddy told him as I began opening suitcases. Together we began throwing in operational litter, forcing McCord's surplus electronic gear into his black attaché case.

To Liddy I said, "Let's go; the police will be here any minute."
"Why?"

"Barker has our room key."

From the W/T the monitor's voice: "What should I do?"

Liddy grunted. I picked up the W/T and pressed the transmit button. "Keep your lights out and stay out of sight. I'll come over as soon as I can. We're signing off."

I retrieved the long automobile antenna from the balcony, telescoped it and tossed it on the bed, where Liddy was packing the most incriminating items into a handbag. "That's most of it," he said, "except for that damn antenna. Leave it here?"

"Hell no." I thrust it down inside my trouser leg and turned off the lights. "Let's go."

Down the elevator, hearts pounding, we walked past the drowsing desk clerk. Then my leg antenna began to slide onto the floor. Hitching it back under my belt, I kept on going without looking back.

We reached the street, half a block from an assemblage of police cars, flashers playing eerily through the darkness. We got inside my Firebird, which I had parked at the entrance—just in case. . . .

As I started the engine, Liddy said, "My jeep's up the street."

"I'll take you there."

He gestured at the dark Listening Post windows across the street. "What about *him?*"

"I'll come back. Go home and get yourself an alibi."

Silently we drove four blocks toward the city, and Liddy got out. "Got the emergency money?"

"I'm going to get it now."

"Okay." He swallowed. "Good night, Howard. I'll be in touch tomorrow." We shook hands and he walked toward his green jeep. I made a U-turn and parked two blocks from the motel. Within pistol range of the police cars, I reflected.

From the motel lobby I took the elevator to the seventh floor and knocked on the L/P door. It opened a crack and I saw a man with a crew cut indistinctly against the dark background. "Are you—?" he asked, but I handed him the W/T and went inside, locking the door behind me. Offering me binoculars, he said, "Hey, take a look; the cops are leading them out."

"Listen," I said, "it's all over. Pack up and get going."

He looked around uncertainly. "Lotta heavy gear here. What do I do with it?"

"Load the goddamn van and shove off."

"Where should I go—McCord's house?"

I stared at him incredulously. "That's the *last* place to go. I don't care if you drive the van into the river; just get the stuff out of here. Understood?" Turning, I strode toward the door.

Plaintively he called, "What's going to happen?"

"I don't know—but you'll be contacted." From the room I took the elevator to the lobby and walked casually to the sidewalk. On the far side of the street police were loading the last of the five-man entry team into a white paddy wagon. It seemed so damned final, I thought as I walked back to my car.

From there I drove to the White House annex—the Old Executive Office Building, in bygone years the War Department and later the Department of State.

Carrying three heavy attaché cases, I entered the Pennsylvania Avenue door, showed my blue-and-white White House pass to the uniformed guards and took the elevator to the third floor. I unlocked the door of 338 and went in. I opened my two-drawer safe, took out my operational notebook, found a telephone number and dialed it. After several rings the call was answered and I heard the sleepy voice of Douglas Caddy. "Yes?"

"Doug? This is Howard. I hate to wake you up, but I've got a tough situation and I need to talk to you. Can I come over?"

"Sure. I'll tell the desk clerk you're expected."

"I'll be there in about twenty minutes," I told him and hung up.

From the safe I took a small money box and removed the $10,000 Liddy had given me for emergency use. I put $1,500 in my wallet and the remaining $8,500 in my coat pocket. The black attaché case containing McCord's electronic equipment I placed in a safe drawer that held my operational notebooks. Then I closed and locked the safe, turning the dial several times. The other two cases I left beside the safe, turned out the light and left my office, locking the door.

From the Executive Office Building I crossed the street and entered 1700 Pennsylvania Avenue, the building that housed Mullen & Company. A night guard was sitting at a desk in the lobby and I signed in, using the name Bob Wait. Bob had succeeded Doug Caddy as the General Foods representative in Washington, and I knew that he was away from Washington this particular weekend. I chose his name because it was listed among the building tenants and because I did not want any lasting record of my own movements that night. Moreover, with Wait provably out of Washington that night, there could be no blowback affecting him.

From my office I dialed Barker's home in Miami and spoke with his wife, Clara.

"Clarita," I said, "things have gone wrong and Macho's been arrested."

I heard a muffled shriek. Then, "Oh, my *God!*"

"He's got bail money with him," I told her, "so maybe he'll be able to get out before dawn. I don't know how these things work, but I think he ought to have an attorney. I've already called one and I want you to call him too."

I gave her Caddy's name and telephone number and asked that she phone Doug and retain him for her husband.

"Where shall I call him from? Here?"

"No. Go to a pay telephone and do it."

Stricken though she was, Clara Barker focused on what had to be done. "All right," she said decisively. "I'll do it, Eduardo. My God, what happened? What was he *doing* up there?"

"I haven't got time for questions," I told her. "Just call Caddy. That's all you or anybody can do." I hung up and stood for a moment looking around my office for what was to be the last time for many weeks. Then I turned out the light and left the room, went down the elevator and signed out at the guard desk.

From there I drove to Caddy's apartment and told the reception clerk I was expected. He called Caddy on the intercom and directed me to the elevator. Caddy was awake and water was boiling for instant coffee.

"Any milk?" I asked. "My ulcer's getting active."

Caddy shook his head. "Sorry, Howard. No milk."

"Then I'll take coffee." I sat down. "There was an operation tonight, Doug, and five men were arrested. You know one of them, Bernie Barker."

"I remember him," Caddy said. "What do you mean 'operation'?"

I sat back in my chair feeling a great weight pressing down on my shoulders. "It was at Democratic National headquarters in the Watergate," I told him. "I don't know what went wrong, but the long and the short of it is the police came and the men were hauled away. There're five of them, Doug, and they need legal representation." From my pocket I took the $8,500 emergency money and handed it to him. "Could you go down to police headquarters or wherever they take men after they're arrested and see if you can bail them out?"

Caddy looked uncertainly at the money, then at me. "I'm not a criminal lawyer, Howard. You know that. I don't have the faintest idea where police take arrested men."

"Could you call and find out?"

"I guess so. Maybe one of my law firm's partners would know."

"Bernie Barker's wife will probably call you and retain you officially to represent her husband and the other men," I told him.

Caddy looked at his wristwatch, then went to another room to phone. I stood up and paced the floor, looked through the windows at the dark street and wondered what was happening to the entry team.

Caddy came back to the room. Then the telephone rang and he disappeared to answer it. I heard him conclude one conversation, then dial another telephone number. He talked awhile longer, and I made myself a cup of instant coffee and began drinking it.

Caddy approached me and said, "I talked to two of the partners; the other one's out of town. One of the partners will try to get hold of a guy named Rafferty. Joe Rafferty. I don't know him, myself, but he's a criminal lawyer, and if they can reach him, he'll call me." He shook his head. "I'll tell you one thing, Howard, my partners certainly don't like my being involved in this thing."

"I'm sorry, Doug," I said sincerely. "I guess you're the only Republican lawyer I know."

He laughed. "I don't know many myself," he said, and then the telephone rang.

When he returned, Caddy said, "That was Rafferty. He says the men are probably at the D.C. Jail."

"Maybe they're still at the precinct house or the station house or wherever police take prisoners to be booked. Funny thing is, Doug, the cops who arrested them were in hippie clothes—mod clothes, I guess you'd call it."

"No kidding?"

"I saw them myself."

"Where were you when all this was going on?"

"In another building. Doug, this is no time for details. I want those men bailed out and fast. Is Rafferty going to go down to the jail, telephone around or come here?"

"I guess he's going to make some phone calls, then come here.

Anyway, he'll call back when he has some information." He looked at the money again.

"Take it along with you," I told him.

"Okay. Any idea what the charges will be?"

"Whatever they are, they can't be very heavy—maybe something like being on premises without permission, trespassing. The door lock was picked, so there shouldn't be anything like breaking and entering or burglary. They weren't going to steal anything, just photograph some documents. One other thing: Bernie has some false documents with him. They'll show him to be either Edward Hamilton or Edward Warren, I don't know which. Another man —who works for CREP—should show up as George Leonard."

Caddy shook his head. "I don't get this false-document business, Howard. Where did they get them?"

"In CIA," I told him, "information is made available on a need-to-know basis. There are things you don't need to know to bail them out. I want them out of jail and out of town before dawn."

The telephone rang and Caddy answered it. I finished my coffee, stared again at the street and saw a solitary policeman at the far end of the block. For a fleeting moment it occurred to me that I might have been followed to the apartment and there was a stakeout waiting for me to leave. Then I dismissed the thought as ridiculous. I was overreacting to a situation that I felt sure could be contained. All the attorney had to do was to post bond for the five men, after which they would disappear. I had never heard of a criminal-conspiracy law, and as for the electronic part of the operation, I knew that electronic surveillance was conducted under the authority of the Attorney General, and Attorney General John Mitchell had approved Gemstone.

By now, I thought, Liddy had informed at least one of his principals and if—as seemed unlikely—Rafferty's representations were insufficient, the full weight of the White House could be brought to bear to free the five men. Richard Kleindienst was the Attorney General, but as Mitchell's heir and successor, he should be responsive to John Mitchell's guidance. So perhaps Kleindienst could call Police Chief Jerry Wilson and arrange the men's release.

I was not to learn until later that almost without exception every senior White House official was out of Washington that weekend and in or near San Clemente, California. Only John Dean was in Washington, but had I known that, I would have felt reassured. As one of Liddy's original principals, Dean would certainly know what had to be done, and as the President's counsel, he should be able to arrange things without getting Kleindienst involved.

Finally Caddy returned and said, "Rafferty thinks this may take a little time, Howard, so I'm going to get dressed and stand by to meet him. You can stay here if you want."

I shook my head. "No, I'd better go home." Thinking of Liddy, I said, "There may be some calls for me tonight, and home is the only place I could be reached."

We shook hands and I thanked Caddy for his help.

I never saw him again.

When I left the apartment building, I walked out to the parking lot in a semidaze. I felt as though I had been a week without sleep, though I recognized my fatigue came from sustained tension. I drove home confident that sometime before noon Liddy would phone me to say that the men had been released and were on their way to Miami without their true names having been discovered.

Dawn was graying the sky when I reached home and parked my Firebird outside, and I remember the sensation of moving against a strong current of water as I walked from the drive into my house. Leadenly I made my way to my bedroom, swallowed a sleeping pill and lay down. Through the curtains I could see the sky lightening outside. Somewhere in the nearby woods a bird began to sing. I took the sound as a good omen, for I was fully confident that the attorneys would be able to obtain release of the arrested men. I wondered what had gone wrong in the target offices, and my mind went back to McCord's finding his first tapes taken from the garage doors. I reasoned that in view of what had ensued, a guard rather than a mailman had removed McCord's tapes, then called the police. I was puzzled, however, by the casual dress of the officers who had made the arrests. If a conventional police car had arrived in front of the Watergate office building with its roof light flashing, surely McCord's monitor would have been able to warn the team in time to let them flee the building. But no marked police cars had arrived until later when my five associates were being led from the Watergate.

The sleeping pill began taking effect, and I turned over hoping my questions could be answered tomorrow by Liddy or perhaps by McCord after he was freed. For now, there was nothing to do but sleep.

The maid woke me. Groggily I opened my eyes and looked around, then at the dresser clock. The time was about eleven.

"I'm sorry, Mr. Hunt, but there's someone on the telephone who says he must talk with you."

I nodded, said, "Thanks," and got up. That would be Liddy, I told myself as I went to the kitchen telephone. I picked up the receiver and said, "Yes?"

"Mr. Hunt?" The voice was unfamiliar to me.

"Yes."

"Mr. Hunt, this is Bob Woodward from the Washington *Post*. Some men have been arrested, and one of them had your name in his notebook. His name is Barker. Is he a friend of yours?"

"Oh, my God," I said unthinkingly, then hung up. Moments later the telephone rang and it was Woodward again. "Mr. Hunt, is Barker a friend of yours?"

"Sorry, I have no comment," I said and hung up once more.

To the maid I said, "That was a reporter. I don't want to talk to him or any others. The only calls I'll take will be from Mr. Caddy or Mr. Liddy."

As I walked back to the bedroom, I decided I might as well get dressed and face the day. As the effects of the sleeping pill wore off, my mind began to race, and I wondered how much more the reporter had learned. Barker should have left his address book in Miami, I reflected, but now it was too late for that. Far too late. I wondered what Liddy had been doing since our parting nine hours ago. Where was he now?

Dressed, I telephoned Caddy's apartment, but there was no answer. I phoned Liddy's home, but his wife told me he had gone out. After a while the maid told me Woodward had called again. I barely tasted breakfast, feeling as though I were in the center of a vise whose jaws were beginning slowly but inexorably to close. On the other hand, I reasoned, despite what the reporter had told me, the men still might have been freed. Any charges against them would have to be minor, and there would be no reason to deny them bail. None of our operational planning had even considered the possibility that a building guard might call the police. Our assumption had been that if alerted, he would confront the intruders himself and could be bought off. That was why Liddy had given Barker the hundred-dollar bills. Moreover, McCord was an employee of John Mitchell's, and the former Attorney General would move quickly to secure his release and with it the release of the other men.

After a while the telephone rang, and it was Gordon Liddy, voice somber. "The boys are still in jail," he told me. "There are reporters all over the place, and I've just seen the noon paper. It's got Bernie's name in it."

"I'm not surprised," I told him. "A reporter from the *Post* named Woodward told me that a little earlier."

"*He did?*"

"My name was in Barker's address book, his telephone book. I don't know whether they found it on him or in the room. Do you?"

"No. But it doesn't make any difference. Did Caddy come through?"

"Well, he got a lawyer named Rafferty to go down to the jail. I thought by now they'd have been able to get the men out. Where are you calling from?"

"My office. All hell's breaking loose around here. I'm shredding everything I've got. What did you do with the stuff you took from the room?"

"Stashed in my office at the White House. Colson once remarked it was the safest place in town, so let's hope it is."

"Listen, I'm pretty busy right now, but I'll get back in touch later. Trouble is, everybody's out of town, on the West Coast. Just when we need them, too."

"They can't leave the guys in jail, can they?"

"No. It's a question of reaching the right people and getting something done. So far I haven't had any luck, though."

"All right. Call me when you've any news, will you?"

"I will," Liddy promised and hung up.

Toward midafternoon I heard the doorbell ring, and the maid came to my study to tell me that two government men were at the door.

"What kind of government men?" I asked, hoping they would be from the White House.

"They say they're from the FBI."

"Did you tell them I was here?"

"Yes."

I went to the door and saw two youngish men. One of them said, "Mr. Hunt?"

I nodded.

Both men produced FBI credentials and identified themselves by name. The senior man said, "Could we come in and talk to you?"

"About what?"

"Some burglars were arrested last night, and one of them had your name in his address book. We'd like to talk to you about it."

I shook my head. "Sorry, but before I talk to you, I'd want to talk to counsel."

The agent persisted. "After you've talked to your attorney, Mr. Hunt, would you talk to us then?"

"It depends upon what my attorney recommends."

The agents looked at each other. Then one said, "You *will* call your attorney, won't you?"

"I'll call him," I told them and closed the door.

There was no point in asking Caddy what to do, for Caddy was a specialist in labor law. The only lawyer with criminal experience I knew was Gordon Liddy, who had often told me stories about his days as a prosecutor and his years with the FBI.

With some difficulty I reached Liddy at his CREP office, told him of my unexpected visitors and asked him what to do.

"As your attorney, Howard, this is my advice: When they come back to see you or telephone you, tell them you've talked to your attorney and your attorney has told you to have nothing whatever to do with any law-enforcement agency."

"Okay. Is that all there is to it?"

"That's all you can do for now. And let me know if they get in touch with you. Also, their reaction."

From then on, the phone began ringing constantly. During the afternoon reporters visited the house and I denied them entrance, instructing the maid to turn away all callers.

My children returned home and expressed surprise at the presence of reporters outside the house. I told them Bernie Barker had been arrested, and my name had been found in his address book.

That was why the reporters were at the house. I assured them the reporters wanted to learn about Barker, not about me, and Lisa and St. John seemed satisfied.

My house was now resembling a fortress under siege. In an attempt to find out what was going on downtown, I turned on radio and television and listened to the broadcasts. Five men had been arrested in Democratic National headquarters. Cameras and electronic devices had been found. The name of E. Howard Hunt, a White House aide, had been found in a notebook belonging to one of the men.

So it went for the rest of the afternoon, gaining scope and detail as night approached.

To escape the house I took the children to our country club for dinner, returning home afterward and telling everyone in the house to let the telephone ring without answering. I tried to reach Liddy by telephone but his line was busy.

I have no particular recollection of how that night passed, but I remember a feeling of growing concern as more details of the entry operation were made public by the police. I knew that Police Chief Jerry Wilson was a political appointee, and I assumed the White House would be able to order him to a) release the men and b) stop talking to the press. But none of this happened.

Sunday morning I left the house early and drove to the Old Executive Office Building. I entered it as before, went to my office and opened my safe. I put the contents of the two attaché cases into my safe and locked it again, removing the two empty attaché cases from the office and taking them home. As I drove into my property, I could see television cameras stationed on River Road. Reporters followed my car up the drive on foot but I asked them to leave.

Toward midday the maid announced that yesterday's FBI men had returned. I met them at the door and after they had flashed their credentials again, the senior agent said, "Mr. Hunt, have you had a chance to talk with your attorney?"

"I have."

The agent smiled expectantly. "And what did your attorney advise you, Mr. Hunt?"

"He told me to have nothing whatever to do with any law-enforcement agency."

The agent's face fell. "May I ask the name of your attorney, Mr. Hunt?"

"Sure. Mr. G. Gordon Liddy."

"Is he a member of the D.C. Bar?"

"I imagine he is. He's also a former FBI agent."

The agent rallied a final time. "Are you going to take your attorney's advice?"

"I certainly am," I told him and closed the door.

I telephoned Liddy and summarized the Bureau's second visitation.

"Good," he said. "That should hold them for a while until we can get this straightened out."

"Where are the boys?"

"Still in jail."

"Christ, when are your people going to get them out?"

"Frankly, there have been some problems I didn't anticipate. You gave Caddy the ten grand?"

"I kept out fifteen hundred thinking you or I might need it."

"We may, at that, Howard. I shredded all the green I had in my office."

"Caddy was going to call me, but he hasn't made contact yet. I guess with Rafferty on the scene he just bowed out."

But when Caddy called me later in the day, he told me he and Rafferty had gone together to see their clients, who were not particularly happy at being in jail. I said, "Why can't you bail them out?"

"The charges are too heavy. I don't think they're going to be able to get bail."

I felt my stomach chill. "I never heard of anything you couldn't get bail for except murder, and the boys haven't done that or anything close to it."

"Well, they've got hold of your name and found out you were at the White House, so the thing is getting a lot of publicity. Besides, the Democrats are getting interested in this, and things are likely to get worse before they get better."

"Listen, Doug, I want to go down and see them. That's the least I can do. Just tell me where they are."

"Howard, I wouldn't advise it. For one thing, as I understand it, they can see only their lawyers. Oh, by the way, Mrs. Barker is flying up from Miami."

"I didn't suggest it," I told him. "There's nothing she can do, and it's just a waste of money. Anyway, after Bernie gets out, they can fly back to Miami together."

"Howard, my firm's senior partners aren't taking this very well. They're pretty upset about my name being in the papers and I'm getting a lot of flack from them. Do you want to see Rafferty yourself?"

"No. I'm not his client. But if there's nothing more you can do, Doug, then by all means withdraw and keep your partners happy."

Caddy grunted. "It's already been suggested—indirectly—that I resign from the firm."

"Why, for God's sake?"

"That's the attitude they take."

I told Caddy about my two visits from the FBI and the advice given me by Gordon Liddy. Caddy made no comment, but in closing again recommended that I not visit my imprisoned colleagues. I now felt almost completely isolated, shut off from my superiors and my subordinates. Moreover, both the press and the FBI were exceedingly anxious to talk with me. I could no longer conceal from myself that the episode was assuming alarming proportions. However, at that point I still felt the crisis was manageable as soon as sensible people returned to the White House and began doing whatever had to be done.

Instead, the contrary was true.

Never had I so greatly needed my wife's counsel and guidance, but she was in Europe. At least, I thought, she and the other two children were spared the inconvenience of press inquiries and the unwelcome presence of reporters and FBI agents at our home. And although I had kept our Afghan hound indoors for the better part of two days, I decided to release him on our property as a deterrent to casual visitors.

On the fence of my front paddock I had long ago posted a sign— BEWARE OF DOG—so I felt that if uninvited visitors were bitten, I was legally covered against lawsuits.

Whether it was the presence of the dog or the fact that the reportorial search was turning in other and broader directions, my doorbell rang less frequently. Nevertheless, the pryings of the press were a constant annoyance to all of us, in particular to my children, who were unaccustomed to fending off inquiries.

The two FBI visits, plus the advice of lawyer Liddy, began to make me think for the first time that perhaps I might indeed need an attorney. At that point I felt allegations and insinuations of my involvement in the Watergate entry could be dealt with through silence—at least until the White House was able to marshal its forces and undertake remedial action.

Liddy was not in touch with me during the day,* and toward evening I studied my wife's European itinerary, thinking I might place a reassuring telephone call to her in London. I did not, however, do so and that night, despite the intermittent ringing of the telephone, I fell asleep tired from the strain of the day.

On Monday morning, the nineteenth, I drove to Washington, went into the Executive Office Building and visited my office. As far as I could see, it had not been entered since my last visit. The safe was still in place, and the few papers on my desk were undisturbed.

The morning newspaper had carried my name prominently in a story concerning the five arrested men. Since I was in the building, I thought I might as well try to get Chuck Colson's reaction to the publicity, so on the way out I stopped by his office, but Colson had not yet arrived. Joan Hall was at her desk, however, and her eyes widened when she saw me enter.

"Well," she exclaimed, "I'm surprised to see *you* here!"

The tone of her voice irritated me. I went to her desk and said, "Why shouldn't I be here?" and sat down in the chair. "There's one thing I want to tell you," I said, "and you can pass it along to Chuck." I gestured toward the ceiling. "That safe of mine upstairs is loaded."

"I sort of thought it might be," she said. I rose and left the Executive Office Building for the last time.

At Mullen & Company the secretaries and my colleagues were buzzing over the appearance of my name in the paper. I went to my office and began a normal day's work. The Julie Eisenhower public-service television commercial on which I had been working was

---

*Although it was later revealed that Liddy saw Attorney General Kleindienst at the Burning Tree golf club and told Kleindienst that John Mitchell wanted Kleindienst to have the arrested men released at once, Kleindienst refused, and had I known of his refusal, my subsequent actions would have been far different from what they were, for I would have realized that the administration was *not* going to provide the assistance to which we felt we were entitled.

nearly completed, but some postproduction work needed to be done in New York. The positive and negative prints were there, awaiting my viewing and consultation with the postproduction firm.

After a while Bob Bennett came into my office and shut the door. The papers seemed to be full of my name, he remarked, and I agreed noncommittally. Then he told me that reporters had been telephoning him about me, and he had taken the position that he knew nothing about my extraoffice activities.

Not long before, Bennett's name had surfaced as the founder of a couple of hundred political fund-raising committees to several of which my wife and I had lent our names as a matter of courtesy and convenience to him.* For several days Bennett had been kept busy with press inquiries, and I reminded him that hostile publicity was nothing new to the firm. So for the rest of the morning he left me alone.

Then, about eleven thirty, I got a call from Gordon Liddy. His voice was almost hoarse, his words clipped. "Howard, go down to the street and walk west on Pennsylvania Avenue as far as the corner. Turn left, and I'll meet you there. We'll keep walking."

"How soon?"

"Right away. Get going."

I did as bidden and caught up with Liddy, who was ostensibly reading a newspaper at the corner of the USIA building. As I neared him, he fell into step with me and we walked down Eighteenth Street. Tensely, Liddy said, "They** want you to get out of town."

"Out of town?" I was reacting slowly to the unexpected instructions. "Where? I don't get it."

"Those are the orders," Liddy told me. "They want you to get moving, and fast."

"Where would I go?"

"How about Europe? Dorothy's there with your children. Why not spend the rest of the summer over there with them? Or go to Jamaica. An expense-paid vacation."

I shook my head. "Gordon, if I leave town now it will look as though I'm a fugitive—particularly after the two visits by the FBI

---

*These committees were to figure as fronts for receipt of funds from the milk-producing industry.

**Presidential Counsel John Dean, according to later testimony.

guys—and I don't like it. I don't need a vacation: What I *do* need is a lawyer. Can you get me one?"

"We'll work that out later." He glanced at his wristwatch. "I'm due back in a few minutes; are you going to go?"

"If that's what they want," I said dubiously, "but let's get a lawyer for me, Gordon."

"You've got that money from your safe, haven't you?"

I nodded. "Fifteen hundred. Caddy's got the rest."

"Well, go as far as you can on that and I'll get more money to you somehow." He thrust out his hand and gripped mine.

"*Adiós, amigo,*" he said, almost dramatically, clapped my back with the flat of his hand, pivoted and strode back in the direction we had been walking.

When he was out of sight, I retraced my steps to Mullen & Company and went into Bob Bennett's office just as he was getting ready to leave for lunch.

"Bob," I said, "I'll be leaving town for a while, but I'll stay in touch."

He looked at me wordlessly, then nodded.

"I'm leaving now," I told him and returned to my office, where I closed the door, put a dust cover over my typewriter and let myself out by the corridor exit where Liddy and McCord customarily entered.

Half an hour later I was home and throwing things into a suitcase, including my passport. I was still packing when the telephone rang.

Gordon Liddy again. "Howard, the orders have been changed. You don't have to leave town."

For a moment I considered the change in instructions, then said, "I don't know who's giving hard-and-fast orders, then rescinding them in forty-five minutes, Gordon, but I'll say this: It makes me uneasy. Obviously the decision to send me out of Washington had to be made with something approaching thought and wisdom. But then suddenly to cancel it makes me wonder what the hell's going on. I've already told Bennett I'm leaving town, and he didn't ask any questions. I've got some company work in New York and that will be my excuse for leaving. Too, once the children can say I'm not home, the press won't hound them anymore. So I'm going to go up to New York this evening and I'll get in touch with you from there."

"Sounds like not a bad idea."

"In New York I can stay poised either to fly somewhere else —Europe, for instance—or come back here, depending upon circumstances. But your original orders convinced me: I ought to get out of town, and fast."

"I can't argue against it."

"Do one thing for me, will you? And do it now. Get me a lawyer. When I call you tonight or tomorrow, I'll want that lawyer's name, Gordon."

"Okay, *amigo*. I'll get with it."

I hung up and asked the maid to prepare my lunch. While that was being taken care of, I called several airlines and found out that because of a personnel strike, flights to New York had been cut back and there was little choice but to go on a standby list for a six o'clock flight to Kennedy International Airport.

In midafternoon Lisa and St. John returned to the house and I told them I was leaving for New York and asked them to drive me to National Airport. I added that I had some business in New York that could take me several days to take care of and gave them some money to cover household needs.

At the airport I got the last seat on the New York-bound flight. An hour later I deplaned at Kennedy and registered at a motel under an assumed name. From a pay station I telephoned Liddy's office and home, but he was not at either place, and after dinner I went to my room to consider my situation. I pondered Liddy's midday instructions and the abrupt about-face, wondering what had possessed Mitchell or Dean or Magruder to issue the orders in the first place. I was keenly conscious of a need to consult my wife, talk things over with her and receive the good advice of which I knew her to be so capable. But Dorothy and two of our children were in London at Brown's Hotel or at Claridge's, and I was at Kennedy Airport in New York.

For a while I watched the evening news programs, realizing that the Watergate arrests were figuring in all the media—ballooning, it seemed to me, out of all proportion to the reality of the episode. Finally, with the help of a sleeping pill, I got to sleep, awoke early and checked out of the motel.

In Manhattan I telephoned the postproduction offices and spoke with Phil Larschan, who was surprised to learn I had come to New

York without notice. In any case, he told me, I should come over to his office and we would begin work on the opticals. I bought a morning paper and read that my White House safe had been opened and a pistol, variously described as a Colt, Browning, or Beretta, found in it. I did not particularly mind the discovery of the pistol, but the insinuation was clear: I was a gun packer and now a probable fugitive.

What concerned me most was the contents of my files. I had warned Joan Hall about my safe, and she, as well as the Secret Service, had the safe combination. Surely she or Colson had gone through the safe before outside officials had been given access to it. McCord's attaché case was there, by now discovered and inventoried unless it had been previously extracted. It seemed unreasonable to me that White House officials had given the FBI or anyone else permission to open my safe, and yet it had happened.

This, on top of yesterday's demonstration of White House indecision, baffled me. More than ever I felt I needed an attorney and when I reached Larschan's office, I telephoned Gordon Liddy, but again was unable to reach him. I then phoned Bob Bennett and told him I was doing postproduction work in New York and asked him what the Washington atmosphere was like. He described it as excited and ominous and commented on the opening of my White House safe.

"Bob," I said, "I feel I've been put in a false position and made to look like a fugitive—which I'm not. All I want is an attorney. Liddy said he'd find one for me, but I haven't been able to reach him. Would you call Liddy for me? Or, failing that, Doug Caddy?"

Bennett said he would see what he could do for me, and I told him I would be at Larschan's for the next few hours.

After Phil worked with me, he had another client to attend to, and while he was busy with him, I placed a telephone call to my wife in London. Miraculously she and the children were at their hotel and had read my name in the London papers.

I said, "The important thing is for you not to cut short your vacation. I'm sure this whole thing will blow away just as soon as the right people do what they're supposed to do."

"Was Gordon arrested?" Dorothy asked.

"No. So far his name hasn't even been mentioned. Just me—and of course Bernie, McCord and the other men. I don't know why they've let the thing reach the dimensions it has, but it makes me more than a little unhappy. Liddy said he'd get me a lawyer, but I haven't been able to reach him. My photo's in all the papers, and it won't be long before I'm recognized in New York. The night it happened I went to Doug Caddy and he found a lawyer to represent the arrested men, but there's no lawyer for me. The press has been all over the house, and we've been like prisoners."

"What are you going to do?" she asked calmly.

"Get out of New York today." A thought came to me. "Maybe I'll go to Tony Jackson's for a while. He's a lawyer, and he could help me. At least I'd have the benefit of a friend's advice. So I don't want you to come back. There's no need to, and this thing will work itself out."

In the background I could hear the children talking to each other. Finally my wife said, "All right, darling, we've been having a wonderful time, and if you don't need us, we'll stay and continue the trip."

As I hung up, Phil Larschan returned and said we could resume our work together. We lunched in his apartment, then while Phil was on another telephone, I called American Airlines and reserved under an assumed name a seat on an afternoon flight to Los Angeles.

We worked for another hour or so, then I left with my bags for Kennedy Airport.

It was after dark when I landed at Los Angeles, and I phoned Jackson's home from a telephone booth.

"Tony, this is Howard."

"I've been reading about you. Where are you?"

"In Los Angeles. Tony, I'm not a fugitive, and I want to know if you can put me up for a few days. I don't have any alias documentation with me so the only way I can register at a hotel or motel is in my true name."

"Okay. Take a taxi to my office building and I'll pick you up there. There's sort of a progressive family wedding going on and Nancy's down in Texas. From there they go on to Mexico, and I'll be joining them in a couple of days, so I'm all alone here right now. After that the place is yours."

In his home, talking over drinks, I told Jackson I felt I needed legal advice, and as he was already my attorney from previous commercial and family dealings, I would appreciate his advice. He told me that he was not really equipped to counsel me, for many years had passed since he had handled anything resembling criminal practice. One of his partners, however, might be able to advise me, and in the meantime Jackson suggested I make myself comfortable in his home.

It was an attractive place, high on a crest in Beverly Hills, handsomely furnished in teak acquired in Bangkok; outside there was a large swimming pool. His cook-maid was Mexican, and I had no difficulty communicating with her in Spanish.

From Jackson's home I telephoned Liddy and told him where I was. I asked if he had retained a lawyer for me and was told that that was "in the works."

"Anyway," he said, "Tony can take care of you for now, can't he?"

"I suppose. But he's leaving in a day or so for Mexico. What do I do then?"

"Sit tight, *amigo*, and I'll get back to you."

"Great," I said acidly. "Opening my safe was a charming affair, and I'm delighted to be known as a gunslinger. Whose bright idea was that? Who the hell's in charge back there?"

"Take it easy," Liddy said in an attempt to soothe me. Then, "All hell's breaking loose here in Washington."

"Did Bob Bennett call you?"

"No. Was he supposed to?"

"I asked him to. What's with the boys?"

"Still in jail."

"When are they going to get out?"

"Christ only knows. You can't imagine what this thing's like, Howard. It's ballooning all over the place. The office is crawling with reporters, and I haven't had any sleep in two nights. If you think you've got troubles, think of mine."

"There's a difference," I told him. "You're located at the seat of power and I'm three thousand miles away. Everything's come apart."

"Well, one of the problems is that everyone was on the West Coast—you know that."

"I know it now, but Christ, Gordon, that was over the weekend, and now it's Tuesday night. I'm not criticizing the response to the crisis; I'm saying there hasn't been any response at all."

"Listen," he pleaded, "just take it easy for a while. Okay?"

"What else can I do?"

Liddy mumbled more assurances and I reminded him of his promise to obtain counsel for me, the matter uppermost in my mind.

It was clear to me that Liddy himself was in a tormented situation. He had been in charge of Gemstone, and it had gone awry. I could image John Mitchell's fury, but at the same time I believed him too intelligent and capable a man to permit anger to interfere with his obligation to extricate the arrested men. Surely it was also to Mitchell's interests to put an end to such alarming episodes as the violation of my White House safe and revelation of its contents. So, although I could appreciate Liddy's situation, I did not believe that in the long run he or I would be made to suffer.

Next morning my host left for his office while I had a late breakfast and enjoyed his pool. At midday he arrived with his secretary, whom he introduced to me, and said that during his absence she was to assist me in any way she could. That evening Jackson returned home and brought Los Angeles newspapers for me to read. I felt awed by the attention paid to Watergate and was profoundly concerned by a report that the FBI was looking for me in all fifty states and two foreign continents. I was rumored to be simultaneously in Spain and Mexico while reports from Europe indicated that I had been seen strolling the boulevards of Paris.

As I put aside the papers, I hoped that Dorothy and the children were in some Cornish village, isolated from the metropolitan press, but it seemed unlikely that my family could long remain unaware of escalating interest in my whereabouts.

Jackson and I had a drink, then the telephone rang. The maid called him away, and when Jackson came back, he said, "We've got a visitor coming here."

"Anyone I know?"

He nodded. "Gordon."

"I'll be glad to see him," I said. "Where is he?"

"Downtown. He'll be here in, oh, half an hour."

The news cheered me, for I interpreted it to mean that solutions had been found for the main and satellite problems caused by the arrest of my five associates. And the fact that Liddy was still free to travel and not publicly implicated in the affair was a further source of encouragement to me.

Presently Liddy arrived. He greeted us effusively and joined us in a drink. Jackson excused himself for a period of transcendental meditation, and Liddy and I were alone.

"Well," I said, "what's been happening?"

"You wouldn't believe it." From his pocket he drew a sheaf of bills and put it in my hand. "This is for Tony—a thousand bucks as a retainer. He's your attorney."

"He's been my attorney for a long time," I reminded him, "but Tony's not a criminal lawyer."

"I know that, but have him represent you for now."

I shook my head. "He's going to Mexico tomorrow, Gordon. Meanwhile I'll be alone here with the FBI scouring the world for me."

"Let me tell you this, *amigo*, you're better off here than back in Washington. What I've gone through this past few days is unbelievable."

"At this point I can believe anything," I told him. "All I have to do is read the papers—or watch television. I can't help but get the impression that the White House is *cooperating* in the investigation. For God's sake, Gordon, that's unreal!"

"I don't know what went on over there," he said with a trace of bitterness, "but they certainly haven't helped."

"Tell me one thing: Who's in charge now?"

"Well, when I left this morning, it was Bob Mardian. As of now, God knows."

"This is five days after the arrests," I reminded him. "I can't believe that isn't long enough for someone to take charge and bring this thing to a screaming halt."

He shrugged. "You read the papers, Howard. The next story will be my resignation."

I stared at him. "From the committee?"

He nodded. "Yeah. As of the first of the month."

His announcement baffled me. Then it occurred to me that Liddy, Magruder, Dean and Mitchell were going to make a clean breast of their responsibility for Gemstone, the five prisoners would be released and the affair thus closed. As I looked at Liddy, he seemed to sag. "I'll be out of a job now," he told me, "and that's bad."

I began to grapple with the new facts. "You don't mean they're abandoning you?"

"Oh, no. Anyway, Howard, everything's going to be taken care of—just like in the Company."

"Company" was a euphemism for the Central Intelligence Agency. "There's no problem about money," he went on. "Do you need any now?"

I shook my head. "I've got enough for now, but I read that Bob Bennett gratuitously announced I'd been fired from Mullen & Company. I'm depicted as a fugitive who was probably responsible for what is now called a burglary, and to top it off, it's been announced to the papers that my firm has dispensed with my services summarily. I get the uneasy feeling, Gordon, that I'm being made a scapegoat. Let's face it, I can't stay out here forever. A few days more, maybe, but eventually I have to go back to Washington. That's where my family is—at least part of it—and my home. Before I get there, I want competent counsel to represent me. Highly competent," I added.

"This may be the last time I'll see you for quite a while," Liddy said. "Macho had my name in his notebook, and that's going to be announced to the press probably by tomorrow. I'm sure your home phone has been tapped and probably mine as well."

"How do you know that?"

"We're getting reports," he said without amplifying. "Just take it from me."

Jackson emerged from his retreat and joined us. I handed him the ten one-hundred-dollar bills and said, "Tony, this is a retainer."

Jackson took the money. "Let's go out for dinner, Gordon. Feel like some steak?"

After dinner Liddy took me aside and asked me to fly to Miami the next day and try to see Clara Barker. "She's going bananas," he told me, "and nobody's been able to get in touch with her. In fact, no one dares to. How about it?"

"I can try," I said reluctantly, "but how do I know she isn't in Washington trying to get Barker out of jail?"

"That's possible, but it's better than sitting around here twiddling your thumbs, isn't it?"

Jackson and I drove him to his hotel, and Liddy left us saying he was flying back to Washington in the morning.

Next day Jackson flew to Mexico, and I took a nonstop flight from Los Angeles to Miami. It was dusk when I arrived at the airport, and by the time a taxi had taken me to Barker's neighborhood, darkness had fallen. As we neared Barker's house, I could see the glare of photofloods illuminating the front of his duplex house. Along the sidewalk and partly up his drive were onlookers, most of whom appeared to be reporters. There were television cameras and cassette recorders in evidence. I had my driver circle the block, then drop me at a phone booth, where I called Clara's telephone number. There was no answer despite repeated rings, so I returned to the airport, checked my bag and waited for the next flight back to Los Angeles. I spent most of the night dozing in the airport lounge, read early editions of the Miami *Herald* and tiredly boarded the plane.

The Jackson home was locked, but I knew where the spare key was concealed and went inside, falling asleep almost immediately.

The following day I called Caddy's office and left a fictitious name by which he might recognize me. Soon my call was returned, and Caddy informed me that my wife and children had returned from Europe. I groaned, then asked him about the jailed men. He said some progress was being made on raising money for the inordinately high bail bond that had been set for each of them. I said I was sure that Gordon Liddy could raise the money if he knew it was needed, but Caddy told me he was withdrawing from the case following pressure from the senior members of his law firm.

I realized that Caddy had already done more than could reasonably have been asked of him, and so I thanked him for his help and asked him to let Dorothy know where I was. He agreed to do so and a little later I telephoned Bob Bennett's office, only to find him out. Eventually Bennett returned my call, and I said, "Look, Bob, I'm out on the end of a slender limb, and the tree is shaking violently. I don't know why you had to fire me publicly and without notice, but we'll skip that for now. What I need is an attorney in Washington. You ought to know most of the capable Republican attorneys around town. Can't you get one for me?"

Bennett muttered something vaguely about not wanting to get involved in the affair.

"All right, then, but at least do this for me: Call John Dean and tell him what I need. If anyone should know Republican lawyers, it's the President's counsel. Right?"

Bennett acknowledged that it was a reasonable supposition. Even so, he made me no promises, and when I concluded the conversation, I felt I might as well have been talking to a mirror.

Grim outlines of the expanding affair were now apparent to me. With myself a supposed fugitive, Liddy fired from the committee, and the Gemstone principals—Mitchell, Dean and Magruder—remaining aloof from their responsibilities, I was reluctantly beginning to feel that perhaps no succor would be forthcoming. The continuing imprisonment of the arrested men astounded and dismayed me. Nevertheless, I had Liddy's recent reassurances that everything would be taken care of, "Company-style." To me that meant heroic efforts to right the situation, financing legal defense if it came to that and certainly income replacement for those of us who had lost or would lose our jobs as a result of the unflattering publicity.

For the next couple of days I made full use of the pool and spent evenings at a movie or watching television. Then a call came from Tony Jackson: Several of his children were returning to his house, and he and his wife would be coming back soon. Accordingly, I would have to vacate and—though he regretted it—make other plans. I thanked him for his hospitality to date and assured him I would be off the premises in the next day or so.

So far I had not been in touch with my wife, and I was reminded of her cousins in suburban Chicago, the Carlsteads. Hal, like myself, had been a Naval officer, moreover, over the years he had become aware of my CIA connection and was not likely to ask questions if I applied to him for lodging. In any case, Chicago was a halfway point in the inevitable return to my home, and from the Carlsteads' I would be able to reach Dorothy and decide what my future actions ought to be.

So it was that I left Los Angeles for Chicago, phoned my wife's cousins from the airport and asked if I could spend a few days with them. They met me at the airport, commented about the publicity attached to my name and confirmed what I already knew: that Dorothy had come home from Europe. They remarked on the government's revelation that I had been a career CIA officer and wondered at this breach of trust.

To me it was inexplicable that after my having spent twenty-one years under cover, the government—perhaps the CIA itself —should have revealed the secret, as it were, of my life. Such a revelation benefited no one, I felt sure, and had been amplified by the press into what amounted to sinister implications.

Next day Phyllis phoned my wife and suggested she come to Chicago for a brief visit. Dorothy understood at once, and soon we were reunited at the Carlstead home.

I explained the sequence of events and described the situation —particularly my personal one—as I perceived it to be. We agreed that my priority need was for counsel in Washington, and I told Dorothy I was still hopeful that either Liddy or John Dean would come through. I told her of the specific commitment Liddy had given me in Los Angeles, and after twenty-one years as the wife of a CIA officer she understood the scope of the obligations and commitments that had been made.

Dorothy informed me that she had been in touch with Douglas Caddy, not knowing where else to turn, but had been, in effect, rebuffed by him. She remarked that Liddy had been unavailable to her, and I informed her of his pending forced resignation. Dorothy did not burden me with recriminations or take me to task for my involvement in Liddy's operation. Instead her thoughts were positive and in refreshing contrast to my own after-the-fact musings.

She stayed one night with me, returning to Washington in the morning, and after her departure I tried again to reach Bob Bennett by telephone. When that effort failed, I called Tony Jackson in Los Angeles and asked him to recommend counsel to me. He agreed to inquire among his colleagues and phone back.

On July 2 Jackson phoned me and gave me the names of two Washington attorneys. Alphabetically, the first name was that of William O. Bittman. The name of the second I have forgotten, for it was unnecessary that I reach him. I telephoned Mr. Bittman, identified myself and asked if he would consider representing me. Bittman said that after talking with Jackson he had been expecting my call and had given my situation some thought. I told him I resented being cast in a fugitive role and had only been awaiting the retention of competent counsel before I agreed to speak with such government authorities as might legitimately desire to discuss the case with me. On that understanding, Bittman agreed to accept me as a client, and we agreed to meet at his home the following night.

Purchasing a ticket to Washington at O'Hare Airport, I gave a false name, and as I went through the airlines checkpoint, I was selected at random—in view of a recent rash of hijackings—to be checked. When the ticket agent asked for identification corresponding to the name on my ticket, I said I had none and he asked me to step aside. Two security men—sky marshals, I suppose—invited me into a stairwell, where I was competently frisked and my baggage examined. When they asked why I had no identification, I said simply that my wallet had been stolen in Chicago and I was temporarily without credit cards, driver's license or other normal forms of identification. After examining me, the marshals permitted me to board the plane, and with a sense of relief I settled back for the flight to Dulles, where Dorothy and Kevan met me.

We drove directly to Mr. Bittman's home, which was only about a mile from my own in Potomac, Maryland. With Bittman was his associate, Austin Mittler.

For the next several hours I told them and Dorothy what I thought they needed to know in terms of a case I still hoped would somehow be swept under the carpet. As a retainer I gave Bittman $1,000 of the $1,500 I had taken from the emergency funds in my White House safe. Bittman then placed a telephone call to Assistant U.S. Attorney Earl Silbert, told him he was representing me, and that in the event Silbert wanted to interview me, no subpoena would be necessary; Hunt would see the assistant U.S. Attorney at the latter's convenience.

That much completed, I returned home with my wife, and we discussed the present situation and the future until far into the night. We feared, but did not dare to think, the worst.

18 INDICTMENTS; THE DEATH OF MY WIFE

BY now the Democratic National Committee had initiated lawsuits against the Republican Party, the Committee to Re-elect the President, myself and the five arrested men, four of whom were now out of jail and at their homes.

Douglas Caddy had been invited to appear before the federal grand jury but had declined to reveal our discussions following the Watergate arrests. Threatened with contempt, he had retained counsel and was resisting judicial pressure on the grounds of the heretofore-inviolable confidentiality between attorney and client.

I was interviewed in Silbert's office, with his assistants, Messrs. Campbell and Glanzer. Bittman was present and advised me to decline to answer questions, citing my constitutional rights under the Fifth Amendment, which I did.

On July 7 Bittman informed me that he had received $25,000 as a retainer in my representation. My wife was with me, and almost as an afterthought, Bittman told of a curious telephone call he had received. "Some guy—I don't know who he was—said he wanted to talk to 'the writer's wife.' He said his name was 'Mr. Rivers' and that he wanted to talk only to the writer's wife."

Bittman looked at me. "Howard, you're the only writer I know, so this Rivers fellow must want to talk to Dorothy. Anyway, that's how I put it together. Is there any reason he couldn't just call your house?"

"Well, I suppose he assumes, as I do, that my line has been

tapped by the feds, but if he's an agent of Liddy's principals [Mitchell or Dean or Magruder] I think we ought to hear what he has to say."

After leaving Bittman, Dorothy told me that upon her return from Europe she had called Caddy on several occasions and received what she considered were unsatisfactory responses. She had been unable to reach Liddy. Confronted with this situation, and not knowing where I was or what faced me, she went to CREP headquarters and demanded to see the general counsel, an attorney named Paul O'Brien. Dorothy went on to say that O'Brien had blanched when she told him of my involvement with Gordon Liddy, and he said he would look into the circumstances at once. Mr. Rivers' call, she theorized, was in response to her enlightenment of Paul O'Brien.

Presently Bittman reported that during a conversation with CREP's attorneys—in connection with the DNC civil suits against us—he had been assured that Mr. Rivers was an appropriate person for him or Dorothy to deal with.

On the following day Dorothy received a phone call from a man identifying himself as Mr. Rivers. He said he did not want to hold any discussions with her over our home telephone line, but if she would be at a particular phone booth in Potomac Village, he would call her half an hour later.

When my wife returned, she told me that Mr. Rivers had instructed her to obtain from the arrested men, Liddy and myself an estimate of monthly living costs and attorneys' fees. This she was to do by the following day, when she was to be at a different phone booth to receive a call from Mr. Rivers. Accordingly, she telephoned James McCord, then Bernard Barker, asking the latter for a combined estimate covering all four Miami men. These figures she delivered to Mr. Rivers during their subsequent telephone contact, after which he said, "Well, let's multiply that by five to cut down on the number of deliveries."

Dorothy asked him why he was using a multiple of five—aware that five months represented the interval to the national Presidential election—and was told by Rivers that five was a convenient figure for him to multiply by.

Within a day or so Dorothy was instructed by Rivers to drive to National Airport, go to a particular wall telephone in the American

Airlines section and reach under it for a locker key taped to the underside. This she did and opened a nearby locker to find in it a blue plastic airlines bag, which she brought home.

Later she told me that the contents had been considerably less than the figure agreed upon by Mr. Rivers. In fact, she told me, the monthly budget had been multiplied by three rather than five, so on that basis she set about distributing the funds. Liddy, she told me, was to receive his support funds and attorneys' fees directly through a separate channel.

The transaction represented verification of what Liddy had told me during his dramatic appearance at Jackson's home in Beverly Hills—that everyone would be taken care of, Company-style—and so I faced the future with renewed confidence that all obligations would be kept.

However, there was no letup in media coverage of the spreading Watergate involvement.

On July 13 Douglas Caddy was in court, and that same day grand jury summonses were served on every member of my family with the exception of David, who was only eight. On the eighteenth Dorothy, Kevan and St. John were interrogated by the federal grand jury, and on the following day at the federal courthouse I was fingerprinted by the FBI and submitted samples of my handwriting to them—a process which took several hours. While this was going on, Caddy was testifying before the grand jury after having been briefly in jail. As for myself, I spent long hours each day with my attorneys.

On Saturday the twenty-third I went to the Mullen office building, but was denied entrance by the guard until he telephoned Bob Mullen, with whom I spoke. I told Mullen that I simply wanted to remove my personal possessions from my former office and he agreed.

Over the weekend Gordon and Frances Liddy dined with us and intensively discussed the deteriorating situation.

On Monday FBI agents appeared at my home to interrogate our Guatemalan maid, who was terrified by them, I might add.

Soon afterward I changed my telephone number to a different and unlisted one to avoid further harassment by the press, and in the following days I spent most of my time with my attorneys at their offices or in Bittman's home at night.

In early August I wrote a letter to Chuck Colson saying that I understood his position to be a difficult one and, in effect, apologizing for the fact that my identification as an employee of his had brought his name into prominence. He did not reply.

On August 10 Dorothy and I took Lisa and David to Orlando, Florida, for a visit to Disney World. The following day we met the Barkers in Miami and drove to Marathon in the Florida Keys for a fishing vacation which we felt would do all of us some good. On Sunday the thirteenth, when we had returned from a day's fishing, the motel manager told Dorothy there had been a person-to-person call for her. He supplied the operator number, and from a phone booth across the highway Dorothy placed a call to Joan Hall. When Dorothy's conversation was concluded, she turned over the phone to me, and Joan told me that Chuck had received my letter and wanted me to know that he remained my friend and hoped that everything would be cleared up in the near future.

This indirect communication from Colson encouraged me to believe that the highest levels of government were keenly aware of our situation and were taking all necessary steps to secure relief.

We returned to our Potomac home on August 17, and I resumed my daily consultations with Bittman. On the twenty-ninth I appeared at the law offices of Edward Bennett Williams, who was taking depositions from the defendants in the suits initiated by the Democratic National Committee. On that occasion—my first semipublic appearance following the massive publicity to which I had been subjected—I found the press and television corps filling the lobby of the office building. After I had given my deposition, I attempted to leave by a rear exit, only to encounter television reporters there as well. For relief I walked across the street to the Army and Navy Club, pursued by cameramen and reporters, lunched at the club and did not leave it until midafternoon when the media men had dispersed.

Next day Tony Jackson appeared before the Washington grand jury, and I saw him briefly while I drove him to Dulles airport for his return to Los Angeles.

On September 8 Manuel Artime appeared before the grand jury, evidently as a result of his name, address and telephone number having been found in either Barker's or my address book. On the eleventh Kevan began her sophomore year at Smith, and on September 15 the seven of us were indicted on multiple counts.

We were arraigned on September 19, and my bond was set at $10,000, of which I needed to pay only $1,000 in cash to the courthouse clerk. From that time on I was required to telephone the bail agency each Tuesday and give an account of my whereabouts and anticipated travel.

On September 22 I was telephoning attorney Bittman from my home when I heard a whisper just after my attorney had spoken. The intruder voice said, *"That's Bittman,"* as though to identify the person to whom I was talking. This slipup by the monitors convinced me—if I needed further convincing—that my telephone line continued to be tapped. Consequently we filed a motion alleging government eavesdropping on a privileged attorney-client conversation, but the government denied the charge.*

By the end of the month my attorneys' fees had greatly exceeded the $26,000 retainer, and I discussed with Bittman and Mittler my understanding of the assurances that had been made not only to me but to the other six defendants as well. I knew that the attorney for the Miami men was carrying a delinquent account, as was Liddy's attorney, this information having been given to Dorothy by Liddy.

On October 4 Chief Judge John J. Sirica issued an order enjoining everyone connected with the Watergate case from commenting publicly on it. Even so, the Los Angeles *Times* began publication of Al Baldwin's disclosures that he was McCord's monitor in the motel Listening Post and had himself delivered transcripts to the reelection committee prior to the unsuccessful entry. But despite Sirica's ruling, Baldwin's "memoirs" continued to be published by the Los Angeles *Times*.

As soon as I heard of Baldwin's declarations, I telephoned McCord and berated him for Baldwin's conduct. To my surprise, McCord defended Baldwin, saying that Baldwin, after consulting with attorneys in Connecticut immediately following his flight from Washington, had been advised to return to Washington and consult with CREP attorneys. According to McCord, Baldwin had done so, but had been turned away by the attorneys, who professed igno-

---

*McCord filed a similar affidavit which was also rejected by the government.

rance of his affairs, much less his involvement with James McCord. This reaction, McCord maintained, freed Baldwin to act independently of the rest of us, and this he had done. McCord then said he was feeling a monetary pinch and wondered when financial aid would be forthcoming. I told him that inasmuch as Baldwin had violated my orders and taken the van to McCord's home, the van—which McCord had purchased with money given him by Gordon Liddy—could be sold and the proceeds used for McCord's benefit. In closing, however, I remarked that I felt sure we would not be forgotten.

At this point I did not know McCord had charted an independent course of his own: He had been writing mysterious and Aesopian letters to a friend in CIA's Office of Security, and on October 10 McCord telephoned the Chilean Embassy. He identified himself as a Watergate defendant and requested a visa. McCord's assumption was that the embassy's phones were tapped and that when he filed a motion for government disclosure of any wiretaps on his line, the government would drop its case against him rather than reveal that the Chilean Embassy phone was tapped. This the government later denied.

From the first, my wife told me that her dealings with McCord made her feel uneasy. There was something "wrong" about him, she said repeatedly, and the less she had to do with him, the better, as far as she was concerned.

About this time Bill Bittman approached Assistant U.S. Attorney Silbert and suggested a "deal" by which I would testify fully to my knowledge of the events in return for Silbert's recommendation to Judge Sirica that I be given a suspended sentence.

Silbert's response, as reported to me by Bittman, was that he did "not need" my testimony, as he had sufficient evidence to convict all seven defendants. In any case, Silbert told Bittman, he was going to avail himself of the Kelly case precedent and, whatever the outcome of our jury trial, immunize each of us and force us to talk before the grand jury under penalty of contempt of court.

I was depressed by the negative results of my first experience in plea bargaining and became increasingly pessimistic over my future. The episode, however, was to bear an even greater significance when allegations were made that money had been paid me to "buy my silence." On the contrary, I had offered to talk freely but was peremptorily refused by Prosecutor Silbert. Second, the U.S. Attorney's Office knew that immunizing us would force us to testify. These facts were certainly known to the highest levels in the Department of Justice and to the White House in turn.

Accordingly, there was simply no silence to "buy."

On the day after my fifty-fourth birthday Chief Judge Sirica denied our motion that he disqualify himself from presiding over our trial on the grounds that as chief judge he was also presiding over what had now become known as the Watergate Grand Jury. Sirica then set a trial date for November 15, scarcely a month away.

On the twenty-second Dorothy called Joan Hall to ask Colson's intercession in the matter of long-overdue payments to the defendants. Mrs. Hall told her to call back on the twenty-fourth, but when Dorothy did so, there was no answer. On the following day Judge Sirica denied all motions made by the defendants, and the next night Dorothy received a call from Mr. Rivers telling her he would call on the following day.

That day, on advice of his physician, Judge Sirica postponed our trial to January 8, 1973, and though Dorothy waited all day for Mr. Rivers' call, no contact was made. On the thirtieth, however, I answered the telephone and heard a man's voice. He said he was "a friend of Mr. Rivers" and wanted to speak to "the writer's wife." In this fashion contact with Liddy's principals resumed.

I was at Bittman's law offices on the evening of October 20 when Bittman answered the telephone and told me a messenger was on his way—theoretically with money. In due course a package was delivered to the then-vacant reception desk, and after Bittman handed it to me, I opened it and turned over its contents to him and Austin Mittler. The precise sum I have no way of recalling, but I remember that it was far less than what was owed my attorney. And of course there was nothing in the package for family support for myself or for Liddy, McCord or the Miami men.

Dorothy now expressed to me her great dissatisfaction at the role she had been asked to undertake by Mr. Rivers. It was he who had solicited budget figures from her; they had been agreed to, yet the payments had never been fully met. Now Dorothy was dealing with "a friend of Mr. Rivers," and she felt that with the election won, the White House would be less inclined to live up to its assurances. Moreover, she had the lingering feeling that because she was a woman, her representations were given less weight than those of a man—myself, for example. For these reasons she suggested that I call Colson and attempt to explain the situation to him. On instructions of Mr. Rivers, she had given specific financial assurances to the Miami defendants, but the money had been only partially forthcoming. And their lawyer was making disquieting sounds.

So I phoned Colson's office on November 13, speaking with his secretary, Holly Holm. After checking with her boss, she told me I could call Colson the following day from a phone booth—not my home phone. The hour was, I believe, twelve o'clock, and after salutations I congratulated Colson on the electoral victory and suggested that with the election out of the way, people in the White House ought to be able to get together and concentrate on the fate of us seven defendants. I informed him that despite all previous assurances—some of which had been met—financial support was greatly in arrears, particularly payment of legal fees for the defendants. I believed the seven of us had behaved manfully and remarked that this was "a two-way street." I told him that, in the language of clandestine service, money was the cheapest commodity there was. By that I meant that men—the Watergate defendants—were not expendable, but money was. And money was badly needed for legal defense and the support of our families.

Dorothy had once suggested my writing a memorandum to Kenneth Parkinson, one of the CREP attorneys, summarizing the financial situation of all seven men in terms of the assurances given her by Mr. Rivers. I had not done so, but, for effect, I now told Colson I was planning to write a memorandum and "lay it on Parkinson" in the near future. I suggested that a week or ten days hence ought to be sufficient time for Liddy's principals to make up the arrears and expressed my strong hope that this would be done.

Interjecting from time to time, Colson's responses were cagey. He put it to me that he had not been involved, was not involved and did not want to be involved: From this posture, he explained, he could be of more assistance to me. In sum, Colson's responses were unsatisfactory, and I left the telephone with a distinct feeling that the White House had now washed its hands of us.*

On the twentieth I mentioned my telephone call to Colson and told Bittman that I would neither mortgage nor sell my home to meet the cost of my defense. I stated that I would rather face trial without an attorney than beggar my family by depriving it of its limited economic base.

Ten days later, no payments having been received, my wife met with James McCord at his request and told him that our principals (Mitchell, Magruder and Dean) had not come through. She described McCord as philosophical over the news as though he had been expecting it, a reaction she found incomprehensible.

On November 7 I had voted in the national election at my home town of Potomac, Maryland, and on the following day accompanied Bittman and Mittler to the U.S. Courthouse, where I was allowed to examine evidence that had been seized from my violated White House safe. I searched the seized material for my operational notebook, files and telephone list, but did not find them.

Bittman asked Silbert if he was holding them in another area, but Silbert declared that what I had reviewed was all there was. It was sufficient to convict me, *but any material that could have been used to construct a defense for me was missing*: my operational notebooks, telephone lists and documents in which I had recorded the progress of Gemstone from its inception, mentioning Liddy's three principals by name: Mitchell, Magruder and Dean.

On December 4 all defense lawyers met for a pretrial meeting at Bittman's office. Some of the defendants were present for varying periods of time, and I encountered Bernie Barker, with whom I had a brief conversation. I told him that Dorothy and I were going to take the children to Key West before Christmas and asked him to make reservations for us there beginning the fifteenth. He agreed and added that he and his wife might join us there for a day or so.

On the night of the seventh I received a special-delivery letter addressed to me from McCord and immediately took it to Bittman at his home. Its thrust was to accuse me of planting press stories

---

*Some nine months later I was shown what purported to be a transcript of our telephone call. It had been recorded by Colson for purposes I could only interpret as self-serving.

charging McCord with having recruited the Miami men, and its tone was threatening. After reading the letter, Bittman told me he had received a similar telegram signed McCord, but had declined to accept the telegram on the grounds that anyone could sign his name to a telegram without having been the actual sender.

From Bittman's home I phoned Bernie Barker, who had been mentioned, by implication, in McCord's letter and asked if he had received anything similar. Barker told me that although he had not, his attorney had, and together they had been trying to interpret its significance.

The episode left all involved with a sense of bafflement and a concern that McCord's eccentricities might somehow endanger his codefendants.

Some days earlier Dorothy had suggested to me that she fly to her cousins' home in suburban Chicago and deliver Christmas presents she had selected for them, their children and their daughters-in-law. While there, she said, she would like to leave $10,000 in cash with Hal Carlstead for investment.

For some time she and I had been discussing our financial future and had decided that we would invest a portion of our savings in a motel-management company formed by Carlstead and some of his associates. A $10,000 investment would give us an equity in a company controlling two already-built Holiday Inns in the Chicago area and a third under construction. Granted the investment was relatively small, still, I had been jobless for six months, and my prospects for future employment were, to say the least, diminished. Perhaps the investment would enable me to work in some capacity at one of the Holiday Inns after my trial.

Her plane reservation to Chicago was on United Airlines Flight 553 to Chicago's Midway Airport, with a return on Sunday the tenth. There had been no economy-class seats available, so while she was in the process of making the reservations, she turned to me and said, "Could I travel first class, Papa, just this once?"

"Of course," I told her. "I don't know why you bothered to ask."

Since early fall I had been working on a novel, *The Berlin Ending*, based on counterespionage cases I was familiar with from work with CIA. The novel was nearing completion, and—as with all my other work—I discussed problems with Dorothy as they arose. From day to day she had been typing the final manuscript, and as I drove her to

National Airport on the morning of the eighth, she turned to the ending of the book.

"The way you have it," she pointed out, "the good guys win. But, Howard, you know it isn't always that way in real life. More often than not, the good guys lose—so why not end it that way?"

"What are your ideas?"

"Well, the girl for one thing. The hero doesn't get the girl. And the villain, well, he gets away. That's how I'd end it if I were you." She smiled. "Besides, if you don't do it that way, I won't type it for you."

"That's the clinching argument," I told her as we drew up before the United Airlines entrance. "Shall I come in?" I asked.

She shook her head. "You don't need to. I'm early and there's some shopping I want to do for some of Phyllis' grandchildren. I'll just wander around the shops until it's time to leave."

We kissed, and a skycap took her bags. From the curb she turned and waved at me and I waved back. I saw her enter the doors of the airlines ticket office.*

Driving home, I considered Dorothy's words and by the time I reached my study had decided to end the book† the way she wanted it. This meant only a small amount of rewriting, and I became engrossed in it for the next couple of hours until I heard David running down the stairs and realized he was home from school.

"*Papa, Papa!*" he called and ran to me at my desk.

"What's the matter?"

"Papa, in the car radio coming home I heard that Mama's plane crashed and she's dead!"

---

*Where, I later learned, she purchased $250,000 in flight insurance payable to me.
†*The Berlin Ending* (New York, G. P. Putnam's Sons, 1973).

19 A CHANGE OF PLANS

I glanced at my watch. By now Dorothy's plane should have landed in Chicago. Frantically I dialed Phyllis Carlstead and heard her voice. "Phyllis, there's been a crash at Midway Airport. Is Dorothy all right? Is she with you?"

"Oh, Howard, Hal's at the airport and he just called. There's been a crash and he thinks it's Dorothy's plane. He said he'd call back."

"Can you call the airport and find out what happened?"

"I'll try, dear. Oh, Howard, this is awful!"

"I'm going to start for the airport here," I told her and hung up. I dialed United Airlines but the switchboards were jammed. Helplessly I stared at David, who turned from me and walked toward the steps. Moments later I heard him sobbing, went to him, picked him up in my arms and carried him upstairs. I tried to comfort him, though my own mind was ungovernable. I tried to choke back my own sobs, but after unsuccessful efforts I felt David's hand patting me comfortingly. He looked up at me and dried his eyes. I kissed him and he returned my embrace. He was never to cry again.

I turned on the radio and told the servants what had happened, and in a moment or so the telephone rang. It was Kevan calling from college. She knew of her mother's flight plans and had heard of the crash. I told her I was leaving for Chicago and she said she was coming home.

I left David in the charge of Lisa and St. John, who were on the verge of tears, and began driving through a heavy rainstorm toward National Airport, not knowing whether my wife was alive, dead or injured. She had been forward in the first-class section, I reminded myself, and unless the plane had been in a nose-down attitude, chances were the tail had struck first, enhancing her chances of survival.

The traffic was maddeningly slow as the rain increased. When I reached National Airport, I found the United Airlines section besieged with worried relatives and managed to single out a passenger-service agent. I identified myself, told him my wife was on the crashed plane and asked for an immediate seat to Chicago. While arrangements were being made, I telephoned home, then our cousins in Chicago, but learned only that a morgue had been set up in a nearby hangar and attempts at identification of the bodies were being made. Hal was there now, according to Phyllis, and because he had not yet phoned her, she was still clinging to hope that Dorothy had survived.

It seemed hours before the plane took off, and I spent the time calling my home and that of our cousins.

Finally we landed at Midway Airport after dark. From the air I could see distant fire engines beyond the end of the field and police cars with their flashers whirling eerily. As I left the plane, Hal found me and before I could speak, he said, "I don't know yet, Howard. There are too many bodies, and most of them are burned beyond recognition."

"What about the injured?"

"They've been taken to hospitals. No one knows where they are."

A United passenger agent approached us and introduced himself. Hal did the talking for me, and the agent suggested we leave the area and he would phone us as soon as he had any information. There seemed nothing else we could do.

At the Carlstead home Phyllis and I embraced tearfully, then she led me inside. She and her husband alternated calling United Airlines for further information, but by two o'clock in the morning, when I finally went to bed, there was still no definite word. I fell asleep with the lingering hope that Dorothy was a patient in one of several hospitals to which the injured had been taken, that she had not yet been identified and tomorrow I would be able to see her alive and smiling.

In the morning available information was inconclusive. Few of the dead had been identified, and not all of the injured.

At midday an attorney who was a partner of Hal's in the motel-management firm joined us to use his good offices with the Chicago police and coroner. I told him that Dorothy was travelling with $10,000 in cash for the investment and had perhaps $700 in her purse besides. He suggested I sketch some of the jewelry she was wearing, and I did: wedding ring, family signet ring, engagement ring and finally a large solitaire diamond that had been my mother's.

A party had been planned for Dorothy, and Phyllis telephoned the invited guests to cancel the affair. Since the day before I had eaten nothing and slept little; from time to time I began crying uncontrollably.

Kevan telephoned me from our home but I was unable to tell her whether her mother was alive or dead. I spoke with the other children, all in highly emotional states, which increased my own. The United Airlines passenger agent who had given us his card seemed to be unavailable and we could get no information from other United offices.

Toward midafternoon the attorney returned to the Carlstead house and suggested that we go to the Cook County morgue, taking the sketches I had made of Dorothy's jewelry.

It was a long ride through gathering dusk to the ugly and solitary old building, and when our party had identified itself, we sat down for a long wait. Finally a functionary returned with a plastic bag containing scorched jewelry. This he emptied onto a table and I stared at it unbelievingly. Everything I had sketched was there —except my mother's diamond solitaire.

The wedding ring.

I picked it up and held it in my hand; ashes dropped from it, smudging my palm. The charm bracelet, half melted by the heat. Her signet ring had not been harmed.

The man said, "Can you identify these, Mr. Hunt?"

I nodded wordlessly. To another functionary he said, "That takes care of body eighteen," and gave me a form to sign. "Where was she born?" he asked me. "What year?"

I shook my head, unable to speak. Finally Phyllis said, "I can tell you what you need to know."

They had been brought up almost as sisters, and Phyllis was the only living person who knew Dorothy better than I.

That night radio and television carried reports that $10,000 in hundred-dollar bills had been found in my wife's purse, but I was unprepared for the barrage of innuendo and insinuation that was to follow. The FBI checked the bills' serial numbers against their many lists, particularly that of the cash given Barker in return for one of the Mexican checks, but no connection could be established. On one of the bills was a handwritten "Good luck, Frank," and this was interpreted as a reference to Frank Sturgis, one of the arrested Miami men.

Of such unsubstantial material is the web of fantasy spun.

As I flew back to Washington, I realized I could not stand the stress of a four-to-six week trial now less than a month away, and convinced that the government was still concealing the only documentary evidence that might establish that I had been acting in good faith, I decided to plead guilty in the hope that leniency would be accorded me. In fact, as later revealed, John Dean and Patrick Gray *had* destroyed this material.

At home my daughters had taken over almost completely, rising to meet this new tragedy with a fortitude I was later to admire. The house filled with faces—relatives, friends and visitors, and I have no clear recollection of the ensuing days except that, to my surprise, James McCord stopped by to express his sympathy.

Meanwhile I informed Bill Bittman of my decision and my reasons for making it. My attorney did not attempt to dissuade me, but said he would communicate my intention to Assistant U.S. Attorney Silbert and see if he would agree to let me plead guilty to all but the electronic charges against me.

My wife of twenty-three years was buried in a small Catholic cemetery near our home in Potomac, and at the suggestion of cousins who lived in Largo, Florida, I took my four children there for the Christmas period, which would have been unbearable to us in our home.

Aware of my extreme mental depression and physical exhaustion, Bittman summoned me to Washington to undergo physical examination by government physicians as well as my own. And although my personal physician of many years concluded that I should not have to appear in court, the government physicians felt otherwise, and I was ordered to appear at federal district court on Monday, January 8, one month to the day after Dorothy's death.

Meanwhile, my codefendants and their attorneys had been informed of my decision to plead guilty. I personally notified Bernie Barker, who, when he arrived in Washington some days in advance of the trial, called on me to explore my motivations more fully. He could see and understand my mental depression, and I pointed out to him that the evidence against me was overwhelming: McCord's briefcase had been found in my rifled safe, but the notebooks and other papers which could have substantiated a defense that I acted under duly constituted authority had not appeared.

In consequence, I told him, I was defenseless.

Barker said, "Well, Eduardo, you're pleading guilty and you weren't even arrested. The five of us were caught red-handed in the office, and I haven't been able to find out yet from our attorney what our defense is going to be. He tells us he's a law technician, and he'll get the judge so mad that he'll commit reversible errors and we can have the case thrown out on appeal." Barker looked at me thoughtfully. "Does that make sense to you?"

"I don't know enough about law to even guess," I told him. "Besides, my situation is different from yours. I've got four children to take care of, Bernie, and if I have to go to prison, I'd rather spend the last few weeks with them rather than in a courtroom every day. I've got to provide for their future, and there's no way I can do it with so many other things on my mind."

I had written a letter to Colson on December 31, asking him to see my attorney, Bill Bittman. I thought Colson might find my guilty plea out of character, and I wanted Bittman to explain to him the reasons for it. Too, some weeks before, I had heard that the U.S. Attorney's Office was undertaking research to determine in what manner my CIA annuity could be terminated, and I wanted Colson's help in staving this off.

For his part, Bittman wanted to discuss with Colson our motion for disclosure of evidence that had been taken from my White House safe. If the White House resisted the motion, then it was hopeless to proceed, and Bittman needed to know the White House attitude. Thus, Colson gave Bittman an appointment on January 3.

As reported to me by Bittman, Colson said that he understood the reasons for my plea of guilty, that he would have research done on my position vis-à-vis my CIA annuity, and as for the disclosure motion, he asked Bittman to return the following day.

Following Bittman's second interview with Colson, my attorney informed me that the White House was taking the position that I had "abandoned" my office and safe; therefore, the White House had every right to enter my "abandoned" property.

While this position was useful to the White House, it nevertheless conflicted with the actual circumstances: My employment contract with the White House was open-ended; I had never resigned my White House consultancy, nor had I been discharged. Also, I had visited Room 338 frequently, my last visit having been on June 19. My White House pass and the keys to my office remained in my possession and had not been asked for by the Secret Service. Despite all this, the White House was going to resist our motion.

Bittman had told Colson that I was naturally concerned about the sentence I might be given and its length. He and Colson had discussed this area briefly, each of them agreeing there were mitigating circumstances, and particularly because I was pleading guilty, I might well receive a lenient sentence, if not probation. Colson had added, according to my attorney, that whether in or out of the White House he, Colson, would continue to be my friend and would help me any way he could in his *personal* capacity,* even to taking my children into his home should that be necessary. Beyond this, according to Bittman, there had been nothing of substance to the meeting.

Colson's message did nothing to alleviate my burdens, and I recalled that he had not even come to the funeral home before my wife's interment, sending Joan Hall, instead, with a handwritten letter of sympathy. So I now realized that there was a growing gap between Colson and myself, though I could still appreciate his position.

Over the weekend Barker told me that the four of them had been discussing a possible guilty plea with their attorney, who was resisting the change. I neither encouraged nor discouraged him from these discussions, and when Barker asked whether I thought our financial support would continue in the event we were imprisoned, I

---

*This was to amount to an unsolicited letter sent by Colson to the probation officer who was conducting my presentence investigation.

could tell him only that I hoped so—based on the fact that the assurances given us had so far been reasonably well honored.

That Sunday afternoon, the day before the trial, Bittman told me that Judge Sirica had repudiated the agreement entered into by Silbert and Bittman: that I would plead guilty to the three nonelectronic charges. Sirica's attitude was—if Hunt wants to plead guilty, let him plead guilty to everything.

This was a further heavy blow, but I was so far along the road at that point that I numbly said I would plead guilty to all seven counts. Bittman told me he would enter my changed plea before the trial got under way and before the jury was selected. In my attorney's view, any leniency accorded me might be greater if I pleaded *before* the government prosecutors outlined their case against me and my codefendants.

But even that was not to be.

20 END OF A COMMITMENT

MONDAY morning, January 8, 1973, was cold, windy and overcast. Bittman and Mittler helped me elbow my way through the throng of waiting reporters and cameramen into the federal courthouse and to the ceremonial courtroom on the fourth floor. There I took my place at a table with my attorneys, the other defendants and their lawyers. Liddy, McCord and their attorneys faced us from another table.

At ten o'clock Chief Judge John J. Sirica strode to the bench while we rose, the court clerk intoning the formula. Sirica banged his gavel and said court was now in session.

Bittman approached the bench, stating that his client wished to withdraw his not-guilty plea and enter a plea of guilty. Brusquely, Sirica told him—and me—that he would entertain no deviation from set procedure until the jury had been selected and the prosecution had outlined its case.

This was the first of countless courtroom exchanges I was to lose over the ensuing eleven months, and I felt a chill come over me. I looked at the Miami men, wondering what decision they had reached concerning their plea. I studied the face of their attorney, but he was smiling and unperturbed. So, apparently, was Liddy.

Almost as though neither attorney Bittman nor I existed, Sirica began jury selection. I was astonished when one woman in her eighties was accepted, she having maintained *under oath* that she had never heard *anything* about the Watergate case. She was, however, one of only a few whites on the panel, since juries in the

District of Columbia reflect the capital's overwhelmingly black population.

I found myself scanning the courtroom, spotting reporters whose faces were by now familiar; relatives of the Miami men; and federal marshals who guarded the door. Over the next year I was to become intimately familiar with the U.S. Marshal Service, whose members transported me from place to place like so much dead meat.

I refused to let my mind focus on the courtroom proceedings; I was not going to stand trial, and there was no point in my becoming emotionally involved in what was going on. Instead, I began making notes of things to do, matters to take care of affecting the household and my children.

At one o'clock court recessed for an hour, and with my attorneys I walked across Pennsylvania Avenue to the National Art Gallery, where we had a hurried lunch in the cafeteria. While I was eating, Barker came over to my table and said, "Eduardo, we've got a problem with the attorney."

"What kind of problem?"

"Well, he says he refuses to let us plead guilty."

I stared at him. "How can he? He's your attorney. If that's your decision, I don't know how he can fail to honor it."

Barker shifted uneasily. "I don't know about these things, Eduardo, but the others agree with me: The evidence against us is overwhelming; we were caught on the premises and you weren't. If *you're* pleading guilty, then that's enough for us."

"Bernie," I said, "you know I can't tell you what to do, but you saw what happened in court this morning. Sirica not only repudiated the agreement Silbert made with Bittman, but he's twisting the knife by refusing to let me plead until *after* the government's presented its case. That makes it look as though I didn't decide to plead guilty until I was overwhelmed by what Silbert intends to prove."

"I heard it, but I guess I really didn't understand what was going on. Bad, huh?"

"It's certainly not good."

At 2:10 P.M. court was again in session, and the dreary process of jury selection continued until 4:35, when court was recessed until the following morning at 11.

With my attorneys I pushed and shoved my way out of the

courthouse to a taxi commandeered by a young law associate. Then, in Bittman's office, we discussed the day's negative results, and finally I made my way home.

That night Manuel Artime visited me and comforted and reassured my children. For the next year he was to prove a closer and more reliable friend than a blood brother, and I was deeply grateful for his presence.

As I remember, the following day in court was occupied with jury selection. Then, on Wednesday the tenth, Earl "the Pearl" Silbert began to present the government's case. He showed blowups of the Watergate complex and renderings of DNC floor plans and described the evidence that had been captured and seized by government agents. Finally, at 2:15, I was permitted to enter my plea of guilty.

Judge Sirica attempted to question me about my involvement in the case, but my attorney interposed, stating quite properly that the questions the judge wanted me to answer could be more appropriately responded to before the grand jury that had handed down the indictments.

Sirica said he would consider the matter overnight; and in the morning, after the opening of court, he announced that he was accepting my plea on all seven counts and ordered that I be jailed in lieu of $100,000 cash bond. He added—gratuitously, I thought —that he would want to know the source of any monies that might be raised for such a bond.

A bond of this size—in *cash* rather than collateral, as is customary—is almost unprecedented except in murder cases.

Marshals led me from the courtroom and into a small elevator reserved for prisoners. There, for the first time in my life, I was frisked and handcuffed. Taken below, I was photographed, fingerprinted and booked and directed finally into a cell with a metal bench. The Felony Tank. My handcuffs were removed, and I was alone for the first time in a jail.

Fatigue, ever present for the preceding months, swept over me. The metal bench was unyielding, so I rolled up my coat and made a pillow of it. There was a washbasin and seatless toilet, nothing more. Ceiling lights were recessed, and though I did not realize it at the time, the yellow-tiled cell was the cleanest and largest I was to occupy in any of the jails and penitentiaries where I was imprisoned over the next year. I felt detached from the judicial proceedings that were continuing five floors above me. While they went on, I would have time to organize my household in a way that would endure, hopefully, for the period of my expected sentence.

I thought back to the day when Liddy had first approached me in the White House citing the Attorney General's desire to establish the program—Gemstone—and what had befallen us, and it. Liddy, I knew, was not going to plead guilty, nor was McCord. As a lawyer, Liddy understood my reasons, and because he was a lawyer, I understood his. To me, McCord was always an enigma, and his later conduct was to prove even more baffling.

All these things revolved in my mind, then an incongruous sense of peace came over me and I fell asleep.

I was awakened by keys rattling in the lock, the hearty voice of a marshal saying, "Wake up, Mr. Hunt, your lawyer is here."

Blinking, I sat up and rubbed my eyes, wondering how long I had slept. I was stiff and my mouth was dry. The time was two o'clock. I put on my coat and followed the marshal down the corridors to the attorney interview room, where I found Bittman, Mittler and a notary public from their law firm.

"Howard, we'll have you out of here in a little while," Bittman said heartily. "Just sign these documents here and endorse these checks from Dorothy's insurance proceeds. We'll deposit them to a joint account with the surety company. After that's done, we'll go with you up to the clerk's office, and you'll be released."

Still not grasping the mechanics of what was being done—or really caring—I endorsed two checks made out to me from insurance companies and signed documents that were attested by the notary. Bittman chomped on his ever-present cigar, put on his coat and said, "We'll have you out of here in no time."

They departed and I was led back to my cell. There was no point in trying to sleep anymore; the prospect of freedom was too enticing. I tried to smooth wrinkles from my coat, and in a quarter of an hour the marshal took me back to the interview room, where Bittman and Mittler were waiting. Accompanied by a marshal, we rode an elevator to the clerk's office, where my cash bond was filed and I signed a paper containing the terms of my release, and when that was accomplished, Bittman drew me aside.

"The press is all over the place, Howard, and they want a statement. They've been bugging me for weeks, and I think the best thing to do is to say something now. Do you want me to try my hand at something, or do you feel you—?"

"I don't want a press conference, Bill, and I don't want to answer any questions. Let me make a simple statement, and the hell with it."

Bittman gestured to Mittler, who went off to inform the media representatives waiting outside the courthouse door. I sat down for a few moments to compose myself, then nodded to Bittman. "Okay, let's go."

On the courthouse steps bright lights and flashbulbs made me wince, and a dozen microphones were thrust at me.

One of the commentators, apparently briefed by Mittler, said, "Mr. Hunt, now that you're free on bond, do you have a statement you'd like to make?"

"I do," I said. "Thank you." The glare of the lights was painful to my eyes after nearly four hours in the dimness of my cell.

"Anything I may have done I did for what I believed to be in the best interests of my country," I said and stepped back from the microphones.

"That's all there is," Bittman told them, took me by the arm and guided me to a waiting car.

I have no further recollection of that day, but I suppose I went home as soon as I could to be with my small son when he returned from school.

Next day I lunched with Kevan and Bill Bittman at the City Tavern Club and that evening, for the first time, I gave an interview: to Dave Beckwith of *Time*'s Washington Bureau. The following day *Time* photographed me in my home, and on Monday, for the first time, I reported to the probation officer charged by Judge Sirica with preparing my presentence report.

His name was Frank Saunders and his lair was Room G6417 in the federal courthouse. He was a cautious, rather oily bureaucrat, who I soon realized was an extension of Judge Sirica. Saunders was far less interested in learning my background, employment and family ties than in trying to weasel from me fresh information about Watergate. I did not care for him, and I'm sure, like his master, he viewed me as an Enemy of the State.

That afternoon Bill Buckley phoned to ask if I could tape a *Firing*

Line segment in San Francisco the following Thursday. I told him that I felt it would be against my best interests to discuss Watergate, and he said that he had no intention of putting me in so difficult a position. On the contrary, he told me, he wanted to discuss the CIA and foreign policy with Dr. Mario Lazo, a distinguished Cuban-American lawyer whose book, *Dagger in the Heart*, had recently been published. I had read the book and knew that Lazo and Barker were longtime friends, dating back to a period in Cuba when both were cooperating with the American Embassy. I agreed in principal and Bittman called the clerk of the district court, who confirmed that I would be able to participate in the program.

On January 15, with the appearance of a court-appointed lawyer, my four Miami friends pleaded guilty as charged in the indictments and were sent to D.C. Jail to await sentence. (After I joined them, Barker told me the four had written a joint letter dismissing their original attorney, who even then, Barker told me, refused to withdraw until the four men turned to the prosecutor for help.)

On January 17 I flew to San Francisco and was met by my college classmate and former fellow musician, Frank Rollins, who spent the night with me at the Palace Hotel.

Next morning at station KQED I appeared for the first time on an hour-long television program, before a group of students from Mills College. Nervous at first, I soon found myself absorbed by Buckley's questions and in the internal dynamics a friendly debate can generate. That night I went to the Rollins' home in suburban Marin County and from there enplaned to Washington once more. The day after my return from San Francisco President Nixon was inaugurated for the second term. I was not invited to the inaugural festivities. But Manuel Artime was.

On January 30, after relatively brief deliberation, the Watergate jury found Gordon Liddy and James McCord guilty—the former on six counts and McCord on eight. Their trial had lasted sixteen days.

On February 2 probation officer Saunders visited my home and strongly suggested I give him any information I might possess concerning Watergate. I reminded him that the trial was over, five men having pleaded guilty and two convicted. Sixty-two witnesses had been heard, and as far as I was concerned, that was the end of it. Moreover, I pointed out, all of us would be summoned before the grand jury, which, I felt, was a far more appropriate forum than the sort of *sub rosa* confidences he was inviting.

On the seventh the Senate voted unanimously to establish a select committee to investigate the Watergate break-in and related campaign activities.

Bittman told me it was inevitable that I would be called as a witness before the select committee, though at that point no one could estimate when I might be called. And on Bittman's recommendation, I retained a Chicago attorney to represent my wife's estate in suing United Airlines for her wrongful death.*

On the seventeenth my daughters returned from a week's vacation in Nassau, and the President nominated L. Patrick Gray as permanent director of the FBI. That day I wrote the nominee as follows:

Hon. Patrick Gray
Acting Director
Federal Bureau of Investigation
Washington, D.C.

Dear Mr. Gray:

I noted Senator Byrd's announced opposition to your confirmation with a certain wry amusement, one of his reasons for opposition being the Bureau's alleged failure to investigate the Watergate Case.

From my own experience I am able fully and freely to testify that the Bureau left no grain of sand unturned in its investigation. My late wife and children were interrogated, blackmailed, threatened and harassed by Special Agents of the Bureau. . . . My relatives, friends and acquaintances, however remote, were interviewed exhaustively and embarrassingly by FBI personnel across the country, their inquiries extending as far back as my

---

*Because of my "conviction"—even though I was not yet sentenced—Maryland state authorities removed me as executor of my wife's estate and I was replaced by my successor —according to Dorothy's will—William F. Buckley, Jr. Thus stripped of even the right to engage in litigation, I realized that I was on my way to becoming a nonperson, though still very much a taxpayer.

primary school days. Threats and intimidation were not
the least of the investigative tools employed by SA's under
your direction.

For whatever assistance the above might be to you in
realizing your professed desire of being confirmed in your
present post, feel free to utilize it. Should the occasion
arise during my projected appearance before the Ervin
Sub-Committee I will be eager to make the thoroughness
and savagery of the FBI's Watergate investigation a matter
of public record.

From time to time Bittman had been keeping me apprised of the
mounting fees owed his firm for my defense. Even though I could
have paid the legal charges from the proceeds of Dorothy's life
insurance, I believed responsibility for these payments was not
mine. Neither Liddy nor anyone else had ever revoked the assurances he had made me on June 21; on the contrary, the contacts with
my wife by Mr. Rivers and his successor and the initial retainer to
Bittman of $25,000 all persuaded me that my expenses would con-
tinue to be met. I was never privy to the total support money
provided, but was struck by John Dean's admission that he had used
some of it to pay for his honeymoon.

Since Dorothy's death I had received no support money and had
been in contact with no one other than a chance contact with Paul
O'Brien of CREP in the corridor outside Bittman's office.

I had asked the children's former governess to become my housekeeper during my expected absence, bringing her to Washington
from Buenos Aires to renew her life with my family, and her salary
was substantial. I thought of mortgage payments and insurance
premiums, college tuition for both daughters and private school for
David, and I realized that I would need additional family support
money beyond my legal fees.

A hundred thousand dollars of my own funds was tied up indefinitely with the surety company—at least for as long as I remained
unsentenced.*

_____

*Eventually a large portion of it was to go for legal fees and expenses.

I requested Bittman to arrange a meeting between Paul O'Brien of CREP and myself so I could review the financial situation with him in person, O'Brien having been the CREP official Dorothy had approached on her return from Europe. Accordingly, O'Brien and I met privately in early March and I told him that Mr. Rivers' deliveries of funds had never been sufficient to meet the figures originally agreed to between him and Dorothy and that as the months progressed, the arrears were constantly mounting. Now, faced as I was with a prison sentence, I hoped funds could be supplied before I was in prison and unable to make prudent disposition of them. O'Brien said he understood the problem, but felt himself becoming less and less effective as time went on. I responded that inasmuch as he was the sole remaining contact with the unknown source of funds, I was obliged to turn to him. I added that he might or might not be aware of certain seamy things* I had done for the White House and that if anyone was deserving of support—in view of those activities—it was myself. I went on to say that if the White House was now planning to abandon me, then I would have to consider my options. O'Brien told me he would relay my conversation, but suggested I write a strongly worded memorandum to Colson. This suggestion surprised me, for I associated O'Brien with John Mitchell, not Colson.

"Why should I do that?" I asked.

"Because some of us feel it's time Colson got into it—got his feet wet like the rest of us," O'Brien told me.

I gave a noncommittal reply, and after O'Brien departed, I revealed portions of our conversation to Bill Bittman, telling Bittman I had no intention of writing to Colson, but felt that Colson should be apprised of O'Brien's recommendations.

Presently Bittman informed me that I could see Colson's law partner, David Shapiro, at the latter's office on March 16. I went there believing that the Shapiro appointment was merely to disguise a meeting between Colson and myself. However, when Shapiro showed me into his office, he declared that he was Colson's attorney and was acting in that capacity. I found his manner both arrogant and

*The "seamy things" were later identified in the press in reporting on grand jury testimony as the burglary of Dr. Daniel Ellsberg's former psychiatrist, the forging of State Department cables and the political dirty tricks of Donald Segretti.

offensive and told him frankly that I had expected to see Colson and
not a surrogate. Shapiro then told me that Colson greatly admired
me and wanted to help me any way he could in his private capacity,
but I was tired of these banalities and recited Paul O'Brien's suggestion, then outlined our funding difficulties since the preceding
June.

Despite Shapiro's stated unwillingness to hear my full exposition,
I insisted on telling him that I wanted two years' family support plus
legal fees in hand before March 23, my sentence date. Shapiro said
he would pass along to Colson such portions of our conversation as
he saw fit. Rather angrily I told him he should pass along the *entire*
conversation or none of it, and when I left his office, I felt that
nothing useful had been accomplished.

From time to time I was visited by Clara Barker and her daughter,
Maria Elena. Frances Liddy told me that Gordon had been sent to
the Federal Correctional Institution at Danbury, Connecticut,
pending sentencing and gave me his address. I wrote both Barker
and Liddy and received restrained replies because all prisoner mail
was censored. Then, at the recommendation of Tony Jackson, I
began taking a course in transcendental meditation which, I hoped,
would make prison more endurable.

Sentencing was set for March 23, a date whose finality conditioned my every move and thought. Bittman remained somewhat
hopeful that in view of my exemplary life, I would be given probation rather than a prison term, but the little I had seen of Judge
Sirica made me pessimistic.

After St. Patrick's Day I gave a party for David and his school
friends, and Artime arrived to visit the four imprisoned men and
myself. He told my four children that they were to look on him as a
father and assured them they could turn to him for any and all
things.

On the night of March 21 I received a phone call from Bittman,
who said he had received an envelope for me. In the morning I went
to his house to retrieve it, took the envelope home and there opened
it. The contents were $75,000—a sum far less than my previous
estimate of $60,000 for two year's family living expenses plus
$60,000 for attorneys' fees already owed. The $45,000 deficit, I
knew, I would have to make up myself.

I now realized I could count on no further assistance, financial or otherwise, from Liddy's principals—Mitchell, Dean and Magruder—or their successors. And while I hoped that provision had been made for Liddy and the Miami men, I had no way of knowing what, if anything, had been done in their behalf.

21 SENTENCE AND JAIL

I slept little the night of March 22 and in the morning packed a small kit with toilet articles and a change of underwear. I removed the family signet ring I had worn since the age of twelve and left it in my home, said good-bye to my children, whom I had asked not to be in the courtroom, and was driven by Bill Bittman to the federal courthouse.

At ten o'clock Judge Sirica appeared, and McCord's attorney handed Sirica a sealed letter from McCord. This unexpected move produced an uproar in court, which the judge quickly silenced, then announced that he would suspend sentencing McCord.

Sirica now read a self-serving statement having to do with the care with which he had considered the defendants' presentence reports, and while McCord remained seated, Liddy, Barker, Martínez, González, Sturgis and myself were summoned in front of him. Sirica explained that he was going to hand down provisional sentences pending further "evaluation" of our cases—sentences that might be lightened depending upon our cooperating with the Senate committee and the grand jury.

Liddy's sentence, however, was a final one: twenty years.

The judge posed the pro forma question: Did anyone wish to make a statement?

Acutely and uncomfortably aware of Sirica's "Maximum John" nickname, and urged by my attorneys to plead with Sirica for leniency, I had, with their advice, prepared such a plea. Although I was reluctant to request mercy for myself, the fate and welfare of my motherless children took precedence over my personal reluctance. Besides, it was a possibility—however remote—that this prosecutor/judge, who had shown not the least interest in the defendants as human beings caught in a web of circumstances, might reverse his own harsh judicial tradition and exhibit a semblance of humanity.

Besides, I reflected, I had nothing to lose.

So, with the court's permission, I stepped forward and began:

"Your honor, I stand before you, a man convicted first by the press, then by my own admissions, freely made even before the beginning of my trial. For twenty-six years I served my country honorably and with devotion: first as a Naval officer on the wartime North Atlantic, then as an Air Force officer in China. And finally as an officer of the Central Intelligence Agency combating our country's enemies abroad. In my entire life I was never charged with a crime, much less convicted of one. Since the seventeenth of June, 1972, I lost my employment, then my beloved wife, both in consequence of my involvement in the Watergate Affair. Today I stand before the bar of justice alone, nearly friendless, ridiculed, disgraced, destroyed as a man. These have been a few of the many tragic consequences of my participation in the Watergate Affair, and they have been visited upon me in overwhelming measure.

"What I did was wrong, unquestionably wrong in the eyes of the law, and I can accept that. For the last eight months I have suffered an ever-deepening consciousness of guilt, of responsibility for my acts, and of the drastic penalties they entail. I pray, however, that this court—and the American people—can accept my statement today that my motives were not evil.

"The court is about to impose sentence on me. It is my understanding that three principal factors are taken into consideration in arriving at an appropriate sentence. The first is the character of the offender—whether his life represents a cycle of criminality or whether he is a first-time offender. The second factor, as I understand it, is the extent to which the offender represents or is likely to represent a danger to society. Third is the deterrent effect —whether the offender is likely to repeat his offense and whether his fate serves as a deterrent to others who might consider a like offense.

"As to myself, Your Honor, the offenses I have freely admitted are the first in a life of blameless and honorable conduct. As a man already destroyed by the consequences of his acts I can represent no threat to our society, now or at any conceivable future time. And as to the factor of deterrence, Your Honor, the Watergate Case has been so publicized that I believe it fair to say the American public knows that political offenses are not to be tolerated by our society within our democratic system. The American public knows also that because of what I did, I have lost virtually everything that I cherished in life—my wife, my job, my reputation. Surely, these tragic consequences will serve as an effective deterrent to anyone else who might contemplate engaging in a similar activity.

"I am entirely conscious, Your Honor, that what is done to me from this time on is in your hands alone. The offenses to which I pleaded guilty even before trial began were not crimes of violence. To be sure, they were an affront to the state, but not to the body of a man or to his property. The real victims of the Watergate conspiracy, Your Honor, as it has turned out, are the conspirators themselves. But there are other prospective victims.

"Your Honor, I am the father of four children, the youngest a boy of nine. Had my wife and I not lost our employment because of Watergate involvement, she would not have sought investment security for our family in Chicago, where she was killed last December. My children's knowledge of the reason for her death is ineradicable—as is mine. Four children without a mother. I ask that they not lose their father, as well.

"Your Honor, I cannot believe the ends of justice would be well served by incarcerating me. To do so would add four more victims, young and innocent victims, to the disastrous train of events in which I was involved. I say to you, in all candor, that my family desperately needs me at this time. My problems are unique and real, and Your Honor knows what they are. My probation officer has discussed them with me at some length.

"I have spent almost an entire lifetime helping and serving my country, in war and peace. I am the one who now needs help. Throughout the civilized world we are renowned for our American system of justice. Especially honored is our judicial concept of justice tempered with mercy. Mercy, Your Honor, not vengeance and reprisal, as in some lands. It is this revered tradition of mercy that I ask Your Honor to remember while you ponder my fate.

"I have lost everything, Your Honor—friends, reputation —everything a man holds dear—except my children, who are all that remain of a once-happy family.

"Since the Watergate Case began, I have suffered agonies I never believed a man could endure and still survive. I have pled guilty as charged, of my own free will. Humbly, with profound contrition, I ask now that Your Honor look beyond the Howard Hunt of last June 17 to my life as a whole. And if it please this court, to temper justice with mercy.

"My fate—and that of my family—my children—is in your hands."

Rolando Martínez spoke movingly, and so did Bernie Barker. But we might as well have remained mute.

Seven counts times five years each gave me thirty-five years, and the four Miami men received forty years apiece. I felt stunned, sick. Sirica revoked my bond and marshals led me off.

"Maximum John" had more than lived up to his somber sobriquet.

For a while I was held in the courthouse Felony Tank, then taken in a locked and guarded van to the old stone complex near RFK Stadium that made up D.C. Jail.

Just outside the gates the van stopped while the marshals turned over their revolvers to a guard in a tall watchtower. The van moved up to the gate; a marshal got out and phoned ahead. Moments later the barred gate slid open and the van entered, the gate closing behind us.

We were in the outside courtyard now, and when the van stopped, I was ordered out. Marshals marched me to a metal door that opened into a barred corridor, one side of which formed the central-control office. My handcuffs were removed and I was left alone. After a while a loudspeaker told me to enter the next section of the corridor—the procedure reminding me of canal locks. Walk, stop. Door closes behind me. Wait. Door ahead opens. Walk, stop. Door closes. Door opens. Through Plexiglas windows, guards, officers and trusties stare at me. Their lips move, but I hear nothing.

A gray-shirted guard motions me to follow.

I follow. Down steps, down, down, heat increasing until I'm in a low-ceilinged room; guards in khaki, convicts in blue dungarees and denim shirts behind old, scarred tables. Beyond a wire mesh screen other convicts are lined up at four pay phones. Those would be the ones Barker told me about, and I've concealed dimes so that I can call—if I ever get a chance at a phone.

A guard positions me in front of a camera; photos are taken in quick succession. Fingerprinted again. On command I strip before two guards, step to a yellow line, raise arms, open mouth, extend tongue, run fingers through my hair, bend and turn, spread buttocks, raise testicles, show bottoms of feet, and now my clothing is inventoried by a convict in a hip singsong.

"Burn him" means a lighter added to my inventory. After my shoes are searched, they're returned to me with my pipe and tobacco pouch—also thoroughly searched. Nothing more.

At the clothing-issue counter I'm given unpressed denims, white socks, two sheets, blankets and a pillowcase. Except for the crudity I'm reminded of Annapolis and Ft. Dix.

This is R&D—Receiving and Discharge. From it I follow a guard to the "hospital," where, after a long wait, blood and urine samples are taken. I turn medical statements *re* my ulcers and skin cancers over to a disinterested doctor—almost the first white I've seen.

Finally I'm led to cellblock 4, third floor, where, I know, the four Miami men are kept.

Word of my arrival preceded me, and I'm met with *abrazos* and handshaking. Liddy is there, too. "Welcome, *amigo*," he tells me as the deck guard points out an empty cell not far from the guard desk. Friends help make my bed. I mop the floor, clean the basin and toilet. Martínez tells me the canteen is about to open and asks what I need. "Toothpaste, a brush, soap and writing paper," I tell him, and Barker suggests candy bars. "It's a long time between meals, Eduardo."

I nod, grateful to be among friends, and let myself be led along the corridor, where I shake hands with twenty to thirty black fellow prisoners.

By now I've noticed that everyone is wearing starched, pressed denims. Liddy tells me a contact can get me clothing in my size and deliver it pressed and starched twice a week for a couple of packs of cigarettes—prison currency.

"It's not bad here," Sturgis tells me and takes me to a large corner cell with two double bunks and a makeshift card table. "Here's our home—the Watergate Hilton."

Villo provides an orange and I begin to eat it, starting to relax for the first time in days.

Then I hear the deck guard bay my name.

At his desk stands a gray-shirted guard from central control. He sees me, snaps, "Let's go."

"Where?"

"C'mon, get going. Bring your bedding."

Okay, I won't argue. My friends repeat my question, though, and finally the escort guard says, "CB One."

Sturgis says, "That's where we were kept last summer—it's rough, Eduardo."

Liddy: "There's got to be a mistake. Listen. I'll try to work something out. This is the only place to be."

I unmake my bed and roll up the bedding, follow the guard through a dozen doors he unlocks and locks behind me. Finally I'm in the bowels of the prison again. The Lower Depths.

Through a small steel doorway I enter CB 1. There's a desk manned by a guard and convict assistant. "This here's Hunt," my escort announces.

The desk guard hardly looks at me. The convict says, "Cell Seven," and I walk toward it.

Electrically the barred door slides aside and I enter. The door slides shut.

A double bunk, both mattresses filthy, no pillow. I select the cleanest mattress—narrow choice—and start to make my bed on the upper bunk. Tension must have been blocking my hearing and sense of smell, for now raucous sounds assail my ears, the stench of urine and old vomit fills my nostrils.

I'm on the lower tier of four, facing a sort of hall as large as a jai alai court. From its walls hang six TV sets all "tuned" to the same discordant channel.

I look around for a light bulb but the socket is empty. Even so, I can see accumulated filth on basin and seatless toilet. Moving, I step on something that squashes underfoot. My first roach victim.

Psychological fatigue overcomes me. I climb to the upper bunk and stretch out, but the noise is too much: Dinner is being served to

prisoners not in deadlock, as I am. Wetting toilet paper, I mold it
into earplugs and lie down again. After a while a paper plate is
shoved at me through a slot in the bars, a plastic spoon and a paper
cup of Kool-Aid. Sauerkraut and a frankfurter on the plate. No,
thanks, not really hungry. Ice cream comes later. I eat it and lie
down again. Even with earplugs the noise is a lot more decibels than
I'm used to. For half an hour I sit on the edge of my bunk and
meditate, feeling better afterward, less exhausted, my mind partially unburdened.

An inmate sweeping the catwalk in front of my bars pauses.
"*Pssst!*" You Hunt?"

"Yeah."

"The cats in CB Four want to know what you need."

"Soap and a towel. A light bulb. Toothpaste and a brush." It
seemed a large order.

"I see what I can do, man." He grinned at me. "Don' go 'way."

"I'll be here. What about showers?"

"Once a day. Too late now. Tomorrow afternoon." He swept on
and in an hour returned with everything I'd asked for.

Using the towel for insulation, I got the metal base of a former
bulb out of the socket, then screwed in the new bulb. I blinked in
the sudden light, saw the walls appear to melt, turn green from
brown as roaches scurried away. My nostrils were accommodating
to the rancid odors of my cell, but the TV sets blared on. I lay face
down on the bunk, peered through the bars and tried to watch
television on the far wall, but the angle was wrong. A guard paused
and peered at me. Satisfied I was alive, he passed on.

I heard voices in a high-pitched chatter, then half a dozen
female-appearing creatures swished along the catwalk. They wore
towel skirts and turbans; two appeared to have breasts. They stared
in at me and giggled, stopped at the next cell and made sex proposals
to the two occupants.

Late that night the TV sets were silenced and the noise level
lowered enough that I could sleep. But before then I pondered
McCord's private letter to Sirica and felt betrayed. Unwilling to
accept his conviction and desperately grasping at anything that
might save him, my onetime CIA colleague had chosen to step to the
head of the line instead of waiting, as the rest of us were, to tell the
grand jury those facts of which we had knowledge. In most circles

McCord was a hero, but I wondered how history would finally view him.*

The meal attendant woke me before dawn. "Diet tray," he called and shoved a plate through the slot in my bars. The plate held a cold fried egg, pears and bread, reasonably close to the bland diet I had been following for years. As I ate, I reflected that apparently the physician's letter had had some effect on the jail sawbones.

The light bulb kept the roaches at bay while I meditated, then made my bunk and anticipated the luxury of a shower. Today was Saturday, and the TV sets were turned on while other inmates breakfasted in the area beyond my catwalk. The queens were out there in all their makeshift glory, being goosed unresistingly from time to time by interested inmates. By now I realized that I was in the jail's disciplinary section under deadlock, something reserved normally for only the most hardened and refractory prisoners. It was like the hold of a slave ship.

I made fresh earplugs from toilet paper and tried to sleep, but the cacophony was far too great, so I lay in a half-conscious daze until midmorning, when, without notice, my cell door slid open. I stepped onto the catwalk and the guard beckoned me toward him. "You got a visit," he said. "Wait here for a convoy."

The rotunda was a high-domed room with windowed booths along one end. The rest of the large space was given over to rows of tables, where, already, attorneys had gathered with their clients. I was led into a booth occupied by four other prisoners and told my visit would last half an hour. After a prolonged wait I saw Lisa and St. John walking toward me. They looked fresh and cheerful, and I tried to suppress my emotions as I picked up the telephone and spoke through it to theirs. I asked them to tell Bittman I had been taken to solitary for no apparent reason and said in great understatement that I would much prefer being with my five friends in CB 4. They told me David was well, and we talked about household problems until a guard came up and ended my first family visit.

Returned to CB 1, I learned that the shower period was over, and I would have to wait until the next day. The TV sets now featured an Aretha Franklin concert—if concert is the word—followed by *Soul*

*McCord, as matters developed, had been more practical than the rest of us, for his accelerated revelations spared him from serving another day in prison.

Train through the long afternoon. A prisoner stopped by and leered at me. "Well, Dad, you done joined the Blue Denim Brigade. Right on. How you like them mothahfuckas?"

"Not much," I told him and turned over on my bunk.

"You'll like 'em less when you been here long as me."

True words, I was to find, but hardly a revelation even then.

Then I began to muse—as I did every day I was imprisoned—on the singular cruelty of Judge Sirica's sentence. First offense, a spotless record, twenty-six years of service to the government, my wife dead less than three months, four motherless children—the sentence was nightmarish, unbelievable. But—it might be lessened, depending on my cooperation.

Only that had been decided long ago—in October, when the prosecutor told Bittman all of us would be immunized and taken before the grand jury. When would that be? How soon would I be called? Hell, I was *eager* to talk.

I gazed at my filthy surroundings and saw, scratched on the wall: *If I was God I'd quit!*

The legend depressed me. To rouse myself from despondency I got up, pulled off one of my shoes and began killing roaches. It was a task for Tantalus, but it focused my mind and kept me physically active. The futility of trying to eradicate a never-ending supply of roaches was all too evident, and after a while I surrendered.

A steam hose was needed to clean the cell, rid it of long-accumulated filth—and so far I had not even managed a shower.

My cell is faced with fifteen vertical bars about an inch and a quarter thick, flaked with old green paint. . . .

22 JUDGMENT

ON monday the twenty-sixth my diet breakfast arrived late and cold. I ate the applesauce and two oranges slipped me by a passing prisoner. At ten thirty I was taken out for a "Rotunda Visit," which meant I could sit at a table with my attorneys.

I had a lengthy discussion with Bittman and Mittler, who promised to contact jail authorities with regard to my deadlock confinement. They left, and at one o'clock Captain Black, a large, burly ex-D.C. policeman, tersely informed me that I could return to CB 4.

There I was greeted by the four Miami men, who informed me that Gordon Liddy had been provoked into a fistfight early that morning when passing through an adjacent dormitory en route court. Liddy had recognized his stolen brush and comb, demanded their return and was punched, the blow tearing his ear. A good boxer, Liddy was well on the way to felling his larger opponent when guards broke up the rumble. Liddy received medical treatment, delaying his court appearance.

Once moved into a cell, I visited the four Miami men in their large cell, met other inmates, had a decent diet dinner, and that evening Liddy returned from court in time to watch the TV Watergate summary with us. I wrote my children and turned in early after a welcome (and needed) shower.

At 4:30 I was wakened for court call. I dressed, shaved, had breakfast and was escorted to R&D, where my civilian clothing was returned. About 7:00 I was handcuffed and taken in a large bus

307

with thirty other prisoners to the subterranean entrance of the federal courthouse, a fifteen-minute journey from the jail. Sequestered in the Felony Tank, I meditated, then killed time by dozing until noon, when my attorneys arrived. They had me write a brief statement for the grand jury, and at 2 P.M. I was again handcuffed and taken up to the grand jury room, where I was asked one question.

According to the preset formula, I declined to answer on grounds of my constitutional rights to remain silent and was excused for the day. Back to the Felony Tank until 7 P.M., when I was returned to D.C. Jail. Dinner was over and the canteen was closed, so I subsisted on potato chips and an orange given me by Villo, then lay on my bunk and considered the grand jury and its novel—to me —procedures.

The room itself was perhaps twenty by twenty feet and smoke-filled. The twenty-three jurors comprised a cross section of the D.C. population, and facing them at a long table were Assistant U.S. Attorneys Silbert, Glanzer and Campbell. After the foreman administered my oath, I had been seated at the end of the table facing jurors and prosecutors and near the female court stenographer. Silbert informed me that I could ask the foreman of the grand jury for permission to consult my attorney at any time—a right I was to avail myself of frequently during my many subsequent interrogations.

The next morning's court call established a pattern that was to become burdensomely familiar over the next two months. But on arrival at the courthouse with my five fellow Watergaters, we were taken to Judge Sirica's chambers, where we were granted "use immunity" on application of Earl Silbert. Then I was led to the grand jury room and subjected to four hours of intensive interrogation by all three prosecutors—each with his own style and preconceived notions—and by grand jurors, as well.

By now McCord had testified before the Ervin committee in "secret" session and the grand jury. What he said appeared in the press, verbatim or in substance—Jack Anderson's column, for instance, published whole sections of secret transcript, normally a criminal offense.

Because of this unprecedented leakage of grand jury proceedings, I considered my replies carefully, for it seemed improper that any hearsay testimony of mine involving Mitchell, Magruder and Dean should be publicized and so damage men whose innocence before the law was (in theory) still presumed. Only Gordon Liddy could give direct testimony to his commission from those three men, and Liddy declined. For this he was held in contempt by Judge Sirica and sentenced to an additional eighteen months. Liddy's legal position, however, as I perceived it, entitled him to remain silent. He had undergone a trial which was a mockery of American justice, and he and his attorney believed that his conviction would be reversed on appeal. Consequently, for Liddy to testify, even under immunity, could fatally prejudice the outcome of his appeal. Gordon was to maintain this posture before the House of Representatives subcommittee, and in May, 1974, he received an additional year's sentence for contempt of Congress.

Day after day I was taken from D.C. Jail to the federal courthouse, either to testify or to wait uncalled in the Felony Tank, my only diversion an occasional newspaper borrowed from the U.S. marshals who were my guards. Missing meals brought about weight loss and fatigue. I was disturbed by reports that John Dean and Jeb Magruder had approached Silbert's office with offers of cooperation. Meanwhile, McCord, free, seemed to be enjoying his role as repentant conspirator. His new attorney, a leading local Democrat, was much in the news, and both the grand jury and Ervin subcommittee investigations assumed an alarming extrajudicial character that was to deteriorate into almost open competition for the admiration of the media.

The form of my sentencing was a constant preoccupation. Its "provisional" aspect called for an "evaluation" to be performed on me and my Miami colleagues by the Federal Bureau of Prisons. But the device was no more than a transparent and cynical method of exacting from us the final drops of blood. The D.C. Jail had no facilities for the prescribed evaluation, so it was only a question of time before we would be transferred to a federal institution—the time to be determined by Silbert's and Ervin's investigators' arbitrary need for our availability to testify.

On April 5 the White House withdrew the nomination of L. Patrick Gray as director of the FBI, and on April 9 the New York *Times* reported McCord's allegations to the grand jury that my late wife had delivered cash to the Watergate Seven in return for their silence and pleas of guilty. These allegations—and their publication—enraged me, for what my wife had done—at the request of our sponsors—was simply to join in a humanitarian undertaking to provide legitimate legal defense and family-support funds to the defendants. Nor, as McCord was later to allege, did my wife ever speak with anyone about clemency or pardons. Had she been so authorized, she would certainly have informed me, and this she never did. Moreover, on John Dean's orders, McCord had been offered clemency by Jack Caulfield, *not* by my wife, and for the White House to have employed a channel to McCord less official than Caulfield seems unlikely under the circumstances described by Caulfield in his Senate testimony.

Bill Bittman, my attorney, brought galley proofs of *The Berlin Ending* to the D.C. Jail and stayed in the rotunda with me while I read and corrected them. Then, some days later, John Dean revealed our entry into Dr. Fielding's offices in Beverly Hills, and I was taken before the grand jury to give a lengthy statement about the operation. Silbert sent the transcript of my testimony to Judge Matthew Byrne in Los Angeles, who was presiding over the trials of Daniel Ellsberg and Anthony Russo. After reading the transcript, Judge Byrne promptly dismissed all charges against the two men.

President Nixon addressed the nation on April 30, assuming general responsibility for the Watergate entry, though denying personal knowledge of it. This official assumption of responsibility, I felt sure, would absolve the Watergate Seven, but the President's words were so couched as to establish his own innocence rather than ours. During this same televised address the President indicated awareness of an attempt to "conceal the facts" and announced he had given Acting Attorney General Richardson power to appoint a Special Prosecutor.

Then, on May 2, after my return from another day at the grand jury, Gordon Liddy asked to be transferred from our cellblock and was sent to CB 1. He did so out of resentment for my continuing to testify before the grand jury, and a jail order was promulgated separating him from me at all times. Previously I had discussed with Gordon the fact that our legal positions were entirely distinct. Liddy had chosen to go to trial and been convicted; he was filing an appeal.

I, on the other hand, had pleaded guilty and so apparently lacked grounds for appeal; moreover, my attorneys had consistently counseled cooperation with the authorities, and this I had been providing day after day. (It was not until L. Patrick Gray and John Dean confessed their withholding and destruction of my White House safe documents that I was able to appeal on the basis that their actions had deprived me of a legitimate defense to the charges against me.)

Bud Krogh resigned as under secretary of the Department of Transportation on May 9, manfully assuming responsibility for the Fielding entry operation, though Krogh denied that any of his White House superiors had knowledge of the operation.

The historic Senate Watergate hearings began on May 17, and on the following day Harvard law professor Archibald Cox was named Special Prosecutor. This appointment disturbed me, for Cox had served the Kennedy Administration as Solicitor General and was hardly a nonpartisan figure. I predicted that he would staff his office with Kennedy anti-Nixon revanchists and was proved right during my many subsequent grillings by those ideological bravos. Cox and Richardson were sworn in on the twenty-fifth, during whose early hours I was awakened, told to pack my few belongings and informed that the four Miami men and I were being transferred to the Federal Correctional Institution at Danbury, Connecticut.

For the long trip we were individually handcuffed, the cuffs linked to a chain around our waists, and leg irons clamped on our ankles. As if this did not sufficiently restrict our freedom of movement, we were chained together in the rear of the van, whose windows were protected by steel mesh. Adding to our discomfort was the van's hard metal bench and the overt hostility of the two young escorting marshals, one white, one black. As we bumped painfully along, they began bickering, calling each other "red-neck" and "black motherfucker." When a revolver flashed, I began to think our escorts had decided to kill us, then claim we had tried to escape. They permitted us only one comfort stop en route, leading all five of us, still chained together, into the rear of a filling station, where the limited movements of our hands made urination a challenge. The marshals lost their way three times before the van pulled into Danbury.

Although the evening meal was over, prison officers who received us ordered coffee and sandwiches for us while we were processed in. This meant fingerprinting, more mug shots, a search of our cardboard boxes from D.C. Jail and issue of clean, military-type khakis, black shoes and clean sheets and blankets. The prison was constructed as a two-story hollow square within which was a baseball diamond, running track, green grass and weight-lifting facilities. Visiting permission was liberal, and after the drabness and squalor of the D.C. Jail, FCI Danbury seemed close to paradise.

There, as the days went on, we found ourselves being treated as men rather than animals, though prison authorities were frank to tell us that not within memory had they been asked to perform an "evaluation" of the type Sirica had ordained for us. (As it turned out, the process was similar to World War Army screening: basic intelligence tests and an interview with a resident psychologist.) The "evaluation" was, of course, a sham, but it nevertheless served to keep us docile and subservient to the whims and demands of the prison, the Office of the Special Prosecutor and the Ervin committee. And, one never knew, the "evaluation" might just persuade Sirica to lower or suspend our sentences. Later we learned that the prison's report to the Federal Bureau of Prisons and Judge Sirica did *not* recommend incarceration for any of us.

Hardly settled in at Danbury, I was brought back to Washington, a shuttle process that was to continue for months, and lodged in Cell Block 1 of the D.C. Jail. Late at night on June 11 a new arrival was shoved in with me. The cell was almost unbearably hot, and I dozed rather than slept, aware from time to time of rustling noises from the bunk below. When a guard roused me for court call, I began to dress, but could find neither shoes nor sox. From my manila envelope many essential legal papers were missing; the toilet was choked with their fragments. While the guard stood outside, I woke my cellmate and demanded my possessions. His response was to strike me and break my glasses. A scuffle ensued before the guard ordered me onto the catwalk and said, "I didn't see nothin'." However, my shoes and sox were repossessed, and with my nearly empty envelope I was taken down to R&D to dress out for the courthouse, where I arrived tired and shaken.

Apprised of the incident, Bill Bittman asked the Senate committee that I be held in a less hazardous place, so at the end of the day I was taken to the Arlington County Jail, where I spent the night. Following my next day's testimony I was moved to the Montgomery County Detention Center, a ten-minute drive from my Potomac home, and was never again held in the District of Columbia Jail during my many trips from Danbury to Washington.

Along with Bernie Barker and Rolando Martínez I was subpoenaed by the Los Angeles County grand jury. During our testimony—for which the district attorney had granted us immunity—we were held in the maximum-security cells atop the Hall of Justice. Those very cells had held killers Charles Manson and Sirhan Sirhan, and though the cells were bleak, the deputies did all they could to make us comfortable. The West Coast attitude toward us was a welcome contrast to that of the East. After a week in Los Angeles we were returned to Danbury, assigned prison jobs and began integrating into the usual life of prison "population."

Among other Danbury prisoners was Clifford Irving, the only other writer, and we frequently ate together, discussing the publishing business, agents and our plans for the future. Cliff was an ardent baseball player, even then recovering from a nose broken by a misthrown ball. The fact that both of us had lived in Spain provided another conversational link. Cliff was a good companion and well regarded by our fellow inmates.

Toward the end of June I learned that Messrs. Silbert, Campbell and Glanzer had "withdrawn" from the Watergate inquiry. Their departure gave me a minor measure of satisfaction, for Silbert's unwillingness to plea bargain with me was, I felt, responsible for my incarceration. Moreover, their hostile interrogation of my wife, daughter and son had been unpardonable. (In 1974 McCord was publicly to oppose Silbert's confirmation as U.S. Attorney for the District of Columbia, a gesture I felt to be in poor taste.)

My prison job was as one of three librarians, who served on different shifts. The fact that I spoke Spanish helped me aid many of the inmates, for about one-third of the prison population was Spanish-speaking and literate only in that language.

Since childhood I had been a reader of Eric Ambler's stories of intrigue and espionage. Now I came across a dog-eared paperback of Ambler's *Judgment on Deltchev*, one passage of which, I felt, had singular relevance to what I had undergone: "His trial, therefore, is no formality, but a ceremony of preparation and precaution. *He*

*must be discredited and destroyed as a man so that he may safely be
dealt with as a criminal.*"*

All that had happened to me.

These memories were reinforced by occasional views of the televised Senate hearings. I watched John Dean and McCord testify,
and I felt that while they had interesting stories to tell, their em-
broidery was unnecessary. Much testimony was reproduced in
newspapers to which I had access, and so I managed to keep abreast
of what was happening outside my prison's hollow square.

On July 4 my children paid me a holiday visit, and I was emotionally overcome by having them see me in prison garb. But unlike in
the D.C. Jail, we were able to sit together and embrace, and when
they left Danbury, I felt deeply depressed over their future and
mine. The constant disruptions of my Danbury routine, caused by
almost weekly trips to Washington, were taking their toll of my
health. Nervous tension, the strain of being grilled hour after hour,
the daily uncertainties of my location, the difficulty of sleeping in
different jails and the frequent loss of meals all added to my mental
depression. Then Bill Bittman announced to me that he had been
asked to cease representing me by Special Prosecutor Cox.

First shocked, then indignant over this interference with what I
assumed to be my basic right to counsel of my choice, I resisted
Cox's demand, but was persuaded to permit Bittman to withdraw by
a group of his senior partners. All along I had felt that Bittman was a
skilled and vigorous defender who had done his utmost for me, and
his concern for my family and other personal affairs had made me
dependent upon him and his advice. Worse, the Cox demand was
based upon the Special Prosecutor's alleged perception of a possible
conflict of interest between Bittman and myself—a situation, I
might add, that was never to arise. So I lost the services of the man
most knowledgeable of me and my relation to Watergate at a critical
time, for now I was scheduled to appear before Senate committee
cameras, and this unexpected change meant long, expensive hours
with new counsel, familiarizing him with aspects of the case that
were by now subliminal to Bittman and myself.

Sidney Sachs was recommended to me and became my new

---

*Italics mine.

attorney. A former assistant U.S. Attorney and onetime president of the D.C. Bar, Sachs was a prestigious local figure who served me through the televised Senate hearings, after which I could no longer afford his fees. By then I had spent nearly $70,000 of my personal money on litigation, money derived from Dorothy's flight insurance, and I resolved not to further reduce my children's financial base, much less beggar them through legal fees which still continue, though at a lesser rate.

As summer gave way to autumn, I was becoming numb to shocks and unpleasant surprises, docilely accustomed to being hauled hither and yon to testify before one body or another. The House Armed Services Sub-Committee on Intelligence, for instance, kept me before it for nine hours with only brief respite for a hamburger and coffee. Then, back to the Montgomery County Detention Center, where cell TV ended at 2:00 and I was usually awakened at 4:00 to dress in civilian clothing and await the 9:00 arrival of my escort marshals. This exhausting regimen so weakened me that only two days before my scheduled Senate appearance on September 24, it was obvious to even the Senate staff that I could not long continue. At the request of my attorney, the Ervin committee asked the U.S. Marshal Service to keep me in a safehouse at Ft. Holabird, Maryland, near Baltimore, only a forty-five minute drive from the U.S. Senate.

There, in an informal but closely guarded barracks, I was assigned a BOQ-type room with bed, shower and writing table. Other prisoners helped me move in, and I learned that they were white-collar criminals, con men and the like, who were valuable to the government as witnesses and had relatively brief sentences to serve. Cooking and cleaning chores were shared among the safehouse occupants, and when I bedded down for the night, it was after the first decent dinner I had enjoyed in many weeks.

My stay at the safehouse was leaked by unfriendly (were *any* friendly?) members of the Senate staff, and *Newsweek* printed a report that I was living in Maryland on the estate of a friend. At once the Bureau of Prisons hustled me out of the safehouse to the already-too-familiar County Detention Center, but further negotiations returned me to the safehouse, where I was to stay until my final sentencing by Judge Sirica in November.

My petition to the U.S. District Court to withdraw my plea of guilty and dismiss all charges against me was entered by my attorneys on September 17. In part my petition said:

> Whether or not the evidence, unexposed because of now notorious corruption by Government officials, would have established the defendant's innocence, such misconduct so gravely violated his constitutional rights as to require dismissal of the proceedings.

In short, if Ellsberg's constitutional rights had been violated by the government because of the Plumbers' entry into the office of his psychiatrist—and the case against Ellsberg dismissed—then the burning and destruction of my White House safe materials by Counsel to the President John Dean and Acting FBI Director Patrick Gray was equally violative of mine. In simple justice, then, the charges against me ought also to be dismissed.

On the morning of September 24 I was driven to the Senate and escorted into a small room off the Rotunda gallery where my handcuffs were removed. My attorneys were there, as were Lisa and St. John. It had been a year and one week since my Watergate indictment had been handed down.

We had some minutes together before the marshals led me down and into the guarded doorway of the immense Caucus Room, where America's attention had been riveted for the past four months. As I was moved toward the witness table, television lights turned on me, flashbulbs exploded and photographers crowded around to photograph my face. When I took my seat, the photographing continued from in front, and I closed my eyes for a moment's rest from the relentless glare. In that brief space the thought came into my mind that I should conduct myself with the same dignity as my father would have under similar circumstances, and the memory of his courage braced me as I opened my eyes to face again my harassers.

Presently committee members and counsel took their places around the curved podium before me; Senator Ervin called the session to order and swore me in. Then I was allowed to read an opening statement, prepared by my attorneys and myself, which I hoped would place my life in reasonable perspective to my questioners. It went as follows:

"Mr. Chairman and members of the committee, my name is E. Howard Hunt. I am here today to answer questions bearing on your current investigation. I have been informed that it is permissible for me to make a preliminary statement, and I want to take advantage of that opportunity. I will describe my personal background, my relationship to the Watergate entry and the events which have befallen me since that day.

"I was born in 1918 at Hamburg, New York. My father was a lawyer and judge; my mother was a pianist and a housewife. I was educated in the public schools of Florida and New York, and in 1940 graduated from Brown University. Six weeks later I volunteered to serve in the armed forces. While a destroyer officer on the North Atlantic convoy run before Pearl Harbor, I was injured and medically discharged. Later I volunteered and became an Air Force intelligence officer. In 1944 I volunteered for the Office of Strategic Services, the forerunner of CIA, and was sent to China, where I was engaged in partisan warfare until the end of the war.

"In 1949 I joined the Central Intelligence Agency, from which I retired on May 1, 1970, having earned two commendations for outstanding contributions to operations ordered by the National Security Council.

"During the twenty-one years I spent with CIA I was engaged in intelligence, covert action and counterintelligence operations. I was trained in the techniques of physical and electronic surveillance, photography, document forgery and surreptitious entries into guarded premises for photography and installation of electronic devices. I participated in and had the responsibility for a number of such entries, and I had knowledge of many others.

"To put it unmistakably, I was an intelligence officer—a spy—for the government of the United States.

"There have been occasions, as one might expect, when covert operations by the United States or other nations have been exposed. Such episodes have not been uncommon. When such mishaps have occurred, it has been universally the practice for the operation to be disavowed and 'covered up.' Usually this has been done by official intervention with law-enforcement authorities. In addition, the employing governments have paid legal-defense fees. Salaries and family living expenses have been continued. Former CIA Director Helms has testified before this committee in regard to some aspects of this practice.

"After retiring from CIA, I was employed by a firm whose officials maintained a relationship with CIA. Some months after I joined the firm, I was approached by Charles W. Colson, special counsel to the President, to become a consultant to the Executive Office of the President. Mr. Colson told me the White House had need for the kind of intelligence background which he knew I possessed. This was the basic reason for my employment, which I understood at the time was approved by John D. Ehrlichman and now understand was approved also by H. R. Haldeman, both assistants to the President of the United States.

"From the time I began working at the White House until June 17, 1972, the day of the second Watergate entry, I engaged in essentially the same kind of work as I had performed for CIA. I became a member of the Special Investigations Unit, later known as the Plumbers, which the President had created to undertake specific national-security tasks for which the traditional investigative agencies were deemed by the President to be inadequate. In this connection I was involved in tracing leaks of highly classified information.

"These investigations led to an entry by the Plumbers into the office of Dr. Lewis Fielding, Dr. Daniel Ellsberg's psychiatrist. The entry was authorized by Mr. Egil Krogh, deputy to John Ehrlichman. It was considered necessary because of the belief that Dr. Ellsberg or his associates were providing classified information to the Soviet Union. The operation was carried out with my assistance, under the direction of G. Gordon Liddy, a lawyer, former FBI agent and member of the Plumbers unit.

"The Fielding entry occurred in September, 1971. In late November I was told by Mr. Liddy that Attorney General John N. Mitchell proposed the establishment of a large-scale intelligence and counterintelligence program, with Mr. Liddy as its chief. Mr. Liddy and I designed a budget for categories of activities to be carried out in this program, which came to be known as Gemstone. It was my understanding that the program had been approved by Messrs. Jeb Stuart Magruder, a former White House aide, and John

W. Dean III, counsel to the President. Later I learned that Charles W. Colson, special counsel to the President, had approved it, too.

"In April, 1972, Mr. Liddy told me that we would be undertaking the Watergate operation as part of the Gemstone program. He said that he had information, the source of which I understood to be a government agency, that the Cuban government was supplying funds to the Democratic Party campaign. To investigate this report, a surreptitious entry of Democratic National headquarters at the Watergate was made on May 27, 1972, and a second entry on June 17. The second entry was accomplished by a group two of whose members had been among those who accomplished the Fielding entry. I was indicted for my part in the Watergate entry.

"Following indictment and prior to my guilty plea, the court ordered the government to produce all material taken from my White House safe and other evidence. Some material was produced, but significant material was withheld or destroyed. Because the government had withheld evidence, I knew there was no chance of proving my defenses. In addition, my wife had been killed in an accident in December and I was deeply depressed and anxious to devote myself as quickly as possible to the welfare of my children. Accordingly, I had no alternative but to concede that I was legally wrong and so I pleaded guilty, hoping for merciful treatment by the court.

"Instead, on March 23 of this year I was provisionally sentenced to prison for more than thirty years. The court stated that my cooperation with the grand jury and with this committee would be considered in determining my final sentence.

"Since being sentenced, I have been questioned under oath on more than twenty-five occasions, often for many hours. I have answered thousands of questions by innumerable investigators, prosecutors, grand jurors and staff members of this committee. I am informed that such intensive and repeated interrogation is a most extraordinary procedure and of dubious legality. Even so, urged by the court to cooperate fully, I have not contested the procedure. In fact, I have answered all questions, even those which involved confidential communications between my attorneys and myself.

"After my plea I learned of obstruction of justice by government officials. I learned of willful destruction and withholding of evidence and perjury and subornation of perjury before the Watergate grand jury. This official misconduct deprived me of evidence which would have supported my position that (a) my participation in the Watergate was an activity authorized within the power of the President of the United States and (b) if my participation was not so authorized, I justifiably believed that it was.

"Within the past few days, therefore, I have asked the court to permit me to withdraw my plea of guilty and to dismiss the proceedings against me. I believe the charges should be dismissed because, based on revelations made public since my plea, evidence is now available to prove that my participation was not unlawful and because, to quote Judge Byrne when he dismissed charges in the Ellsberg case: 'The totality of the circumstances of this case . . . offend a "sense of justice." The bizarre events have incurably infected the prosecution of this case.'

"It has been alleged that I demanded clemency and money for my family and for those who helped in the Watergate entry. I did not ask for clemency. Mr. Liddy assured me that in accordance with the established practice in such cases, funds would be made available. I did seek such funds, but I made no threats.

"Now I find myself confined under a sentence which may keep me in prison for the rest of my life. I have been incarcerated for six months. For a time I was in solitary confinement. I have been physically attacked and robbed in jail. I have suffered a stroke. I have been transferred from place to place, manacled and chained hand and foot. I am isolated from my four motherless children. The funds provided me and others who participated in the break-in have long since been exhausted. I am faced with an enormous financial burden in defending myself against criminal charges and numerous civil suits. Beyond all this, I am crushed by the failure of my government to protect me and my family as in the past it has always done for its clandestine agents.

"In conclusion, I want to emphasize that at the time of the Watergate operation I considered my participation as a duty to my country. I thought it was an unwise operation, but I viewed it as lawful. I hope the court will sustain my view, but whatever that outcome, I deeply regret that I had any part in this affair. I think it was an unfortunate use of executive power and I am sorry that I did not have the wisdom to withdraw. At the same time, I cannot escape feeling that the country I have served for my entire life and which directed me to carry out the Watergate entry is punishing me for doing the very things it trained and directed me to do.

"Mr. Chairman, honorable members of the committee, I thank you for your attention and your patience. I will now undertake to answer your questions to the best of my ability."

Committee Counsel Dash was my first interrogator. Shrewd but courteous, and aware of my physical limitations, Dash led me over familiar ground as I recounted my friendship with Charles Colson and my acceptance of a White House consultancy. Minority Counsel Thompson was next, then Senator Ervin, followed by Senator Baker and the other five Senators, the sequence determined by party affiliation and Senate seniority.

As the morning wore on, I found myself tiring rapidly, not grasping questions as well as I had at the beginning, and I welcomed occasional quorum calls, during which I conferred with counsel and tried to avert my eyes from the now almost-painful glare of the television lights. At lunch recess I ate with my children in the witness room, where I had met them on arrival, and even managed a few minutes' rest in an easy chair. Then back to the Caucus Room again.

When the hearing resumed, Sid Sachs engaged in a technical discussion with several of the panel concerning possible violations of my attorney-client privilege, pointing out that although I was testifying with a grant of immunity, nevertheless, I was doing so under the coercion of Judge Sirica's provisional sentence—a sentence which Sirica might lighten if I cooperated satisfactorily with the committee. This colloquy continued for some time, then Dash resumed his questioning, and the other panel members in a sequence that became drearily familiar. Senator Ervin had a disconcerting habit of addressing me in an uninflected voice that left me in doubt as to whether he was making a statement or asking a question. Senators Baker and Inouye were, I felt, on an intellectual par: both keen questioners, well versed in the subject matter. Senator Montoya's questions startled me, for I had answered most of them when posed by previous questioners. Senator Talmadge, my erstwhile wartime cabin mate, had done his homework and I did not sense him as particularly hostile. Republican Senator Gurney appeared bored by the proceedings, lofting an occasional question, but retreating before any resistance by Democratic counsel or Senators.

That night I again slept at Holabird—in a bed in a noise-free room—and in the morning, despite the drain of my first day's testimony, I felt that I could make it through another day.

September 25 was largely repetition of my first appearance, with few memorable moments to recall. Senator Weicker savagely attacked my theory that Al Baldwin might have informed DNC officials of the pending entry, but by then I had become somewhat accustomed to Weicker's belligerence. Rereading transcripts of my testimony months later, I remain struck by the little I can recall of either questions or answers. Perhaps the experience was so traumatic that even now, nine months later, my mind continues to resist full recollection of the episode.

At Holabird I rested and began to regain weight. I was allowed to wear my personal clothing and use a portable typewriter and began to attack the mounting piles of unanswered mail. The Senate received several thousand telegrams and letters in the wake of my testimony and those were answered by a small committee William Buckley established in my behalf at his *National Review* offices. Well aware of my deepening financial plight, Buckley solicited funds to pay for my legal defense and, when returns were disappointing, suggested my retaining his personal attorney, C. Dickerman Williams, at no cost to me.

Meanwhile, a young Baltimore lawyer, William Snyder, Jr., who had been handling my wife's estate at Buckley's request, also came to my aid and eventually assumed all of my legal representation save that of my appeal, which Dickerman Williams, a senior member of the bar, volunteered to prepare and argue.

On November 9, 1973, Barker, Sturgis, Martinez, Gonzalez and myself were brought to Judge Sirica's courtroom for final sentencing. McCord, still free, was there, also awaiting sentence, and had the effrontery to try to shake my hand. As I stood with my companions before the bench, Sirica handed down our sentences: one to three years for the Miami men, deferred sentencing for James McCord (what else?) and a staggering eight years plus ten-thousand-dollar fine to me, no parole before serving thirty months! Dazed, I declined to make any statement, although Rolando Martinez made a moving speech—moving to everyone present except Judge Sirica. I was taken to the Felony Tank and joined in the bowels of the courthouse by Sid Sachs, whose usually cool demeanor was shaken by my sentence. I thanked him for his counsel, reiterated I could no longer afford his services and later in the day was returned to the Ft. Holabird safehouse.

Over the next two weeks I took care of family business, resigned from several clubs and from time to time talked with Buckley, Dick Williams and Bill Snyder. Manolo Artime visited me with St. John and Lisa, and a decision was made to sell my house and have Artime care for David in his own Miami home.

On Thanksgiving no family visitors came to share the abundant board with me, though Kevan arrived that night for a long and affectionate talk.

Then, on the twenty-ninth, I was abruptly told to pack for transfer to the Federal Prison Camp at Allenwood, Pennsylvania, and allowed to inform Bill Snyder of my destination. He was later to pick up my no-longer-needed personal effects at the safehouse and keep them for me.

Allenwood, inaccurately hailed as "the country club of prisons," turned out to be a forced-labor camp. Absent were the walls and bars I had grown accustomed to, and although prisoners could walk freely in the vicinity of camp buildings, there were limits beyond which an inmate could not pass without being considered an escapee.

As a new arrival, I was housed in a large, decaying wooden dormitory of World War II vintage, with broken showers and drafty windows. Rations were on a palatability level between D.C. Jail and Danbury, with heavy emphasis on pasta offerings and their hollow calories.

There in southern Pennsylvania winter had begun. Without regard to my age or physical condition, I was assigned to a work force on Farm II which raised cattle. I offered my services to the library and the education section, only to be told that the camp superintendent, a cocky young buck named Max Weger, had decreed my farm assignment lest he be accused of favoritism. There was a shortage of boots and warm work clothing for us outdoor laborers, a lack felt keenly by those whose job it was to muck out the cattle barns, set fence poles and string cable fencing to retain the 1,200-head herd.

At Lewisburg Prison hospital my arthritic shoulder condition was confirmed, and after yet another trip to Washington for further interviews by the Office of the Special Prosecutor, I was reassigned as clerk at the farm. There, in the farmhouse, there was some warmth and protection from the winter winds, and at least I was working with my mind rather than solely with my back and hands.

During Washington interviews I became the special target of Richard Ben-Veniste, a curly-headed, abrasive young man who had been a federal prosecutor in New York and was much in the news during continuing litigation over the Presidential tapes.

Prior to my being sent to Allenwood, Ben-Veniste had mused, in the presence of my attorneys, that long-term criminals such as myself were usually committed to Atlanta or Leavenworth penitentiaries. His threat was clear. Then he launched into renewed efforts to try to shake my previously sworn testimony on an area of particular interest to him: the alleged offer of executive clemency to me. He asked me over and over again whether I had been promised clemency or given some signal that clemency would be given to me; when I continually replied in the negative, he said, "Bullshit," and hammered on me some more.

Christmas at Allenwood was bleak. By then I was in a warm cinder-block dormitory among whose occupants was former Representative Cornelius Gallagher of New Jersey, who gave me heavy clothing for my farm work, a gesture I appreciated greatly. Earlier I had come to know the husband of our former Korean ward, Stella Kim, and he, too, did much to ease my dismal life at Allenwood.

Three days after Christmas I was at work on the farm when I was called to the camp superintendent's office and chewed out for having accepted an emergency call the night before from our family housekeeper. The call had been monitored, Weger informed me—not to my surprise—and in the monitor's opinion the call was not of an emergency nature. Weger warned me against abusing telephone "privileges" and sent me back to the farm. Then, just after the midday meal, I was again recalled from the farmhouse and told to call William Snyder in Baltimore. When Snyder answered, he told me the Court of Appeals had ordered my release pending formal arguments in my case, and I was to be brought expeditiously to Washington. I greeted the announcement in stunned silence, then tears welled in my eyes. After all these months I could hardly bring myself to believe the good news. I could see my children again, live at home—at least until the Court of Appeals, which had reversed Sirica's contemptuous rulings, decided the merits of my case.

Euphoric, I told friends the news and received congratulations even from prisoners I did not know.

Snyder, however, had reckoned without bureaucracy: It was then Friday, and official notification of my release would not arrive at Allenwood until mail resumed after the New Year's holiday. Still, I had a release date—only four days away. With the exception of the time I'd spent in solitary at D.C. Jail, those were the longest days of my life.

I worked on the farm until the marshals came for me on Tuesday, January 2, 1974. They arrived late, having lost their way, and I was due in court at Washington no later than four o'clock that day. Having prepared for this moment, I had only to say last-minute good-byes to friends, walk down the hill to central control and receive an ill-fitting suit of street clothes. Then I was turned over to two marshals, who manacled me hand and foot and drove at between eighty and ninety miles an hour to the federal courthouse, where a crowd of photographers was awaiting my arrival. The marshals tried to remove my leg irons and handcuffs without being seen, but a few vigilant journalists noticed, and some news stories were to remark the paradox.

Able now to walk without hobbling, I was led into the courthouse and to the office of the clerk of the Court of Appeals. There I was read the court's decision and the terms of my release: no bond, report monthly to the probation officer and no travel outside the metropolitan area without his permission. Bill Snyder arrived and stood beside me while I took an oath to comply with my parole. Next we went to the office of the chief probation officer, an impressive gentleman named Frank Pace, who explained the conditions of my parole to me and made Snyder and myself comfortable until I could compose a brief statement to give the hungry press.

Emerging on the steps, I expressed satisfaction that the Court of Appeals had found sufficient merit in my appeal to warrant my release, then thanked my attorneys and the thousands of well-wishers whose telegrams and letters had made life more endurable over the long prison months. In closing I said I was anxious to be reunited with my children, and with Snyder I pushed through the crowd to his waiting car.

As we drove away, Snyder told me Kevan was in New York and that he and Buckley had decided I should go there before joining

David in Miami. Moreover, a deathwatch of photographers was patrolling my Potomac home, and Bill had clothing for me at his place in suburban Baltimore. Our car was followed by two carloads of press representatives and a network motorcyclist. While I was showering, reporters came to Snyder's door and asked for further statements, which Bill declined on my behalf. Robin, Bill's wife, had prepared a gourmet dinner for us, and I indulged in a highball before my first family-style meal in nearly eleven months.

Later I placed phone calls to friends, wrote out checks for accumulated bills and turned in for a dreamless sleep.

In the morning Snyder and I took the Metroliner to New York, reaching Buckley's town house at noon. There I found Kevan with Pat and Bill Buckley and Dick Williams. After a notable lunch we discussed my situation and decided that for the present I would make no public statements or appearances. That night Kevan and I flew to Miami, where a mob scene of photographers waited at the airport. Artime met and took us to his car, then to a motel near his home where we were registered under aliases to avoid the attentions of the media.

Artime's home was also staked out by the press, which was convinced I would have to go there to see my son. But Artime brought him to me, and he stayed with me at the motel for several days—until media interest waned and I could go in person to Artime's home.

After a week of sunshine and good food I left Miami for Potomac, where our housekeeper turned over the keys to me. A few days later she returned to Argentina with my heartfelt thanks for performing a difficult and often trying office.

Alone in my home, for Snyder had rented a nearby house for Lisa and St. John to live in—anticipating my house would soon be sold—I found it difficult to adjust to silence after being so long among prison crowds and noise. And I was lonely, for everything I saw reminded me of Dorothy.

For days I could do little more than prepare my meals and care for my Afghan hound and Siamese cat. Then gradually I responded to invitations of neighbors and found that I could open letters and read them, even begin answering some from the stacks that had accumulated. Within a month I was able to prepare an outline of my memoirs, and in late February I signed a contract with the publisher.

Since then, in addition to dictating the manuscript, I have given a public address—to the Nebraska Press Association in Omaha—been interviewed on Buckley's *Firing Line* and by ABC-TV News, given an interview to *People* magazine and written a short piece for the first issue of *Harper's* revived weekly magazine. In addition, I permitted Swedish TV to film me in my home for a documentary film on my literary life.

This morning Dick Williams called from New York to remind me that he would be arguing my appeal on June 14, a scant two weeks away. Did I want to be present? he asked. I considered, then remembered Buckley's jovial comment that I better hadn't be, for every time I'd been in court I'd lost. So I declined the invitation.

On June 14, 1974, the U.S. Court of Appeals heard oral arguments from attorneys for the original Watergate Seven. Two of the nine judges, however, recused themselves from hearing the appeal (they were known conservatives), thus destroying the court's customary liberal-conservative balance. And Dick Williams, my attorney, was unable to present his full pleading, questioning from the bench subtracting from his allotted twenty-five minutes.

At this writing the court's verdict is still to be made known. Until then I'll live as I did in prison, one day at a time, suspending long-range plans until my future is decided one way or another.

Watergate has cost me as much as anyone involved, and at fifty-six I don't want to go back to prison. But if—and I hardly dare hope—I'm freed, what's left of my life will be devoted to my children, David in particular, and others who may need me.

While I was in prison, President Richard Nixon called me, Liddy and my four Miami friends "idiots" and "jackasses," as the Presidential tapes revealed. Given the many deletions in those transcripts, I feel we were lucky not to have been called much worse.

Even so, during the spring, to my astonishment, I was invited by Presidential attorneys James St. Clair and Fred Buzhardt to confer with them at the White House *concerning the President's defense!* The invitation was outrageously inappropriate for several reasons: A visit by me to the White House would have been noticed by any number of reporters and could have raised serious questions concerning a possible continuation of the "cover-up"; and I was a paroled felon—a category of persons seldom if ever admitted, much less invited, to the White House. But more importantly, I had nothing to contribute to the defense of the President.

After I declined, the same invitation was tendered to my attorney, who not only refused, but at my urging reported the strange overtures to the Office of the Special Prosecutor. Only Colson, I speculated, would have had the *chutzpah* to suggest "good old Howard" as a possible last-resort source of aid and comfort to the White House. The incident had the effect of alienating me even further from the highest office in the land.

Nixon's prospective impeachment subsequently appeared to turn on the crucial question of whether he *thought* he was paying "blackmail" for the silence of myself and others. By giving validity to this sole and unsupported allegation of John Dean's—while disparaging the rest of Dean's testimony—Nixon may have felt that the picture of him bowing to blackmail threats would engender public sympathy and be accepted as a rationale for the cover-up, about which his deception finally forced his resignation.

Still the strident cry remains: "Dean said . . . Dean said . . ." and "Hunt did . . . Hunt did . . ." and for the rest of my life I expect to be known as a man who tried to blackmail the White House.

But let *me* make one thing perfectly clear: I did *not* try to "blackmail" the White House, nor did anyone ever offer me "executive clemency" either spontaneously or as an inducement to remain silent. Indeed one of the real ironies of Watergate was, of course, that there was no "silence" to "buy"; my immunization meant that I *had* to testify to any and all questions or face additional charges of contempt. Lawyers Nixon and Ehrlichman should have appreciated that.

The memoirs set down in this book define my life. It seems both ironic and tragic that I must defend its quality with those two denials—as though nothing else was of importance, not any of my fifty-six years of living, except the Watergate experience. The Watergate horror.

I hope the closing of this book does not mean the end of my useful life and that over the next few years I can be active in enough things of general interest to make a sequel worth the writing.

That's what I'd like.

Potomac, Maryland

INDEX